After Watergate

For Marina

After Watergate

Presidential Scandals from Nixon to Trump

Peter J. Ling

First published in Great Britain in 2024 by
Pen & Sword History
An imprint of Pen & Sword Books Limited
Yorkshire – Philadelphia

ISBN 978 1 52676 482 9

A CIP catalogue record for this book is
available from the British Library

Typeset by Mac Style
Printed in the UK by CPI Group (UK) Ltd, Croydon, CR0 4YY.

Pen & Sword Books Limited incorporates the imprints of After the Battle, Atlas, Archaeology, Aviation, Discovery, Family History, Fiction, History, Maritime, Military, Military Classics, Politics, Select, Transport, True Crime, Air World, Frontline Publishing, Leo Cooper, Remember When, Seaforth Publishing, The Praetorian Press, Wharncliffe Local History, Wharncliffe Transport, Wharncliffe True Crime and White Owl.

For a complete list of Pen & Sword titles please contact

PEN & SWORD BOOKS LIMITED
47 Church Street, Barnsley, South Yorkshire, S70 2AS, England
E-mail: enquiries@pen-and-sword.co.uk
Website: www.pen-and-sword.co.uk
or
PEN AND SWORD BOOKS
1950 Lawrence Rd, Havertown, PA 19083, USA
E-mail: uspen-and-sword@casematepublishers.com
Website: www.penandswordbooks.com

Contents

Illustrations

24. Trump supporters march on the US Capitol. 6 January 2021. Photographer TapTheForwardAssist – Own work, CC BY-SA 4.0. (*Public Domain image, via Wikimedia Creative Commons*)
25. Rudy Giuliani. 31 August 2016. By Gage Skidmore from Peoria, AZ, United States of America – Rudy Giuliani, CC BY-SA 2.0. (*Public Domain image, via Wikimedia Creative Commons*)

Glossary of Acronyms

ABC	American Broadcasting Corporation
CBS	Columbia Broadcasting System
CDC	Center for Disease Control
CIA	Central Intelligence Agency
CNN	Cable News Network
CREEP	Campaign to Re-Elect the President
DNC	Democratic National Committee
EPA	Environmental Protection Agency
EEOC	Equal Employment Opportunities Commission
FBI	Federal Bureau of Investigation
FEC	Federal Election Commission
GOP	Grand Old Party [the Republican Party]
GRU	ГРУ [Main Intelligence Directorate in Russian]
HAWK	Homing All the Way Killer [type of missile]
IAI	Israel Aircraft Industries
IRS	Internal Revenue Service
MIT	Massachusetts Institute of Technology
NSA	National Security Advisor
NSC	National Security Council
OIC	Office of Independent Counsel
OLC	Office of Legal Counsel
MSNBC	Microsoft-National Broadcasting System
NBC	National Broadcasting Corporation
PAC	Political Action Committee
PBS	Public Broadcasting Service
RINO	Republican in Name Only
RTC	Resolution Trust Corporation
S&L	Savings and Loans
SBA	Small Business Administration
TOW	Tube-loaded Optically Tracked Wire operated [type of missile]

Introduction

Most people feel they know a scandal when they see one. For some, there is the sunlight test. If something looks suspect, immoral, or illegal in the cold light of day, it is likely to give rise to scandal, if widely known. Thus, scandal almost always entails something that the parties involved would have preferred to keep concealed. But scandal is also shaped by the position and status of the people involved. Presidential scandals therefore represent a category of scandals that are amplified by the expectations and responsibilities of the American presidency. The main scandals examined in this book – Watergate, Iran-Contra, the Clinton scandals, the 2000 election, Russia's role in the 2016 election, and the subsequent Trump scandals – all entail activities that were meant to be private but became public, and all in different ways speak to the reputation of the president both domestically and internationally. The framers of the US Constitution fundamentally mistrusted power (executive power in particular) and tried to divide it between executive, legislative, and judicial branches with each having a check upon the other. Nevertheless, without a distinct head of state like a constitutional monarch, the president tends to be the symbolic figurehead of the nation for Americans and the etiquette surrounding the White House and the First Lady amplifies this mystique.

President Harry Truman famously placed a plaque on his desk in the Oval Office with the words: "The buck stops here." This signals that the president is ultimately responsible for the actions of the federal government and that the final decision-making must lie with him. Most of the scandals under discussion occur in this context. It forms the basis for the famous Watergate question: "What did the President know and when did he know it?" However, it also illustrates the reality that the millions of actions by the wide-ranging sections of the US government cannot in practice be controlled by a single person. Things go wrong in every administration. Bad things happen. But not all of them give rise to scandal. Perhaps most contentiously of all, there are policies pursued and priorities set that are scandalous in the eyes of some at the time. This is strikingly true in terms of priorities. The AIDS crisis in the 1980s and the failure of the Reagan administration to respond would be one example; Barack Obama's use of drone warfare, his failure to close the Guantanamo detention centre, and the widespread use of wiretaps domestically by Homeland Security illustrate how long the list could be. As a practical matter, a book that documented every incidence of misconduct would be a huge volume whereas this is a slender one. In short, this is an account of major scandals, the ones we have all heard about, and it's a book that would have been finished a lot quicker if Donald Trump had not shown a barely faltering capacity for scandal. The last chapter should be read as an early draft.

Two of the scandals discussed – Iran-Contra and Trump-Ukraine – arise from the president's role in foreign policy. The Constitution makes the president Commander-in-Chief of US armed forces and the nation's top diplomat. Since 1945, the US's role as a superpower has massively extended the scale of its armed forces and interventionist character of its diplomacy. Congress has always contested the President's war-making powers as well as his scope for making entangling alliances. Post-Watergate investigations disclosed the murky activities of the Central Intelligence Agency during the Cold War and some lawmakers wanted Nixon impeached for his clandestine war in Cambodia. Others would point to the CIA's involvement in the coup that toppled President Salvadore Allende of Chile as an unpunished scandal. Arguably since 9/11 in 2001, many Americans have accepted the fact that there will be so-called "black ops" against foreign forces deemed hostile to the United States. Those who are outraged are seen as naïve or unpatriotic. At the same time, while the US president is still referred to as the world's most powerful leader, the presidency itself has repeatedly been termed an impossible job because of this critique of the use of American power.

Observers note that Americans seem to demand powerful leaders yet are suspicious of self-confident figures who view themselves as infallible and above criticism. Another cliché of American politics is that all politicians campaign in poetry but govern in prose. Seeking election, presidential candidates especially evoke ideals and promise positive change. This sets the stage for disillusionment, which contributes to the reality that the high turnout of voters in 2020 (around 66 percent; depending on whether you go by those of voting age or try to exclude those who are ineligible – aliens, felons, etc.) still left roughly a third of the electorate in effect abstaining. These features have contributed to scandals. On the one hand, exercising presidential power in a way that advances their goals led both the Nixon and Reagan administrations into scandalous actions. On the other hand, the perception of a Washington establishment that talks about helping others but spends most of its time working deals for its members has been a persistent feature. The ironic outcome has been that many of Donald Trump's most loyal supporters see him as authentic because he says coarse things and doesn't try to wrap up his opinions in the way conventional politicians do.

Since scandal is intrinsically about placing private things in the public domain, it is as much about the media as it is about politics. Small-scale scandal in daily life is often the spice of gossip in every social group. From the yellow press of the late nineteenth century to the tabloid journalism of the twentieth to the internet conspiracy mills of our own time, scandal has proven its ability to capture attention. Even the most principled of investigative journalists has known that scandal works as a combination of outrage and entertainment. This is most conspicuously demonstrated here by the evolution of the Clinton scandals. While rumours circulated about Bill Clinton's womanizing even before his presidential campaign in 1992, it was his slippery response to questions about his character that made journalists keen to find the truth. Initially what came to light were dubious investments in a scheme called Whitewater, duly reported but not read by the wider public in the way they devoured the Paula Jones suit and the Monica Lewinsky affair. The role of the media and its interaction with party politics in the Clinton saga is a key turning point in the presidential scandals within this book. Alongside the disputed 2000 election, it sets the stage for Donald Trump's emergence and his turbulent term as president.

The continual interaction between politics and the media has also ensured that scandal is a well-honed weapon in partisan warfare. It can be readily argued that Watergate was the product of Nixon's conviction that he had to do to the Democrats what they would do to him; but do it first and more successfully. It was part of the Republican response to Iran-Contra that the investigation and prosecution of those involved was taking policy differences that should be settled via elections and disputing them via litigation. Conversely, with some justification, the Clintons insisted that their travails were born of a right-wing media conspiracy. And of course, more recently, there have been the Trump era cries of "witch-hunt" and "fake news." As a result, there is some discussion below of negative campaigning which includes opposition research that can uncover scandals that will diminish a rival's appeal. This well-established practice has now been extended by the onset of Russian cyber-warfare which uses the openness of the internet and social media to spread messages that deepen domestic American divisions, feeding prejudices in ways that boost support for candidates already intent on tapping such support, and fostering doubt among voters who might otherwise vote for a candidate perceived as hostile to Russian interests. The Mueller Report documented this fact, but the headline was: "No collusion."

Among the mountain of scandal that the Trump presidency created, this book treats the following: 2016 and the issue of Russian interference; the Trump-Zelensky phone call and the first impeachment; Trump's response to the COVID-19 pandemic; his claims of a stolen election in 2020 and the attack on the Capitol Building on 6 January 2021. Completing the book in 2023 has meant acknowledging other legal cases brought against the former president. However, his ability to appeal negative verdicts and the reality that he raises funds from his supporters on the basis of these prosecutions means that there is no sense of the story ending soon. Other issues from Trump's failure to staff federal agencies adequately to his blatant nepotism in terms of White House roles are only mentioned in passing. In examining the disputed presidential election of 2000, I use the term scandal of incompetence to signal that sometimes the outrage is misdirected towards intention. Bush's brother, Jeb, as Governor of Florida did not rig the election in a directly corrupt way; instead, the outcome was more affected by incompetence. The same distinction is entangled in many of the Trump scandals.

In telling the story of presidential scandals from Nixon to Trump, another facet grows in importance. It can be summed up in the question: is a scandal different, if only a certain faction or fraction of the public is scandalized? In 1974 when Nixon resigned, he did so because most Americans were scandalized and accordingly many in his own party felt he had to go or be impeached and ousted. In 2021 when Trump was impeached for the second time and the Senate voted to acquit, many Republican voters were not scandalized and thus it was politically risky (maybe even personally risky given his followers' propensity for violence) for GOP (Grand Old Party being the Republican nickname) Senators to vote to convict. The claim that the 2020 election was stolen by Joe Biden still circulates among Republican believers, even though the hold of Donald Trump over the party's future seems less secure in 2023. As I write, Republicans are still sufficiently wary of Trump that they characterize suits against him as inherently partisan and via their newly gained control of the House, they hope to expose scandals that will damage the Biden administration. In short, the future remains ripe for scandal – and a second edition.

Chapter 1

Watergate – Did it Set the Standard for Scandal?

In any conversation involving presidential scandals, it won't be long before the word "Watergate" appears. Watergate was originally just the name given to a complex of buildings in an area of Washington, D.C. called Foggy Bottom, which is more salubrious than it sounds. Indeed, it's a fashionable neighbourhood, and the complex of offices, apartments, and a hotel quickly became popular with members of Congress and government appointees. The Democratic Party's National Committee (DNC) chose the sixth floor of the Watergate building on Virginia Avenue for its offices, when looking to locate its headquarters in 1967. The Watergate scandal begins with the discovery of a break-in at these DNC offices in June 1972, so it seems fitting that the complex's original design was hailed in the press for, among other things, its elaborate, electronic security system, which would ensure that no intruders could easily get into the premises undetected. The press release was vindicated.

As the scandal unfolded, Watergate was on American lips so often that it became forever linked to political scandal. Conservative columnist William Safire, formerly a Nixon speech writer, was particularly adept at coining names for later scandals by adding the suffix "-gate." Often the controversy thus labelled was far less important than Watergate, and Safire later conceded that his efforts were partly intended to diminish the stain that Watergate had left on his former boss's reputation. A glaring example was "Scalpgate," which Safire coined to ridicule President Clinton's 1996 decision to get a haircut at Los Angeles Airport; he caused multiple flight delays.

Not all the scandals tagged were minor, however. The illegal transmission of arms to Iran and money to right-wing Nicaraguan rebels by the Reagan administration (Iran-Contra) in direct defiance of Congress was sometimes referred to as either Iran-gate or Contra-gate (see chapter two). The Monica Lewinsky affair which ultimately produced the Clinton impeachment was similarly dubbed Monica-gate, Lewinsky-gate or even Sex-gate (see chapter 3). Although the George W. Bush and Obama administrations produced some scandals of their own, they largely escaped the –gate suffix. However, the 2016 election campaign produced Russia-gate as well as Pussy-gate, Stormy-gate and Email-gate. The first three related to Donald Trump (see chapter 4). The first allegation, largely substantiated by US intelligence agencies and by the Mueller Report, was that Russia had interfered in the presidential election in support of Trump and against Hilary Clinton. The second arose because of video footage taken during the recording of a cable TV show *Access Hollywood* in which Donald Trump was heard to boast that since he was a star, women let him do anything: he could "...grab them by the pussy." The third surrounded the disclosure that Trump had made payments via attorney Michael Cohen to suppress publication of details of his adulterous affair with porn star, Stormy Daniels. The 45th President has set a record for scandals since he has been impeached twice by the House (and acquitted by the Senate) over what is already referred to as "Ukraine-gate," and for his role in the storming of the US Capitol Building on 6 January 2021 (see chapter 5). Despite the chants of "lock her up" at Trump rallies, *Email-gate*, the controversy over Hilary Clinton's use of a personal email account while serving as Secretary of State in the Obama administration seems small beer. However, this controversy received so much media coverage in the weeks immediately prior to the election that some see it as the key reason for her surprise defeat.

The significance of Watergate is also reflected in a similar tagging of scandals with the *-gate* suffix around the world. In France, the Angola-gate scandal of 2008, more sombrely known as the Mitterand-Pasqua affair, involved dubious and secretive French arms sales to the war-ravaged African nation during the 1990s. Across the Channel, UK newspapers in 1992 were full of Camilla-gate, following the revelation of a taped 1989 phone conversation between the then Prince Charles and his then mistress, Camilla Parker-Bowles, which irrefutably confirmed their intimate relationship, and justified Princess Diana's charge that there had always been three people in the royal marriage. The Princess's own private life was similarly scrutinized after publication of a further taped call in what was duly called "Squidgy-gate" due to the nickname given her by close friend, James Gilbey. The scandal of phone-hacking by UK tabloids took far longer to be exposed.

Lest the reader think that this was solely an Anglo-French phenomenon, one can point to Choi Soon-sil-gate in South Korea, which hinged on the corrupt influence of Choi Soon-sil, daughter of a noted Korean spiritual leader on President Park Geun-hye, the nation's first female president. As a result, President Park was impeached in 2017 and she and Choi were jailed for corruption. The collapse of Communism in eastern Europe produced Duna-gate in Hungary and Stazi-gate in the former East Germany in 1990 amid revelations about the secret police operations under the Communist regimes. By exposing hitherto hidden transactions, the massive trove of financial details known as the Panama Papers, approximately 11.5 million documents, has triggered multiple "-gate" scandals across the world including Raghat-gate involving the President of Azerbaijan. In Malta and Bangladesh, these scandals exposing corruption among high-ranking politicians are referred to simply as Panama-gate.

And one could go on since the journalistic "-gate" label has spread beyond political scandals, revealing how profoundly American media habits shape news coverage elsewhere. That the afterlife of Watergate is linked so much to journalism is fitting because the scandal itself is seen as a vindication of investigative reporting as a crucial safeguard for democracy. This underlines a basic characteristic of all scandals, not least political ones: namely, that they involve details that were meant to be secret becoming public. The principle that one should never do in private anything one would not want to be publicly known seems to be a maxim honoured mainly in the breach.

Watergate highlights the always fractious relationship between the news media and politicians. In 1906 when President Theodore Roosevelt coined the term muckraking to describe the crusading type of investigative journalism, he was not giving it his approval. He compared journalists in this mould to a character in John Bunyan's celebrated *Pilgrim's Progress.* He quoted the following extract:

> *The man with the muck-rake, the man who could look no way but downward with the muck-rake in his hands; who was offered a celestial crown for his muck-rake, but who could neither look up nor regard the crown he was offered, but continued to rake to himself the filth of the floor.*

Implicit in Roosevelt's rebuke was a common feeling shared, not just by politicians, that critics fail to appreciate the difficulties politicians face and to focus relentlessly on the negative. Virtually all the politicians mentioned in this book, not least Nixon, would echo that sentiment. Trump, never known for understatement, spoke of his media critics as "enemies of the people."

Significantly, professional journalists themselves have embraced Teddy Roosevelt's insulting label and made it a badge of honour, insisting that their tireless fact-gathering to challenge the claims made by public figures is a safeguard against the abuse of power and is done to protect the people in general, and the less powerful in particular. In practice, this noble mission of highlighting failings in the system, or instances of injustice or injury, or more generally, the misuse of power has always been mixed with partisan bias and sensationalistic gossip. Television and radio stations, like newspapers before them, and websites more recently, operate on a commercial basis. Speaking truth to power, as the saying goes, risks costly lawsuits, is itself sometimes expensive to resource, and can alienate valuable advertisers and/or portions of the public. It was recently revealed that staff at *Fox News* were warned that challenging Trump's claims of a stolen election in 2020 would adversely affect ratings. Thus, muckraking is more honoured than practiced, and when it ensnares a politician, his or her immediate reaction can be: "why me? Others do it too." In the case of Nixon and Watergate, his reaction was not indignant surprise, but a fury that stemmed from a conviction that the liberal media had never treated him fairly and were always working against him. His extensive "enemies" list always included a fair number of editors and reporters.

Well before Watergate, Richard Nixon had been a divisive figure. When he entered politics in the late 1940s, he used the "Red Scare" to tarnish the reputation of his liberal Democratic opponents. Elected to Congress in 1946, he served on the House Un-American Activities Committee and gained valuable publicity by challenging Hollywood executives over their failure to make overtly anti-Communist movies. He was similarly conspicuous in pursuit of a former member of Franklin D. Roosevelt's government, Alger Hiss, whom he accused of working for the Soviets. He insinuated that Hiss's presence at the Yalta conference explained what the American Right saw as FDR's appeasement of Stalin in negotiations over the fate of eastern Europe. Southern California, Nixon's political base, was a hotbed of anti-Communism and this enabled the ambitious politician to win his 1950 Senate campaign against the progressive Helen Gagahan Douglas; he labelled her "the Pink Lady," thus smearing her as a Communist "fellow-traveler." All this raised Nixon's profile in conservative circles so much that Dwight D. Eisenhower, a "middle-of-the-road" Republican, felt he needed Nixon as his vice-president to unite the party in 1952. However, Nixon's tactics galled liberals and progressives. In their eyes, he was the embodiment of dirty politics, and his notoriety was set to grow.

Eisenhower's choice of Nixon as his running-mate at the Republican convention inevitably made him a bigger story. The young Senator was part of the California delegation which, on the first ballot, at least, was supposed to back a presidential bid by the state's Governor (and future US Chief Justice) Earl Warren. When this failed, and Eisenhower put Nixon on the presidential ticket, Warren supporters accused Nixon of treachery, and one of them leaked to the press rumours of a Nixon slush-fund. By September 1952, the *New York Post* referred to a "millionaires' club" of backers who ensured that Nixon and his family lived well beyond their means, and there were calls for Eisenhower to drop him. To save his career, Nixon agreed to give a televised address, which became known as the "Checkers speech," because while he denied that he and his family benefitted from political contributions, he did admit that they had accepted the gift of a dog for the children. His children had called the dog Checkers, and since they loved it so much, Nixon was determined to keep it. This homespun tale appealed to what was then the largest television audience in US history (60 million). Nixon remained the vice-presidential nominee and the Republicans took the White House for the first time since 1928. Nixon had escaped a scandal and he himself, fatefully, believed that he had mastered the new medium of television.

Nonetheless, Helen Douglas's mocking labelling in 1950 of Nixon as "Tricky Dicky" stuck, and not just in Democratic circles. He never entirely lost his aura of untrustworthiness, partly because he approached the media warily, which predisposed the press corps to respond in kind. He was the antithesis of his near-contemporary John F. Kennedy in terms of relaxed elegance, charm and intelligence. Kennedy had once tried his hand at journalism, as had his wife, Jackie, and his father's work with the Hollywood studios gave the family an inside knowledge of the press management that made and sustained "stars." Even though he faced no serious challenge for the Republican nomination in 1960, Nixon still treated the press as an adversary to be contained whereas Kennedy saw it as an ally to be cultivated. In return, the press largely ignored various rumours about JFK's health and personal life.

Nixon lost the 1960 presidential election by a whisker, and as we shall see in chapter 4, when we look at the narrow victory of George W. Bush in 2000, there were rumours of foul play in 1960. Nixon chose to concede, but this did not mean that he didn't feel hard done by. In the aftermath, he grew increasingly resentful of what he saw as the press corps' infatuation with the Kennedys and their photogenic image. Election pundits made much of Kennedy's superior performance in the first-ever televised presidential debate, which had come at a time when Nixon was struggling with injury and ill health, which partly explained his sweaty and shifty performance on screen that night. Radio listeners judged the debate a tie. Brooding on his defeat hardly improved Nixon's opinion of reporters, some of whom like Theodore White in his award-winning *The Making of the President* (1961), made no attempt to disguise their preference for Kennedy.

The rawness of his feelings towards the media, which would shape the Watergate scandal, was also evident during Nixon's ill-judged attempt to bounce back by winning the 1962 California governor's race. Ever since 1952, Nixon had had enemies among state Republicans, and so he did not go into the contest against Democrat Pat Brown with solid conservative backing. Some locals simply disliked the idea that he was just using them to get back into national politics. Nevertheless, the polls showed Nixon ahead going into election day so when he lost by a decisive 5 percent margin, the press had its big story. The day after the election, a hundred reporters gathered at the Beverly Hills Hilton to listen to a tired-looking Nixon deliver an intemperate fifteen-minute monologue. He began by saying that he knew they were all delighted that he had lost, described how they had attacked him ever since the Alger Hiss case, and concluded what he termed his "last press conference," by inviting them to "just think how much you're going to be missing. You don't have Nixon to kick around anymore." As a sore loser, Nixon had given the press a further story and the American TV network *ABC* decided to devote a half-hour special to

Nixon's apparent political demise. The discussants included none other than Alger Hiss, who openly admitted his own lasting resentment at being used to advance Nixon's career. But *ABC* had misjudged the public and its switchboard lit up with complaining viewers and several of the program's sponsors withdrew. At this stage, a section of the public felt inviting Hiss, a convicted perjurer and possible Soviet agent, to participate was scandalous.

Some see this moment as the start of Nixon's comeback. Over the next five years, he recovered his personal finances via a New York law firm, sustained his reputation by writing cogently on foreign policy, and developed the basis for his presidential bid by campaigning for other Republican candidates nationwide. He was patient, and by 1968 his political standing was restored. But politics, or "the arena," as Nixon called it, was a harsh environment. He had to fire five members of his campaign team in 1967 when private investigators discovered they were leaking information to potential rivals. At the same time, he hired new managers with television expertise and especially marketing men who could ensure that the "new Nixon" proved more popular. The Vietnam War was the dominant issue, and as "Johnson's War" it threatened the Democrats most. A beleaguered President Lyndon Johnson announced on 31 March 1968 that he would not seek his party's nomination. The assassination of Martin Luther King, which prompted widespread rioting, and of Bobby Kennedy, who had emerged as a more charismatic alternative to the eventual nominee, Vice-President Hubert Humphrey, ultimately boosted Nixon.

To that section of the public that Nixon would later call the "silent majority," the widespread public disorder over the summer of 1968 was so scary that the "New Nixon" seemed reassuring by comparison. Tough times needed tough guys. His campaign slogan – "Nixon's The One" – the epitome of vagueness – began to resonate. His nebulous commitment to end the war and his definite stress on law and order played well in the polls. However, if President Johnson could make a breakthrough and secure Vietnam peace talks, then, the Democratic nominee Hubert Humphrey would receive a potentially crucial boost. It was a risk, and Nixon was not going to give peace a chance. A campaign operative Anne Chennault spoke secretly to South Vietnamese officials advising them that their interests would be better protected by a Nixon administration. Hence, the talks about talks stalled. Nixon always denied involvement and Johnson feared exposing it at the time since his knowledge came from illegal wiretaps. The campaign move was also illegal, but it remained unknown at the time; it foreshadowed the actions of the Reagan team in relation to the Iran hostage crisis in the days prior to the 1980 election.

The state of the nation when Nixon came into office in 1969 is an important prelude to the Watergate saga. Just as recent commentators have talked about polarized politics in the Trump era, there was a profound sense that America was coming apart during 1968. The anti-war protests had grown into a social movement that reflected and reinforced a growing popular mistrust of Washington, as well as other anxieties. Nixon had always recognized that most people voted with their heart rather than their head, and that anger and fear were two emotions that very clearly stimulated the heart. He empathized since he himself regularly nursed a grievance and suspected a plot. But in 1968 he was largely able to leave the overt stirring of negative feelings to others. Independent candidate, George Wallace, notorious as a defender of segregation as Alabama's governor in the early 1960s, was adept at firing up white, blue-collar populism. While Nixon saw Wallace as a threat if he captured potential Nixon voters, he could still use him to prime voters who had previously voted Democratic, both in the South and among blue-collar white voters more widely, and thus reap the benefit if they ultimately decided to back the more experienced national figure in order to beat Humphrey. Compared to Wallace, Nixon positioned himself as a centrist, offering peace and stability.

The Watergate scandal spiralled partly because of the vendetta between Nixon and the news media. But it was far more rooted in Nixon's character, and in particular, his chronic insecurity. In foreign policy terms, Nixon's threat obsession may have been positive; it persuaded him that nuclear weapons threatened human survival and that détente with the Communists was preferable, especially if you could play China and the USSR off each other. But domestically, his obsession fed his malice. As president, he expected the Internal Revenue Service to audit the accounts of his enemies since he believed that any previous audit of his supporters was down to his political rivals. He expected the FBI and CIA to gather information on his enemies and make life difficult for them. Even after Watergate, Nixon would tell David Frost that something might be illegal, but if the president did it in what he perceived to be the national interest (like getting re-elected), it was not. The reason why the Watergate scandal brought Nixon down was not because it revealed one single instance of wrongdoing but because it demonstrated that abusing power in order to have power was fundamental to how Nixon operated. As a travesty of the Golden Rule, Nixon believed that you should do unto others, as they would do unto you, but do it more harshly and ideally before they had a chance to do anything.

Nixon's insecurity inclined him to secrecy because he generally mistrusted everyone. He wanted his foreign policy to be run by himself and his National Security Adviser, Henry Kissinger. All other policies should be managed by his close aides, chief of staff H.R. Haldeman and domestic policy adviser, John Ehrlichman. They formed what became known as the "palace guard," overseeing every transaction between the Oval Office and the rest of government. From the outset, Haldeman and Ehrlichman understood their boss's desire for secrecy and its corollary, his deep-seated hatred of leaks. It was Ehrlichman who set up a team whose purpose was to protect the president not only by providing political intelligence on his enemies but by stopping leaks. So important was the latter task that they were known as the "plumbers."

The plumbers were busy in 1971 probing the background of an MIT statistician, Daniel Ellsberg, who in 1967 had helped to prepare an internal Defense Department study reviewing US policies in Vietnam. Subsequently, Ellsberg turned against the war and became, in effect, a whistle-blower. In June 1971, he leaked the so-called *Pentagon Papers* to the *New York Times*. Since the documents focused on the decisions and public statements of the Kennedy and Johnson administrations, the leak seemed set to damage Nixon's Democratic predecessors. An ex-CIA man, E. Howard Hunt was assigned to read the *Papers* and identify items that could be used against the Democrats in the 1972 election. But Nixon was uneasy. The liberal media was lionizing Ellsberg for making the documents public. Given his propensity for secrecy, Nixon was outraged. Special Counsel Chuck Colson recalled him ranting: "This government cannot survive, it cannot function, if anyone can run out and leak whatever documents he wants to...." But when the federal government sought an injunction to block further publication of the *Papers*, the US Supreme Court upheld the freedom of the press as guaranteed by the Constitution.

This victory emboldened the political media, which saw itself as the people's defender against devious government to an even greater degree than before. It conversely inflamed Nixon's ill-feeling not just towards the media, but towards the FBI and CIA neither of who were being as helpful to him, he felt, as they had been to his predecessors. An Ehrlichman protégé, Emil Krogh was placed in charge of the Special Investigations Unit as "the plumbers" were officially called, and accepted Colson's suggestion that blackening Ellsberg's reputation would be a good beginning. The real political payoff would be to link Democratic opponents publicly to the notion of a clandestine "counter government" (a "Deep State," to use a later term) undermining America's position in the world. This, too, became a recurring feature in policy-related presidential scandals: loyalists, like Oliver North in the Iran-Contra scandal, insisting that they did bad things only to prevent worse, and frequently linked everything to national security. Colson's aggressiveness was bolstered by another emerging figure: J. Gordon Liddy, an ex-FBI agent, whose career with the Bureau had been marked by high-profile drug raids. Liddy's personality may be gauged by his decision to run a full FBI background check on his fiancée before their marriage in 1957 in what he describes as a "routine precautionary measure."

Watergate would expose just how many precautionary measures had become routine in the Nixon White House. On 3 September 1971, Liddy, Hunt and three others broke into the offices of Ellsberg's psychiatrist Lewis Fielding in search of damaging personal information on his patient. Ellsberg's file failed to provide it and the burglars trashed the office before departing to conceal the break-in's target. Ehrlichman subsequently denied Liddy's proposal that the plumbers break into Ellsberg's home. However, at the same time, the FBI had agreed to tap Ellsberg's phone and caught conversations between him and National Security Council staffer Morton Halperin, who was already suspected of leaking information about the secret bombing of Cambodia, which had begun in March 1969. The FBI had been illegally listening in on Halperin's calls since the *New York Times* reported the bombing in May 1969. Had Colson had his way in 1971, the plumbers would have raided the Brookings Institution (a celebrated Washington think-tank) in search of Halperin's papers. Liddy, too, was offering a wide range of operations under the heading "Operation Gemstone," but these were so extreme that even Haldeman had paled. This illustrates how

Watergate was a scandal that revealed not one incident but a sustained pattern of illegal behaviour. Ironically, when Ellsberg was prosecuted under the Espionage Act in 1973, a mistrial was declared when the court heard the extent of the government's illegal actions against the defendant.

Another facet of presidential scandals that Watergate foreshadows is the proliferation of people involved. There is always a lengthy cast list. One key subgroup in the Watergate scandal was the Committee to Re-elect the President, sometimes referred to by the sinister sounding acronym, CREEP. It included not just Colson, Hunt and Liddy but Nixon's 1968 campaign manager and former US Attorney General John Mitchell, who succeeded another campaign official Jeb Magruder as CREEP director in 1972, as well as another CIA veteran, James McCord, who oversaw security, and Donald Segretti, a political operative, who specialized in what were called "dirty tricks." This portmanteau term might involve creating materials that ostensibly showed that an opponent had said something insulting or done something objectionable. The opponent would then have to respond to the allegation, and this would extend the news cycle. It could also involve such fraternity pranks as removing the shoes left for cleaning outside the hotel rooms of campaign staff or putting laxative in coffee. As CREEP's work intensified in 1972, US Commerce Secretary Maurice Stans resigned his cabinet post and fatefully joined to chair its finance committee. He managed a steady flow of corporate donations, extracted by letting businesses know that failing to give would be punished. One says fatefully because Stans, like other key CREEP figures, faced prosecution because of the Watergate scandal. Nixon, of course, was pardoned.

To understand CREEP, one must understand the thinking behind it. First and foremost, it grew from the conviction that the Democrats were doing the same thing: looking at ways to hamper Nixon's re-election; building up funds to win the election themselves and developing intelligence operations to portray Nixon as negatively as possible. The last is still known as opposition research. As Democratic National Committee chairman, Larry O'Brien embodied the threat Democrats represented for Nixon. A veteran of the 1960 Kennedy campaign team, he became DNC chairman in 1968 and at the same time, just as importantly, he became billionaire, Howard Hughes's Washington lobbyist. Nixon had never forgotten that in 1961 the Justice Department (under Bobby Kennedy) had investigated a loan given by Hughes to Nixon's younger brother Donald. Over a decade later, H.R. Haldeman observed that Nixon "seemed to lose touch with reality" when anything involving Hughes came up. J. Gordon Liddy always insisted that the Watergate break-in was largely about finding out if O'Brien had any real dirt on Nixon rather than getting something on O'Brien or the Democratic challengers.

Thus, the Watergate scandal was above all else, a scandal prompted by a desire to avoid a scandal. But it was also part of the vendetta against O'Brien who, for his part, had accurately argued that the administration's decision not to proceed with an anti-trust prosecution against the International Telephone and Telegraph Company, which had pledged $400,000 to cover the cost of the 1972 Republican National Convention scheduled for San Diego, was strongly suggestive of a *quid pro quo*. Such negative campaigning, portraying your opponent as corrupt or unworthy, was, and remains, an integral part of electioneering, thus ensuring that scandals are continuously sought by rival campaigns who then feed information to the press. There will be many more instances in later chapters. In the Watergate scandal, investigators eventually uncovered a trove of clandestine donations from corporate executives that provided funds first for illegal operations and then for the cover-up.

On 17 June 1972, J. Gordon Liddy and James McCord were among five men arrested attempting to break into the DNC offices in the Watergate. Asked about the incident the next day, White House press secretary Ron Ziegler called it a "third-rate burglary;" but the story was not so easily dismissed. A *Washington Post* report on 1 August disclosed that one of those arrested had campaign manager, Howard Hunt's number in his address book and a traceable check in his bank account; this linked the attempted burglary to the president. These news stories, however, did not have traction in the summer of 1972. The nation was barely aware of the Watergate affair and was more interested in the withdrawal of Democratic nominee George McGovern's vice-presidential choice, Tom Eagleton, following revelations that he had been hospitalized on three separate occasions for acute depression. Mental illness should not be a scandal, but its revelation not only forced Eagleton to step down, but called into question McGovern's decision-making at a time when the liberal-leaning Senator was already facing a barrage of conservative criticism, some of it aided by the CREEP team. On 7 November, the 55 percent of eligible Americans who could be bothered to vote, re-elected Nixon by a landslide, but Democrats not only retained their majority in the House but increased it in the Senate. In partisan terms, this set the political stage for the confrontations over Watergate that followed.

One of Nixon's more plaintive comments about the scandal that brought him down was that he could have survived, if he had been a better butcher, swiftly prepared to sacrifice those most directly involved. As the Iran-Contra scandal will show, an essential aspect of containing any scandal from the standpoint of the administration is deciding how far blame can be accepted while still insisting that the president is not guilty. This largely depends on the willingness of others to suffer in order to protect the president. J. Gordon Liddy was ready to do that, and at an early stage (21 June 1972), Ehrlichman proposed to pass the whole episode off as Liddy's maverick scheme. But Haldeman knew that Nixon campaign manager John Mitchell was also implicated. Worse still, Mitchell's wife, Martha, was famed for her indiscreet gossiping to reporters. It would be hard to stop Martha telling the press what she knew. Later accounts of Mrs Mitchell's forcible abduction and sedation in June 1972 when she was attempting to reveal "dirty tricks" to a reporter on the phone confirm the seriousness with which the White House viewed the situation.

Martha Mitchell was not the only problem; so, too, were the ex-CIA men, James McCord and Howard Hunt. Under indictment, Hunt, almost immediately, pressed his White House bosses for cash payments to cover legal expenses and family support not just for himself but for the other defendants. This drew others, including Nixon's personal lawyer Herbert Kalbach and CREEP donors, into a cover-up operation that supplied these payments. Facing conviction in March 1973, McCord wrote a letter to the presiding Judge John Sirica that confessed that he had been pressurized into pleading guilty in what was a government, but not a CIA, operation. Even before McCord tried to save himself, the cover-up was in trouble.

Containing a presidential scandal that involves illegal acts is easier if the law enforcement agencies are prepared to look away. When Watergate happened, L. Patrick Gray was FBI acting director, pending Senate approval. His selection left assistant director Mark Felt angrily disappointed and he would subsequently steer the press towards the scandal using the codename "Deep Throat." Given Gray's naval background and past service to the administration, Haldeman believed that he would accept an order to stonewall the Bureau's investigation of Watergate if urged to do so by CIA chiefs on national security grounds. Fatefully, when Haldeman outlined this scheme to the President on 23 June 1972, Nixon's automated White House tape machine was running. It was this "smoking gun" moment that answered the Watergate investigator's key questions: "what did the President know and when did he know it?"

CIA director Richard Helms and his deputy Vernon Walters proved reluctant to involve their agency. However, the loyal Gray proved responsive to White House Counsel John Dean who insisted that every detail of the unfolding investigation should be passed to him and that he or others should be present during FBI interviews with White House staff members. As head of the Justice Department's Criminal Division, Henry Petersen was in charge of investigating Watergate until a special prosecutor was appointed in May 1973. He too felt obliged to keep the President's men informed of developments. This effectively stymied the investigation in the months prior to the 1972 election as Dean ran the cover-up operation. On 28 June 1972, he passed to Gray the potentially incriminating contents of a safe belonging to E. Howard Hunt. While they were not Watergate-related, Dean recommended that they should disappear. Gray clearly had misgivings about what he was being asked to do because during his Senate confirmation hearings on 28 February 1973 he disclosed that Dean had monitored the Watergate investigation and that he suspected that Dean may have lied to FBI investigators.

Not surprising after this disclosure, the Senate refused to confirm Gray, and in combination with McCord's letter to Judge Sirica in March, the scandal gathered momentum. In February, after weeks of post-election, Democratic rumination, the Senate had established its Select Committee on Presidential Campaign Activities, generally referred to as the Watergate Committee, chaired by the veteran Democratic Senator from North Carolina, Sam Ervin. The Committee's initial investigations were low-key partly to avoid prejudicing the outcome of various pending trials. However, the Senate investigation, alongside the ongoing Justice Department one, made those involved in the cover-up nervous. It dawned on Dean, for instance, that Nixon's 22 March instruction to prepare a report summarizing his own, internal investigation, which would effectively exonerate the administration, was also a good way to position him as the fall guy, if things went wrong. The next day, the lengthy prison sentences and fines handed down to Hunt, Liddy and the other Watergate burglars underlined the risks Dean ran.

In the hope of protecting himself, Dean began cooperating with federal prosecutors on 6 April. He was able to provide them with details of the cover-up, although this required him to plead the Fifth Amendment when he appeared confidentially before a grand jury. In this respect, Watergate set a pattern as future scandals would also often hinge on the readiness of protagonists to give evidence in return for a plea bargain, if not complete immunity. It also meant that Special Prosecutors would come to regard Congressional investigators as obstacles because they could place stumbling blocks in the way of future prosecutions. Once Dean defected, Watergate was likely to point to Haldeman and Ehrlichman and their closeness to the President made it more likely that Nixon himself knew what was being done in his name. By the end of April 1973, the Watergate scandal was starting to claim a growing list of senior White House officials: Gray resigned on 27 April, and on 30 April, under pressure from Nixon, so, too, did Haldeman and Ehrlichman. Although he had refused J. Gordon Liddy's demand to release the Watergate burglars, Attorney-General Richard Kleindienst also resigned. Having changed sides, John Dean was fired.

As Nixon sensed, the removal of these figures was no longer enough to kill off the scandal. There had to be action to show the public that the President wanted to find the truth, and two days after Sam Ervin's Watergate Committee began its televised hearings on 17 May, a prominent lawyer with Democratic ties, Archibald Cox, was appointed Special Prosecutor. Cox was far from Nixon's preferred candidate but the new Attorney General Elliot Richardson (who had agreed to appoint a Special Prosecutor during his own Senate ratification) hoped that Cox's Democratic background would boost his, and hence the administration's, credibility. The Special Prosecutor was to become a fixture of subsequent presidential scandals, but the role was never an easy one since it implied that there was a question-mark over the ability of existing agencies to investigate thoroughly any wrong-doing in the Executive Branch of which they remained a part.

This was certainly the case for Cox who never established a positive relationship with the FBI team of prosecutors who had already begun to piece together the Watergate story. Despite assurances that he would be able to work without interference, Cox also had to wrestle with Nixon's new legal defence team, which insisted that certain documents were protected by what was known as "executive privilege." The concept meant that documents relating to current discussions of policy within the White House must remain confidential so that all staff could speak freely without worrying that their words would reach a wider audience for which they were not intended. Finally, Cox had to navigate an increasingly partisan contest for public opinion.

The decision to televise the Senate hearings was clearly intended by Democrats to ensure that the American people could hear for themselves what the Nixon White House had done in the run-up to the 1972 election. With Carl Bernstein and Bob Woodward of the *Washington Post* taking the lead, fresh stories about the extent of the cover-up were breaking by June 1973, notably about the numerous occasions on which the President had met with John Dean to discuss Watergate. When Dean gave his televised testimony on June 25, he portrayed a White House driven by a paranoid fear of its Democratic opponents. He also offered a memorable metaphor for Nixon's situation, relating how he had told the President that there was a cancer growing in his presidency that must be removed or it would kill it. He provided a detailed narrative of the decision to raid the DNC offices and just as importantly, he recounted the elaborate steps taken to cover up and frustrate the investigation with hush money payments and the destruction of evidence. By the time he concluded his testimony only 46 percent of Gallup respondents said they would still vote for Nixon against McGovern, a drop of sixteen points since the November 1972 election.

The next big story broke on 13 July when Nixon's former appointments secretary Alexander Butterfield revealed to the Watergate Committee that conversations and phone calls were routinely tape-recorded in Nixon's office. If anything could answer the question posed by moderate Republican Senator Howard Baker of Tennessee: "What did the President know and when did he know it?" – then, these tapes could. The tapes also epitomized a recurrent feature of the politics of presidential scandals: namely, that the president normally wishes to limit what investigators get to see and any blanket request for documentation will be denied. The separation of powers built into the US system of government assumes and, in some respects, amplifies mistrust. Thus, when both the Senate and the Special Prosecutor requested the tapes on 23 July, Nixon refused to provide them, and the issue would work its way to the US Supreme Court but would take a year to do so. Along the way it would emerge that there was a gap in one tape of more than eighteen minutes supposedly caused by Rosemary Wood, the White House secretary who accidentally pressed delete. Experts were never able to duplicate her technique.

The summer of 1973 saw a fateful deterioration in Nixon's political position, which ultimately would decide how the scandal ended. Congressional opponents of the conflict in South-East Asia (so-called "doves") were now strong enough to insert conditions on funding for the war into defence appropriations. This complicated Nixon's relations with conservative "hawks" who were more often Republicans and they began to complain that Nixon was selling out to the liberals as he tried to stifle the Watergate investigation. Since the public hearings had secured a growing audience across the three TV networks, voters had become familiar with the unfolding scandal and Nixon's popular support had drained. He tried a counterattack, telling the nation on 15 August 1973, that he had no prior knowledge of the break-in and had neither known about nor participated in a cover-up. He pleaded that the Watergate obsession was "causing this Nation to neglect matters of far greater importance to all of the American people;" an argument that would be regularly replayed in later scandals. His words fell on largely deaf ears: more than 70 percent of those polled believed that he was still withholding key information, and less than a third were convinced that he was not involved in the cover-up.

This increased the demand for the tapes, which Nixon insisted could not be released without jeopardizing the whole confidential basis of government and policy making. Given Nixon's reputation, some pondered why he had not had the tapes destroyed. Watergate committee chairman Sam Ervin detected the workings of providence, but others sensed that Nixon still hoped that executive privilege would allow him to use the tapes selectively in a way that exonerated him personally. With hindsight, both Nixon and Haldeman's successor as chief of staff, Alexander Haig, felt that the revelation that there had been tapes, but that they had been destroyed, would have been taken as proof of guilt. In protracted negotiations about access to the taped material, a compromise was proposed on September 13 that suggested that Special Prosecutor Cox and the President's legal representative could listen to the tapes together. Nixon's counsel, Fred Buzhardt, offered to prepare "written summaries" of the tapes, but Cox responded that at least in the pre-trial phase, only vetted verbatim transcripts would be accepted. Cox's insistence on full transcripts, alongside his pursuit of other issues such as the ballooning federal expenditures on Nixon's San Clemente home, incensed the already deeply distrustful President.

As fall approached, another political scandal briefly eclipsed Watergate, while also having a clear bearing on its outcome. Used by Nixon to attack the press and liberals, Vice President Spiro T. Agnew had never enjoyed any rapport with the President, who was known to joke that Agnew was his insurance against assassination, implying that even an assassin would hesitate to put Agnew in charge. By the summer of 1973, the *Wall Street Journal* had learned of a grand jury investigation relating to Agnew's time as governor of Maryland, which confirmed more than a year of its own probing into the then governor's dubious dealings with state contractors. Initially, Agnew strenuously denied everything, but Attorney General Richardson warned that the Justice Department's assessment was that Maryland authorities had a cut-and-dried case proving corruption. By the end of September 1973, the administration let Congressional figures know that it did not support Agnew's request that, as a sitting vice-president, he should be impeached before Congress rather than prosecuted through the courts.

Already the Justice Department's Henry Petersen had drafted a resignation statement in which Agnew would admit that as Maryland's governor he had received payments from contractors in receipt of state funds. Chief of Staff Haig had also heard that the IRS had spotted irregularities in Agnew's tax returns and recognizing his untenable position, Agnew's own lawyers began plea bargaining. On October 10, Agnew pleaded "no contest" in a federal courtroom to a charge of tax evasion. Several hours earlier he had delivered a written message to the Secretary of State. It read: "I hereby resign the Office of Vice-President of the United States effective immediately." His departure was a double blow to Nixon. Not only did the taint of wrongdoing increase growing public mistrust, but the removal of Agnew removed a brake on impeachment proceedings. As early as July 1973, there was gossip on Capitol Hill that while Nixon might be guilty, the alternative of Agnew as president was just unthinkable. Two days later, following consultation with senior Congressional figures, the White House nominated House Minority Leader Gerald Ford as vice-president under the terms of the Twenty-Fifth Amendment. The choice was approved by both houses by December 6 and Ford was duly sworn in. Nixon's assassination insurance policy was gone.

In the interim, the vestiges of credibility surrounding Nixon had been torn irreparably by what was known as the "Saturday Night Massacre." Even as Ford was named to replace Agnew, the legal struggle over the Nixon tapes turned sharply against him as the Circuit Court of Appeals ruled in favour of Special Prosecutor Cox's subpoena. When Attorney-General Richardson met with Haig on October 15, he learned that while the President accepted that an "authenticated" version of the subpoenaed tapes must be prepared, he had also decided to fire Cox and thereby, as the jargon goes, render the case moot. Richardson warned that if Cox were fired, he would feel compelled to resign himself. In subsequent phone calls the two discussed who would authenticate the tapes and Richardson agreed to confer with the Special Prosecutor. Cox sensed that the underlying aim was to limit his investigations in ways that contradicted Richardson's previous assurances that he would have a free hand.

At a press conference on Saturday 20 October, Cox began by insisting that he was not out to "get the President," but went on to reaffirm the need for Nixon to obey the court order. In Cox's view, any prior evaluation and selection of the taped materials compromised their value as evidence and the administration's request that no further subpoenas be allowed violated the guidelines agreed for the Special Prosecutor's role and made it impossible for him to fulfil the mandate he had been given. Responding to questions, Cox conceded that the president retained the power to dismiss a Special Prosecutor. When Richardson took Haig's call shortly thereafter telling him to fire Cox, he responded by asking to see the president in person. In their meeting, Nixon urged Richardson not to resign amid the unfolding Middle East crisis (Kissinger was engaged in shuttle diplomacy to end the Yom Kippur War). Undeterred, both Richardson and his deputy William Ruckelhaus refused to fire Cox and instead submitted their own resignations. Having considered resigning himself but being urged by his departing superiors to ensure some continuity at an increasingly demoralized Justice Department, Solicitor-General Robert Bork agreed to carry out Nixon's order. Soon televised images of FBI agents sealing the Special Prosecutor's office and barring access to his staff caused consternation across the nation. As a spectacle, the episode deeply damaged Nixon's already tarnished public image; it also foreshadowed later scandals.

The rest of the autumn saw Nixon trying vainly to delay and limit the release of the tapes while making a similarly vain attempt to boost public support. At a press conference on 26 October, he announced that he would appoint a new Special Prosecutor, but complained of "outrageous, vicious, distorted" reporting, and then contradicted himself by saying he did not blame anybody for the inaccurate news coverage. "Tricky Dicky" lacked Donald Trump's gift for vitriol, even if he shared his sentiments towards media critics. When pressed to clarify, Nixon could not resist the urge to lash out. The press should not assume they angered him, he declared, because "one can only be angry with those he respects." His eventual appointment of Leon Jaworski as Cox's replacement restored little trust. Ultimately, the following spring when Nixon refused Jaworski's subpoena for sixty-four taped conversations, Jaworski requested immediate consideration of the constitutional issues by the US Supreme Court, expediting the appeals process. Meanwhile, over twenty impeachment-related resolutions were introduced in the House, culminating in Judiciary Committee Chair Peter Rodino being asked to proceed. Ominously, there were already Republican Congressmen who admitted publicly that recent events had eroded their trust in the President. Privately, they alluded to the absolute storm of negative mail they had received. Despite the televised images of sealed and guarded offices from October 20, new FBI director Clarence Kelley was determined to avoid even the appearance of participating in any cover-up. The Bureau must survive, even if the Nixon Presidency was doomed. By 17 November 1973, when Nixon told television cameras "I am not a crook" – the general disbelief was tangible.

Guilty pleas by former Nixon aides were the main milestones in the scandal in early 1974. Herbert Kalmbach, who had overseen hush money payments to the Watergate defendants pleaded guilty to two charges of illegal campaign activities on 25 February; the latter included essentially auctioning an ambassadorship. More importantly, his testimony to Congress left a strong impression on Republican members of the House Judiciary Committee who would later vote in support of the articles of impeachment in July. They felt Kalmbach's trust had been abused by those above him. On 18 March, the Committee received the sealed report of the grand jury that indicted seven of the President's close associates including Mitchell, Ehrlichman and Haldeman; it named Nixon as an unindicted co-conspirator. Still intent on releasing the tapes only in a form that suited Nixon's cause, the White House offered the Committee edited transcripts on April 30, but only the unexpurgated versions would be accepted.

The released transcripts did not help Nixon; instead, they further scandalized some because they appeared to reveal that in private the President was a veritable "potty mouth." In the transcripts, a belated sense of etiquette meant that all instances of "bad language" were replaced by the term "expletive deleted," which rapidly became the comedic phrase of the moment. Since the term replaced plosives of the mildest variety like "damn" or "Christ!" it gave the impression that the nation's President spent his working day emitting a torrent of foul language. Equally damaging, there were inexplicable gaps in the record. In the *New York Times*, William Safire felt that by revealing Nixon's "dark side," the transcripts were likely to convince the public that he was "guilty of conduct unbecoming a president." By May, the White House had begun to shift from a straight denial of presidential involvement to the broader question of whether Nixon's actions reached the level required for impeachment. House Republicans felt that they needed to have the full tapes to make that judgment.

Particularly after a first term in which he had reopened relations with China, negotiated with the USSR, and implemented several key regulatory policies on affirmative action and environmental protection, Nixon was not cherished to say the least by conservatives of the Goldwater-Reagan stripe. Appealing to a slightly different segment of the American public, perhaps, advance excerpts from Bernstein and Woodward's *All the President's Men* appeared in *Playboy* magazine. Later serialization in more mainstream newspapers ensured that on its June publication, the book was an immediate and enduring bestseller. More surprisingly transcripts of the Nixon tapes also hit the bestseller list. Scandal is frequently a boon for the publishing industry. Party disunity and public disaffection had reached a point that the scandal had now metastasized into a lethal, political threat to Nixon. On 24 July 1974, the US Supreme Court gave its decision in *United States* v. *Nixon*, which ordered the release of the subpoenaed tapes, even as it gave some legal standing to the concept of executive privilege. The next day the Judiciary Committee was ready to consider in public session the articles of impeachment. Ranking Republican Edward Hutchinson noted that impeachment was always a political act and warned that the proven offense must be of sufficient gravity to warrant removal from office.

The first article charged that the President had violated his oath of office by obstructing and impeding the implementation of justice; a process he had sworn to faithfully uphold. This charge would reappear in the later impeachment trials of Clinton and Trump. Article II charged Nixon with abuse of power through a variety of federal agencies and in defiance of his constitutional duty. Shrewd observers listened attentively to the Republicans and Southern Democrats on the committee whose votes might yet save Nixon. Future Senator William Cohen of Maine was forthright, declaring "no man should be able to bind our destiny, our perpetuation, our success, with the chains of his personal destiny." To save himself, Nixon had weakened the republic. Freshman Virginia Congressman Caldwell Butler whose victory had been ascribed to Nixon's popularity with conservative Democrats admitted that he was dismayed by colleagues who seemed ready to rationalize away corruption by saying that the President's deeds were wrong but not bad enough to warrant impeachment. As a party that had so often campaigned for cleaner politics, Republicans should acknowledge: "Watergate is our shame." By the end of July, a third article, focused largely on Nixon's systematic refusal to comply with Congressional requests for information, was added to amplify the primary charge of obstruction. Nixon knew by that stage that he could not rely on the support of his own party and a Harris poll of August 2 showed 66 percent of Americans favouring impeachment.

On 5 August 1974, the White House released the damning tape transcript of 23 June 1972 – the so-called "smoking gun" tape in which Haldeman and Nixon conferred on how to use the CIA to squash the Watergate investigation. To cover themselves, Haig and Nixon's legal counsel James St Clair insisted to Special Prosecutor Leon Jaworski that they had not known the contents of this tape. With eyes anxiously watching the looming mid-term elections in November, Republicans responded to Nixon's tepid words of regret with sorrow and fury. On August 7, Nixon reluctantly met with senior Republicans who bluntly told him that he should resign and do so immediately since the probability was that he would become the first president to be removed from office if he were tried in the Senate. The next day in a televised address, Nixon resigned the presidency. The scandal had brought him down and he remains the only president to resign because of scandal.

However, the scandal was not finished. Gerald Ford took the oath of office on August 9 and spoke to the country about how theirs was a republic in which the people rule through a government of laws not men. He promised openness and presented himself as a model of the honesty and trustworthiness that he wanted to instil. Initially, Ford's performance earned praise from many sides, although below the surface, factionalism inside the Republican Party and between Nixon loyalists and Ford's new team in the administration simmered. Writing in the *New Republic*, Nathan Lewin defined the dilemma that would torpedo Ford's hopes of success. "What possible explanation will there ever be," he wrote, "if history records that those who acted on Nixon's instructions, express or implied, were charged and convicted of crimes and went to jail while their chief spent his retirement years strolling the Pacific beaches, writing about his accomplishments in foreign policy and lecturing to college audiences."

This was largely what occurred after President Ford granted Nixon a full, free and absolute pardon on 8 September 1974. The explanation of history has been to echo Ford's own reasoning and that of Special Prosecutor Leon Jaworski. Ford quickly became convinced that any attempt to prosecute Nixon would consume the nation for probably years to come, delaying the vital task of rebuilding national morale. Jaworski believed that a decent legal team would be able to argue strongly that it was impossible for Nixon to receive a fair and impartial trial as the law required. Ford also believed that accepting a pardon implicitly signalled an acknowledgement of guilt. Historians generally accept that Ford did the right thing, but that he did it hastily and clumsily without cultivating enough political and public support to ensure that it became an act of closure rather than just another twist in the scandal. In his first month in office Ford had achieved a 70 percent public approval rating. The day after he announced the pardon, polls reported, it had plunged to 48 percent.

One is left with the sad paradox that Nixon, who was certainly guilty of many abuses of power, did not suffer the full consequences of his illegal actions, while Ford, whose actions were not, as some alleged, part of a corrupt bargain to secure the presidency for himself, but rather a sincere attempt to hasten a return to normality, was stained with scandal and regarded as little different to his predecessors. Ford's press secretary, Jerry terHorst, whom he had failed to keep in the loop as he wrestled with the pardon decision, resigned in protest, pointedly observing that mercy, like justice, should be even-handed. When Ford appeared in public the day after the pardon announcement, there were cries of "Jail Ford!" The following day, the Senate passed a resolution opposing any more Watergate pardons and the House demanded an investigation. By mid-October, Ford felt compelled to appear in person before a House subcommittee, becoming the first modern president to so testify. He explained that during a meeting with Chief of Staff Alexander Haig on August 1, Haig had outlined the pardon options, but Ford had insisted that he would decide solely in the national interest, and he baldly placed on record: "There was no deal, period, under no circumstances." In the November mid-term elections, despite desperate campaigning by Ford, the Republicans lost heavily to the Democrats who increased their Congressional majorities, gaining four seats in the Senate and forty-nine in the House.

Still trying to clean up the White House's image, while still facing a hostile press, Ford appointed a presidential commission headed by his Vice-President Nelson Rockefeller to investigate CIA activities inside the US. Its 1975 report confirmed that there had been extensive domestic surveillance and harassment. The main outcome was to reveal more scandals and to prompt Congress to authorize its own multi-agency investigation of improper governmental actions – referred to as the Church Committee after its chairman, Idaho Senator Frank Church. This, in turn, and perhaps inevitably, revealed more secret, and morally suspect, actions – the overthrow of governments and the killing of foreign leaders – prompting Ford to issue Executive Order 11905 on 18 February 1976, to improve oversight of the intelligence agencies and to ban the assassination of foreign leaders. The latter has subsequently been "relaxed" to permit the US to target foreign nationals associated with terrorism. The multi-volume Church Report in April also documented the systematic surveillance and harassment of US citizens that the Rockefeller Report had uncovered and left most Americans unsure of their government's trustworthiness. The sense that the outcome of the Watergate scandal vindicated America's democratic institutions was tempered by a sense that many wrongs had gone unpunished for decades.

When Georgia Governor Jimmy Carter won the Democratic nomination in 1976 and ran as a Washington "outsider" untainted by recent events, his promise that he would never lie to the American people resonated and he secured victory. Those Republicans who had survived the Watergate scandal intact, often Ford's appointees, such as CIA director George H.W. Bush, and Defense Secretary Donald Rumsfeld, returned to prominence during the Reagan years. Bush, of course, became Reagan's vice-president and was able to win the 1988 election, despite the Iran-Contra scandal, while Rumsfeld mixed corporate business and international relations in ways that fed rumours about the murky realities of US foreign policy, notably in the Middle East. As president, Bush would appoint Rumsfeld's protégé, Dick Cheney, as his Defense Secretary in 1989 and Cheney would then become vice-president in 2001, playing a large role in the presidency of Bush's son, G.W. Even some of the lower-level operatives within CREEP like Lucianne Goldberg and Roger Stone would reappear in the scandals of the Clinton and Trump eras.

A key part of Watergate's legacy was public mistrust. In 1978 Congress passed the Ethics in Government Act to provide a legal framework for holding government accountable and getting to the truth of alleged scandals. Title VI established the office of Special Prosecutor, whose appointment could be requested by either House or Senate, who would be chosen by an independent legal panel, and who could not be easily fired by the president. Subsequently renamed independent counsels, Special Prosecutors were appointed in every administration from Carter to Clinton. They would vex Clinton, but in 1999 the task of appointing and retaining them was returned to the Justice Department. A celebrated recent example was Robert Mueller who was appointed in 2017 to investigate reports of Russian interference in the 2016 presidential election. Mueller's conclusion that he could not prosecute a sitting president under Justice Department guidelines has not strengthened American faith in government accountability, but the changed levels in public trust wrought by Watergate may well have made that impossible. Alongside Vietnam, and other blows to public confidence, Watergate helped to create a popular belief in "hidden facts," "conspiracies," government "black ops" and the "Deep State." In the contemporary era, the traditional idea that scandal involves exposing the truth exists within a fragmented media landscape where partisans present "alternate facts" and dismiss "fake news."

Watergate remains, however, the classic presidential scandal and the public's partial recollection of it continues to shape the ways in which current scandals are judged. A key part of the memory of Watergate is its celebration of investigative journalism. Although no journalists have achieved Carl Bernstein and Bob Woodward's legendary status, their fame still fuels the search for the next presidential scandal, and the reaction of the Nixon White House has provided a playbook for later presidents. As we shall see, the press is typically accused of inaccuracy and prejudice. As news breaks, denial of the scandal shifts to justification with an emphasis, wherever possible, that what happened was not self-interested but done in the national interest (often national security), and where this is either impossible or not persuasive, the ground shifts again to the twin claims that pursuing the scandal is a distraction from the more important priorities that the president was elected to address and that the specific wrongdoing was a "rogue" or maverick operation by subordinates.

Watergate also showed that the impact of a presidential scandal is affected by the strength of the rival parties. If the 1972 elections had produced a Republican rather than a Democratic Congress, one suspects there would have been less momentum behind the investigation of Watergate. The separation of powers under the Constitution rests on a view of human nature that is rooted in the idea that power corrupts. The Founders were also wary of political parties because they feared that they might create ties that could negate the system of "checks and balances" by making Congress and/or the Court co-dependent on the president. In both the Clinton and Trump cases, impeachment votes went almost entirely along party lines and hence impeachment failed. They were impeached but not removed from office.

Watergate also affected ideas about the presidency itself. It unfolded in the context of the *Pentagon Papers* which revealed that previous presidents had lied about Vietnam. It was followed by revelations of the wide-ranging misuse of law enforcement and intelligence agencies at home and abroad. Together, such revelations produced the idea of an "imperial presidency," dangerous and unaccountable. But Watergate itself was also very much about Richard Nixon. The "New Nixon" of 1968 and 1972 was certainly a more sellable candidate than the Nixon of 1960 but he was never as charming or likeable as Ronald Reagan or Bill Clinton, and he never had as fanatical a base of support as Donald Trump has retained. As the classic presidential scandal, therefore, Watergate confirms that the significance of a scandal always depends on which president is involved.

The Watergate break-in occurred on 17 June 1972, and Nixon resigned on 9 August 1974, and the more than three years in-between reveals another key aspect of presidential scandals: they tend to go on and on, and on. The struggle to expose or conceal what happened not only takes time and resources, but it also affects the public mood. This explains why President Ford wanted to pardon Nixon and move on, and it may also help to explain why the lengthy investigations into Iran-Contra failed to retain general public interest the way Watergate had. In the accelerated news cycle of the internet era, the scandals that have resulted in impeachment – Clinton's and Trump's – have been episodes expedited by party loyalties and in some sense, a public desire to finish the story. But Watergate still provides the blueprint for making a scandal into a major event through the dogged pursuit of evidence, whether by a Special Prosecutor or a Congressional investigation; often both. Evidence of a cover-up is taken as evidence of original guilt; otherwise, why the cover-up? It is sometimes claimed that if a traffic cop stops you, he can always find a reason to write you a ticket. By the same token, if a president is subjected to enough relentless scrutiny, there will be evidence that not every action has been proper. In this way, the different aspects of Watergate continued to work in later scandals. A hostile press, a partisan atmosphere, a cynical public, and a suspect character are more likely to generate presidential scandals because they fuel precisely the kind of scrutiny that undercovers scandal. At the same time, scandals often reveal that the presidency attracts people whose self-confidence can sometimes slide into a belief that the rules don't apply to them as they do to ordinary mortals.

Watergate is often seen as the classic example of "dirty tricks." As we have seen, it was partly driven by Nixon's conviction that his campaign had to use all the tactics that his Democratic opponents might use against him. This suggests that there is something about the process of getting elected that pushes campaign teams to use tactics that they don't want publicly known. Nixon referred to politics as the "arena" and like Donald Trump, or indeed most politicians, he relished the fact that in politics, as in sports, there are clear winners and losers. Winning generates a sense of validation and entitlement. Presidents believe they have been given a mandate to govern, whereas the US Constitution delegates that process across three branches of government. In the next chapter, we will see how the conviction that the president's policy must be implemented can result in scandal.

Chapter 2

Iran-Contra: Some Presidents Have More Teflon Than Others

When it erupted in 1986 during President Reagan's second term, the Iran-Contra controversy was the biggest scandal since Watergate. If Watergate revealed that Richard Nixon had both known and condoned his campaign's efforts to gather information by illegal means to help his re-election bid, then Iran-Contra likewise showed that Ronald Reagan was equally prepared to pursue his foreign policy goals illicitly, when Congress blocked his way. In both cases, therefore, one can argue that the president violated his constitutional oath to uphold the law, and instead used executive powers to escape the legal restrictions placed upon him. The outcome of the two scandals, however, shows a stark contrast: Nixon resigned in disgrace, whereas Reagan saw out his two full terms, was succeeded by his vice-president George H.W. Bush, and continues to enjoy widespread acclaim as the most successful Republican President of the modern era and is a hero for many American Republicans.

The Constitution was designed deliberately to set the three branches of government – Congress, Presidency, and Supreme Court – as checks against one another. This was a recipe for mistrust and coincidentally, for accusations of scandalous behaviour. Every president swears an oath: "I do solemnly swear [or affirm] that I will faithfully execute the Office of President of the United States, and will to the best of my Ability, preserve, protect and defend the Constitution of the United States." This is a binding commitment to uphold the law in accordance with the Supreme Court's judgment of what is constitutionally permitted. Presidents do not get to choose the laws or legal judgments they enforce, but the scrutiny they apply, and the eagerness with which they ensure compliance, has certainly varied. This inconsistency is especially visible when Congress is not controlled by the president's own party or when a Supreme Court judgment is controversial among sections of the public on whose support the president relies. Donald Trump, for instance, showed a strong reluctance to prioritize the staffing of regulatory agencies that clashed with business interests and used executive orders to pursue policies that were unable to secure Congressional backing. His administration assiduously appointed conservative-minded federal judges at all levels, and he openly complained about, and in some cases, fired career government employees in different agencies, if he felt that they showed insufficient loyalty to him.

Iran-Contra was always likely to play differently than Watergate had with the American public because it dealt with foreign policy. Wary of how kings could involve their nations in war, the Founding Fathers tried to ensure that foreign policy was in key ways managed by both Congress and President, although once the US became a nuclear super-power, the latter's position as commander-in-chief and the growing importance of the departments of State and Defense ensured that the initiative mostly stayed with the White House. During the Cold War, new agencies like the National Security Council (NSC) and Central Intelligence Agency (CIA) became powerful instruments of presidential policymaking. The vital issues of war and peace nevertheless remained a source of mistrust and accusation. Typically, the longer and more costly a conflict became, the more likely it was that opposition would grow. Public dissent over Vietnam made it unrealistic for Lyndon Johnson to seek re-election in 1968 and boosted his successor Richard Nixon's innate desire to elude public scrutiny and congressional oversight. As we have seen, it was the publication of the *Pentagon Papers* in 1971 that triggered the Nixon team's pursuit of Daniel Ellsberg, which included having the future Watergate burglars break into his psychiatrist's office. As Watergate unfolded in July 1974, revelations about the secret bombing of Cambodia prompted Congressman John Conyers to introduce a resolution calling for Nixon's impeachment for the unauthorized use of military force, but this charge was never able to get the level of support that alarm over Nixon's domestic wrongdoing commanded. Subsequent revelations in the mid-1970s about the many covert activities of the CIA strengthened the view that an "imperial presidency" had broken free from the congressional oversight that the Constitution required. This anxiety still shaped the political scene when Ronald Reagan became

President in 1981, but as we shall see, Watergate also played a part in his escape from impeachment.

President Jimmy Carter's failure to secure the release of Americans held hostage after the storming of the US Embassy in Iran partly explains his loss to Reagan. It's not surprising therefore that when Iranian-backed militant groups such as Islamic Jihad and Hezbollah took Americans hostage in Lebanon after 1982, Reagan was so keen to secure their release that he was drawn to the idea that elements in the Iranian regime might be induced to facilitate their freedom. Describing the pressures on Reagan to get the hostages home safely, former National Security Adviser Brent Scowcroft recalled the Lebanon hostage situation as a "running sore politically." During the 1980 campaign, Carter had fought the perception that his foreign policy, which had included reducing support for regimes with bad human rights records, had weakened America internationally and allowed the Soviets and others to seize the initiative. Meanwhile, Reagan, known as a staunch anti-Communist, had expressed deep concern about the Communist threat in Central America. He depicted Nicaragua's Sandinista regime as little more than a springboard for Soviet-backed Communist infiltration. Accordingly, he felt that the US must back the Sandinistas' opponents, the so-called Contras, in every way possible. Almost as soon as he took office, he cancelled economic aid to the Nicaraguan government, and in November 1981, he signed a National Security Directive (or finding), authorizing covert support for the Contras. Congressional Democrats complained that this was just the kind of approach that in the 1960s had led to the Vietnam War. They argued that the Communist threat in Central America grew out of the conspicuous social and economic inequality in countries like Nicaragua and its neighbours, and the often-brutal actions of the authoritarian governments in these countries. Reagan regarded all such talk as symptomatic of "Vietnam Syndrome," which now hampered American foreign policy. In his view, a weakened resolve to fight Communism, reflected in the CIA's diminished capability to take covert measures due to post-Watergate reforms, prevented America from defending its vital interests in the continuing Cold War. To the alarm of critics and delight of his supporters, Reagan was determined to reverse this trend. Here lay the origins of Iran-Contra.

Like Nixon before him, Reagan believed that his opponents were damaging the national interests which he defined in his own ideological terms. The reality that the Iran-Contra scandal could not be detached from key policy differences between the White House and Capitol Hill affected the way the scandal was perceived by the public. Presidential scandals are rarely detached from partisan battles. If one selects scandals based on what outrages Democrats or Republicans, then every administration has them. Tax cuts that benefit the richest outrage progressive Democrats, and "Obamacare" or the Iranian nuclear deal have more recently outraged conservative Republicans. But what made Iran-Contra the biggest scandal of the immediate post-Watergate era was that it clearly revealed illegal and unconstitutional behaviour: the use of American governmental power in ways that went outside the constitutional checks and balances. Along the way, it revealed moments of sheer incompetence and corruption that were scandalous in themselves. Yet, the scandal resulted in neither impeachment nor resignation. Despite multiple investigations, Reagan's historical reputation as perhaps the greatest or most influential president since Franklin D. Roosevelt remains intact.

On 15 July 1987, Admiral John Poindexter, who had served as Reagan's National Security Advisor testified to Congress about the decision to operate a highly clandestine policy of support for the Contras and admitted: "I made a very deliberate decision not to ask the President so that I could insulate him from the decision and provide some future deniability for the President if it ever leaked out… "On this whole issue," he concluded, "the buck stops with me." While setting himself up to protect the President, Poindexter also assured his interrogators that he had worked closely with the President and was convinced that he understood his thinking. The diversion of funds to support the Contras, forbidden by Congress, was not "a secret foreign policy," as critics alleged, but simply a way of implementing the President's policy of supporting the Contras that reflected the policies he had promised if elected. Poindexter thus made himself the "fall guy" for misdeeds that may have originated with his boss. Given the way Donald Trump similarly derided criticism of his policies as signifying a failure to put America first, Iran-Contra proved a steppingstone towards a presidency where staff should be loyal to their president rather than to the Constitution.

While Poindexter's testimony served to protect Reagan in crucial ways, it underlined how Iran-Contra resurrected the question that had been made famous during the Watergate hearings: what did the President know and when did he know it? Ironically, the question was first posed by Howard Baker, a Republican member of the Watergate Committee, who later became a key figure in Reagan's scandal-containment efforts. Although Poindexter was the figure most likely to implicate the President, the testimony of Oliver North was also central to how the scandal unfolded in the eyes of the public. An aide on the National Security Council, and a Vietnam veteran, he testified before Congress in his military dress uniform to emphasize his patriotism. North was a key player in both the efforts to trade arms for hostages in the Middle East and to provide vital support and resources to the Contras in Central America after Congress limited aid in 1984. He can be compared to J. Gordon Liddy among the Watergate burglars. Like Liddy, he showed a dogged commitment to his masters' goals and an erratic degree of competence. Both men were prepared to come up with elaborate plans to win their superiors' admiration. Much of the time, their plans produced more problems than solutions. If Liddy's wilder schemes were blocked by senior figures in the Nixon re-election campaign, North was allowed to roam on a loose leash by CIA director, William Casey, whose death amid the scandal left many details lost forever. North admitted acting in ways that were illegal and being involved in the destruction of evidence, yet his public testimony made him a hero in the eyes of many Republicans and instead of imprisonment and ignominy, he has enjoyed a subsequent career of media prominence and renown. In this sense, he, too, is a milestone on the road to Trump.

The Iran-Contra controversy stemmed partly from a persistent problem in the modern presidency: namely, the tension between the State Department, headed by the Secretary of State, and staffed by career international relations specialists, and the National Security Council (NSC), led by the National Security Advisor (NSA), which often looks for more immediate foreign policy successes for the administration. Secretary George Shultz felt compelled to offer his resignation to Reagan on more than one occasion because he felt that the official US policy of non-negotiation with terrorist hostage takers was not being followed. Through its ambassadors and consuls, the US was seeking to deter other nations from selling arms to Iran, which was at war with its neighbour, Iraq. Yet Shultz was aware that the NSC and CIA were simultaneously considering ways of supplying Iran with arms clandestinely via Israel in order to induce the Iranians to pressurize Lebanese terror groups into releasing American hostages. He pointed out the obvious: if a hostage were worth a fortune in weapons, paying that fortune would quickly encourage the taking of more hostages. In much the same way, the State Department was involved in negotiations with the Sandinista government in Nicaragua and neighbouring states to stabilize the region. But President Reagan, and more hawkish figures in the NSC and CIA were determined to back the Contras' paramilitary operations; a fact that greatly hampered diplomatic efforts. Oliver North was part of a faction whose support for the Contras made any improvement in relations with the Sandinista regime seem a setback, even while US diplomats strove to achieve just such an improvement.

In early 1984, North helped to draft an NSC directive that proposed to supplement the flagging US support for the Contras by securing third-nation or private donations on their behalf. The then NSA, Robert McFarlane, realized that such a presidential directive would be seen as deliberately circumventing congressional resolutions, which limited such support, and he dropped the wording, from the directive, but not the idea. In May 1984, he discussed the administration's predicament with Saudi Prince Bandar Bin Sultan, who, "as a humanitarian gesture," agreed to supply the Contras with $1million a month for the remainder of the year. It was North who then advised Contra leader, Adolf Calero, to set up an offshore account for these funds, and this money-laundering operation became the basis for what was known as the Enterprise. The National Security Planning Group (NSPG) discussed the new initiative on 25 June 1984. Defense Secretary Caspar Weinberger and UN Ambassador Jeanne Kirkpatrick endorsed the idea and the CIA's Bill Casey even suggested that Reagan personally solicit donations, even offering increased US economic aid as an inducement to friendly nations. George Shultz, on the other hand, was firmly opposed. He warned that for the president to pursue foreign money in order to evade the appropriation of funds, constitutionally the exclusive prerogative of Congress, was an impeachable offense. Reagan was not dissuaded, and he reminded colleagues that their discussion was highly confidential. If word leaked out about the new initiative, he joked, "they'd all be hanging by their thumbs outside the White House" until the leaker confessed. The arrangement with Saudi Arabia went unreported, and when Congress cut off Contra aid in October 1984, efforts to secure alternate funding were stepped up.

Getting aid to the Contras and enabling them to carry the war to the Sandinistas also involved Oliver North and other US personnel in negotiations with sympathetic Guatemalan and Honduran officials since Contra training camps and stockpiles were in these countries on Nicaragua's borders. In March 1985, North recommended that the Guatemalan army should once more receive US aid considering its "extraordinary assistance," despite the fact that this had been previously withdrawn due to the regime's track record of human rights' abuse. Among the army's acts of assistance was the provision of false certificates to conceal North's arms shipments, which were becoming an important part of his work, not just in Central America but in the Middle East as well. When Congressional committees asked CIA director Bill Casey if the US had approached allies like Israel or Saudi Arabia to elicit support for the Contras, he simply lied. Since not every part of the Reagan administration was in the loop on these activities, State Department officials may not have known the falseness of their claims when they too reassured Congress that the administration was striving to operate entirely within the limit set by the so-called Boland Amendment. In December 1982, Democratic Congressman Edward Boland had secured passage of this measure that reduced aid to the Contras and limited the objectives it might support. Aid could support the Contras' activities as long as they did not seek to overthrow the elected Nicaraguan government by force. Most of Oliver North's work contravened both the letter and the spirit of the Boland Amendment.

National Security Adviser MacFarlane had chosen North to oversee the sensitive task of sustaining the Contras because of his conspicuous dedication. From childhood, North had gotten into the habit of forming quasi-father/son relationships with his superiors, beginning with his boxing coach at the Naval Academy, where he overcame severe injuries sustained in a car accident to win the Academy's boxing tournament. He also showed an early impulse to break rules if they blocked his path. Fearing his medical history might jeopardize his chances of entering the Marines, he broke into the Academy's admin block and removed his medical records from the files. He subsequently fought in Vietnam, suffering several battle wounds, and winning not just medals but the loyalty of the men under his command through his unswerving commitment to them as a team. His obsessive focus on the Marine Corps, however, damaged his personal life and in 1974 when his wife asked for a divorce, he had a mental breakdown and exhibited suicidal tendencies. His commanding officer suppressed details of this episode to ensure that North's career was not adversely affected. But it certainly should have been a concern when he was considered for a sensitive intelligence post. By the time he was assigned to the NSC in 1981, he had gained a reputation as a "can-do" kind of guy who was ready to bend the rules to get the job done.

As with so many scandals, the fate of Oliver North and others guilty of misconduct in the Iran-Contra affair depended significantly on the letter of the law. Congress passed a revised Boland Amendment in October 1984 that declared:

> During fiscal year 1985, no funds available to the Central Intelligence Agency, the Department of Defense, or any other agency or entity of the United States involved in intelligence activities may be obligated or expended for the purpose or which would have the effect of supporting, directly or indirectly, military or paramilitary operations in Nicaragua by any nation, group, organization, movement, or individual.

The elaborate phrasing signalled a determination to stop the Reagan administration from evading the first Boland Amendment. Yet, by claiming that the NSC was not technically an intelligence agency, Reagan officials insisted that the measure did not apply to it. They also supplied highly selective records to the Intelligence Oversight Board in 1985 which concluded that the NSC was neither named in the legislation nor implicitly flagged because it did not implement covert actions, although it might coordinate them. Reagan's Attorney General, Ed Meese, declined to give a definitive legal opinion when asked, conceding instead that reasonable minds might differ on the NSC's liability. This failure to clarify the legality of proposed actions was symptomatic of the Reagan White House's indifference to the technicalities of governance which allowed questionable conduct to proceed unchecked, if it promised to advance desired outcomes.

Reagan wanted to keep the Contras alive as an anti-Communist force with much the same determination that he showed towards recovering American hostages in Beirut. To Oliver North's mind, doing what his commander-in-chief wanted was the essence of patriotism.

By 1985, North had been groomed to oversee covert operations in Central America by CIA chief William Casey, who saw the NSC zealot as just the man to take over, if Congressional oversight prevented the CIA from acting directly in the Contras' favour. Others at the CIA were less impressed than Casey, especially the career Central America experts, who recognized quickly that North was apt to lie if it made him more persuasive or won praise from his superiors. North seemed comfortable with the fact that many of his partners in Guatemala, Honduras, and Nicaragua itself, as well as some of his American contacts, expected substantial financial rewards for their work. North's close associate, retired Air Force Major General Richard Secord, received more than $3 million in personal benefits in both 1985 and 1986 as his payment for arranging illicit arms deals. Some Contra figures were also drug dealers. Quite apart from the fact that the arms sales and military intelligence that North delivered contravened the Boland Amendment, some of the attacks he facilitated, such as the spring 1985 attack on a Managua military depot, resulted in extensive civilian casualties; in this case because much of the bombardment hit the adjoining hospital. More important to insiders was the fact that North's operations were designed to give aid to the Contras without direct CIA involvement, and thus allow Director Casey to deny that his Agency was doing so.

If the threat of Marxist revolution threatened American interests in one part of the world, a comparable threat from the Iranian Islamic revolution did so in another, although the power of Cold War thinking made American policy makers apt to merge the two. Hence, the toppling of the Shah by the Ayatollah Khomeini was presented in NSC policy documents in early 1985 as having served Soviet interests. The close ties between the Shah and the US meant that the subsequent rift with Iran was deep. However, this tension coexisted with hard military facts. In its ongoing war with Iraq, Iran needed spare parts for its large stockpile of American-sourced arms and risked defeat if international sanctions gave the Iraqis a strategic advantage. Accordingly, the NSC considered a proposal to provide military equipment on a selective basis. Plausibly, such an initiative could be used to cultivate moderate elements within the Iranian regime, thus strengthening their position ahead of the elderly Khomeini's death. Formally, both Defense Secretary Weinberger and Secretary of State Shultz opposed the idea. Had Reagan listened to them, McFarlane's initiative might have stalled, but instead Reagan took to heart the idea that his administration could court these as yet unnamed Iranian moderates, who in turn could secure the release of the Lebanon hostages, and that was all the encouragement McFarlane needed.

The potential for scandal grew because of the tensions inside the Reagan administration and the secretive network of contacts that subsequently developed. As NSA, McFarlane was used to ensuring that some of his activities did not come to the attention of Secretary Shultz. For instance, he used a part-time counter-terrorism consultant on the NSC, Michael Ledeen, to develop contacts with Israeli Premier Shimon Peres. Ledeen's conversations with Peres about the possibility of courting Iranian moderates coincided with Peres's learning about the potentially lucrative arms deals. If the US gave its blessing, these sales could go ahead, bringing rich rewards to close associates of Peres and making it more likely that Iran would be able to sustain its war with Iraq. Strategically, Israel saw absorbing these two nations' energies through prolonged conflict as a way of limiting their ability to damage Israel. Peres was also keen to cement his personal relationship with Reagan and warmed to the idea that a great way to test the influence of the Iranian arms dealer promoting the deal, Manucher Ghorbanifar, would be to link the sale to the release of American hostages. The scheme gathered steam when a supposedly senior Iranian official, Hassan Karoubi, joined the chief players in discussions in Hamburg in July 1985. Karoubi was said to be part of Khomeini's "Kitchen Cabinet." While it was never established whether Karoubi or his unnamed Iranian associates were indeed moderates, when Israeli foreign minister David Kimche told McFarlane that they might secure the release of American hostages, McFarlane promptly visited Reagan, who was recuperating from surgery in hospital, and got his blessing to go ahead. Reagan always insisted that he was interested in the strategic dimension of cultivating the moderate faction, but McFarlane clearly stressed the prospect of freeing the hostages.

In a lengthy cable to Shultz, McFarlane discussed the potential and pitfalls of what he presented as a private Iranian/Israeli initiative. Knowing Shultz's scepticism, McFarlane acknowledged that he had qualms but felt it would be foolish to dismiss these overtures. Shultz, while ignoring the fact that the plan involved arms shipments, conceded that securing the safe return of hostages and establishing contact with sympathetic elements in Iran was tempting. But when McFarlane reviewed the proposal at a meeting of senior advisers with the still recuperating Reagan on 6 August 1985, Weinberger and Shultz reasserted their misgivings about any "arms for hostages" deal. Reagan's Chief of Staff, Donald Regan, on the other hand, felt that this opening had to be explored. As was his habit, Reagan left both sides with the impression that he had accepted their arguments, but several days later, according to both McFarlane and Regan, he called them to give his explicit authorization to proceed.

Meanwhile, as a private business transaction, a deal took shape. Ghorbanifar agreed to purchase 100 anti-tank missiles at $10,000 apiece from Israel Aircraft Industries (IAI). Ghorbanifar planned to charge the Iranians $12,000 per missile, realising a profit of $200,000, which he would share with his billionaire Saudi financial backer, Adnan Khashoggi, who was providing the $1 million advance to purchase the missiles from IAI. For their part, the IAI team had haggled with Israeli officials to secure the missiles for less than $6,000 insisting that they would need a 25 percent margin for "payoffs" to "certain Iranians." However, within two weeks of the White House discussion, there were already ominous signs that the promised hostage release would not happen. Neither the Israelis nor Ghorbanifar chose to relay this information to Washington, and so the arms delivery went ahead on 20 August 1985. The failure to secure the hostages' release, Ghorbanifar then attributed to the unexpected seizure of the shipment by a detachment of the Revolutionary Guard at Tehran Airport. His cover story was that his moderate Iranians had not got the missiles and so were unable to keep their side of the bargain on hostage releases. What should have been obvious at this point in the scandal is that US foreign policy was not working within its constitutional framework, nor even towards Reagan's understood goals; but instead, was being exploited by foreign business interests, who were definitely making money from the prohibited arms sales.

Despite this failure, the Israeli and American negotiators, who now included Oliver North, listened when Ghorbanifar proposed a fresh scheme that promised the release of a single hostage in return for a further shipment of 400 missiles. During admittedly stormy meetings in Paris in early September 1985, Ghorbanifar justified his new demands as coming directly from the Iranian government and allowed them to listen in to his phone call to Prime Minister Mir-Hossein Mousavi. Neither North nor any of the Israeli negotiators pondered how Ghorbanifar's ties to the Premier, who was elsewhere identified as a strong supporter of the Islamic revolution, substantiated the idea that they were dealing with a moderate faction willing to re-establish positive relations with the US. Instead, the Israelis prepared to move ahead with a second profitable shipment and the Americans acquiesced.

The delivery occurred on 15 September 1985, and an American hostage, the Reverend Benjamin Weir, was released outside the US Embassy in Beirut, although a connection between the two events was never proven. No other hostages were released and unknown to the Americans, one of them, CIA agent William Buckley, had been tortured to death by his captors over three months earlier. As McFarlane later acknowledged, only a fool would fail to see that the US government was trading arms for hostages and doing so with a rapidly escalating rate of exchange. What made this politically scandalous was its direct contravention of the Arms Export Control Act of 1976, which specifically banned the transfer of weapons to a third country that engaged in or supported terrorism, a category into which the State Department had clearly placed Iran. The Act also required the president to inform Congress of arms shipments. As McFarlane later testified, CIA chief Bill Casey felt Congress should not be advised of the shipment and Reagan agreed. Indeed, McFarlane did not recall any significant dissent from this decision.

This consensus inside the administration that what Congress didn't know couldn't hurt them was equally evident in the unfolding Contra saga that remained North's main preoccupation. Congressional leaders had steadily tightened controls on Contra aid in Reagan's first two years and his NSC supporters had developed a series of secret understandings with foreign nations to try to make up the shortfall. One practical difficulty North faced was devising ways to move large sums of money to the Contras undetected.

An account with a Cayman Island bank, nominally belonging to the wife of a Panamanian lawyer, thus received $8 million in Saudi money in 1984. Both Reagan and Vice-President Bush knew of these donations, but McFarlane did not disclose their source to either Shultz or Weinberger, leading them and Congress to believe that the Contras themselves had tapped wealthy private donors to the tune of a million dollars a month. Reagan's landslide 1984 re-election victory boosted his inner circle's commitment to the Contra cause that Reagan himself so fervently espoused. These "freedom fighters," as he called them, would never be abandoned.

Despite the disappointing outcome of the initial missile sales in terms of hostage releases, both Israel and the US decided not to abandon their efforts with Ghorbanifar and other Iranian intermediaries. Since the Iraqis had strengthened their air force, the Iranians urgently wanted to enhance their air defences with Homing All the Way Killer (HAWK) missiles and spare parts, and the Israeli arms dealers were raking in the cash. Negotiations resumed with McFarlane stressing that any deal needed to rest on the safe return of American hostages. He even told North that the next deal should proceed on the basis of a hostage release first. But during negotiations, North strayed far from this principle, partly because hopes of extracting the hostages by any other means continued to falter. All the same, the level of incompetence in the HAWK transaction verged on black comedy.

First, the Israeli dealers struggled to find a domestic carrier willing to fly into Iran, given the intensity of anti-Israeli propaganda coming from Tehran. The result was a decision to commence the shipment from Portugal. To get the necessary cargo clearances, North turned to his Contra collaborator Richard Secord. But when Secord went to his usual Portuguese contacts, he discovered that they no longer had influence with the foreign ministry due to a recent change of government. When Secord enquired at the ministry, officials there unsurprisingly checked with the US Embassy (which, as a State Department operation, knew nothing about his mission). Embassy staff therefore reiterated that the US had an arms embargo against Iran. Pressed for time, Secord tried to intercept the foreign minister in person on 21 November 1985, at Lisbon airport as the latter returned from Brussels. But he went to the wrong terminal! He did not get close to the minister but his protestations that he was a prominent US representative were so noisy that they prompted Portuguese complaints to the US ambassador. NSA McFarlane intervened at this point with a phone call directly to the foreign minister, who sensibly agreed to allow the aircraft to depart only if his government received a formal notification of its mission, cargo, and itinerary. Given the secret nature of all three details, this was not easily provided. With the problem still unresolved, Secord agreed with the Israelis to fly a cargo plane to Lisbon with the missiles, even though it did not have landing rights. If landing proved impossible on approach, it would simply turn back to Tel Aviv.

Meanwhile, the IAI arms dealers, concerned that their profits were being reduced by rising shipping costs, discharged two of the planes they had leased in the expectation that the El-Al 747 cargo plane would suffice. This news nearly brought the Iran and Contra-supply operations directly together since Secord suggested using a plane that was already scheduled to fly ammunition to the Contras using funds from the project's offshore front company, the Enterprise. At this point, the team learned that another CIA front company, St Lucia Airlines, might be able to deliver the weapons. With Portugal no longer a viable starting point, attention turned to Cyprus. But starting the mission there raised a fresh challenge. The continuing Greek-Turkish conflict over the island's status meant that any flight from Cyprus was barred from entering Turkish airspace. More bizarrely, the plane available had just completed a contract to ship a large cargo of live poultry and an additional twenty-four hours was lost while cages were removed and at least some of the chicken-shit signalling their recent presence was washed away. More importantly, this much smaller plane could only house eighteen missiles; far short of the eighty that Iran expected.

Despite the ban on over-flying Turkey, the CIA's maverick pilot not only bluffed his way past Cypriot customs officers, who demanded a cargo manifest, but proceeded to talk his way past Turkish air traffic control, giving false estimates of his position to ground control until he was safely across the Iranian border. Ironically, given that Iran was a nation at war, there he encountered no challenge whatsoever and landed safely in Tehran in the early hours of November 25. He didn't even have to use the code phrase his bosses had given him: "I am coming for Mustafa." However, this bravura performance was offset by the fact that the flight was three days late and held only a fraction of the consignment for which the Iranians had paid. Worse still, on closer inspection, the HAWK missiles proved to be of an older type, incapable of intercepting the high-flying Iraqi planes that were their intended target. To add insult to injury, beneath residual bird-shit and feathers, the blue Star of David of the Israeli armed forces was still clearly visible. The Speaker of the Iranian Parliament, Akbar Hashemi Rafsanjani, felt that such a glaring sign of Israeli involvement was deliberately left to foment feuding between Iran's rival factions and potentially topple him from power. The deal had gone very badly wrong. It had not secured the release of any hostages and it had worsened rather than improved US-Iranian relations. Since they faced the full brunt of Iran's anger, the Israeli arms dealers were in turn angry and disappointed at their American partners. Surely, this saga of incompetence was scandalous in itself?

The fiasco had further repercussions. Secord's willingness to use his former CIA contacts for a cargo plane had unwittingly exposed the venture. CIA Deputy Director John McMahon, who had been wary of involving the agency too directly in McFarlane's adventures, felt he had to ask the general counsel to prepare a directive for the President to sign retrospectively authorizing the agency to act. This labelled the mission "Hostage Rescue – Middle East" and stated that as part of these efforts "certain foreign materiel and munitions may be provided to the Government of Iran" because of its steps to "facilitate the release of American hostages." Reagan signed the document on 5 December 1985, and when investigators later discovered it, it seemed to prove that his administration had traded arms for hostages since there was no mention of any broader policy objectives. It posed problems in other ways, too. Findings were supposed to authorize future actions; they could not legitimize past ones. Worse yet, the document tried to justify not informing Congress, even while acknowledging that Section 501 of the National Security Act required the president to inform the Congress whenever he signed one. The justification that any disclosure might jeopardize a sensitive operation where lives were at risk was not acceptable since the law allowed sensitive cases to be reported to as few as eight senior Congressional figures with intelligence clearances. In a final irony, 5 December was John Poindexter's first full day as National Security Advisor, and his decision not to notify lawmakers but to hide the finding in his office safe placed him emphatically in the firing line once the scandal broke, even though the disastrous HAWK mission occurred well before he took charge.

Two days later, President Reagan hosted a meeting of senior figures in the White House residence; Vice-President Bush and CIA director Casey were unable to attend. After McFarlane reviewed the project, Secretaries Shultz (State) and Weinberger (Defense) spoke emphatically against it. It clearly contradicted the policy of not dealing with terrorists and if revealed, it would alienate moderate Arab states. How could America supply weapons to Tehran, they would ask, when they refused to give them to Jordan or Saudi Arabia? Weinberger spelt out to Reagan that what had been done was illegal under the Arms Export Control Act in multiple ways, and "washing" the transaction, as he put it, through Israel didn't alter that fact. Reagan's response was that if it meant saving the lives of American hostages, he was ready to break the law. "They can impeach me if they want," he reportedly declared. Despite this outburst, Weinberger and Shultz believed they had scotched the project but in reality, Reagan wanted McFarlane to persist since his initiative seemed the only hope for securing the hostages' safe return.

McFarlane flew to London to talk to Ghorbanifar. Relaying Reagan's message, that there would be no further arms delivered ahead of hostage releases, he returned with alarming news. As Reagan noted in his diary entry for 9 December 1985, the response from the Iranian side was chilling. If this proposal reached the terrorists, Reagan wrote, "they would kill our people." McFarlane's scheme seemed to be not only the sole hope for the release of hostages but now also appeared to be a potential threat to their safety if the Americans backed out at this stage, so Reagan signalled for the negotiations to continue. At the same time, former Admiral, John Poindexter, who, as McFarlane's deputy, had won plaudits for tracking down the terrorists who had hijacked the cruise liner, *Achille Lauro*, became NSA when McFarlane stepped down. McFarlane's departure did not reflect any misgivings about either the covert funding of the Contras or the clandestine efforts to trade arms for hostages in Lebanon. Far from it; McFarlane remained very much involved in the Iranian mission especially. Poindexter, too, was unlikely to change direction. His expertise combined an impressive naval record with a readiness to embrace technological modernization, but no foreign policy experience and no sensitivity to the complexities of democratic government. He was dedicated to achieving his President's policy objectives and saw congressional opposition as simply another hurdle to be surmounted. His technical savviness prompted him to set up an early intranet email system that not only made NSC communications a lot quicker but enabled him to elude the NSC procedures that still assumed hard-copy memos and messaging. He was able to communicate with Oliver North and Robert McFarlane through this unmonitored channel, cutting out the State and Defense departments while still being able to tap into embassies and military bases. Eventually, this switch to electronic messaging helped convict Poindexter since the investigators' search of computer files uncovered digital copies of exchanges that North and others believed they had destroyed.

Senior figures had already raised their concerns about the legality of the arms deal in late 1985. As one of his early actions as NSA, Poindexter had Reagan sign a new intelligence finding in January which spoke of the arms initiative as key to efforts to establish "a more moderate government in Iran," thus giving the project more legitimacy than the "arms for hostages" formula evident in some earlier drafts. It also permitted the arms delivery to come directly from the US and indicated CIA involvement. Attorney General Ed Meese also countered warnings that the actions contravened the Arms Export Control Act by insisting that Reagan as commander-in-chief had inherent powers that superseded this law. Despite contrary opinions from the CIA's legal counsel and a stark CIA warning that Ghorbanifar was not to be trusted as an intermediary, Reagan signed this finding on 17 January 1986. Eventually, the congressional investigation of Iran-Contra would conclude that allowing Ghorbanifar to remain pivotal to the mission, despite multiple negative evaluations by intelligence officials and his repeatedly failed polygraph tests was "remarkable;" others might prefer the phrase "just plain dumb."

Part of the ongoing negotiations was to set a price for the missiles. Ghorbanifar and North set it at $10,000 per TOW (Tube-loaded, Optically Tracked, Wire-operated) missile. The Israeli government had quoted a figure of $5,500 and the US Army's Missile Command was willing to provide the weapons for $3,469. The large profit margin on the deal was partly due to a failure to spell out that the Iranians were expecting a higher-specification, advanced version of the missile, which cost a lot more. However, the surplus of $5 million on the $40 million deal was the foundation for the diversion of funds to the Contras and hence to the larger public scandal. Israeli intermediary, Amiram Nir, was the first person to mention the possibility of diverting the funds according to North. Ghorbanifar, who knew of North's involvement with the Nicaraguan resistance, specifically mentioned the Contras, and used their continuing need for funds as an argument in favour of the Iranian deal. For his part, North later testified that the idea of "using the Ayatollah's money" to help the Contras seemed to him a "neat idea."

Unlike the HAWK shipment, the initial TOW delivery of 500 missiles went relatively smoothly on 17 February 1986. However, when North and his Iranian intermediaries met with Mohsen Kangarlou, a representative of Iran's Premier Mir-Hossein Mousavi, matters deteriorated. The Iranians were unimpressed with the US intelligence on Iraqi manoeuvres, supplied as part of the trust-building process, and Kangarlou immediately warned that more advanced weaponry would be needed to secure the release of hostages, and any release would be phased rather than the previously promised release of all American hostages. A second shipment of 500 missiles from Israel to Iran prompted no release, but North remained optimistic and committed. Meanwhile Congress's slight relaxation of restrictions on the types of aid that could be supplied legally to the Contras emboldened the Reagan administration to press for further concessions while continuing its illegal activities.

By early 1986, getting supplies into Nicaragua was becoming more challenging because its neighbours (reasonably enough) feared being drawn into what was currently a civil war. The Hondurans in particular were not happy, because there was a new President, Jose Azcona Hoyo, whose slender mandate meant that he needed to win popular support by "giving the gringos a hard time" as North's deputy, Robert Owen put it. Under-Secretary for Inter-American Affairs, Elliot Abrams was given the task of placating Azcona and returned with the news that it would take a further $20 million worth of weaponry on top of existing agreements to reactivate the supply-line to the Contras via Honduras. Like so much else in the Iran-Contra affair, this flew in the face of congressional legislation. Already, North was using what were supposed to be humanitarian aid flights to gather intelligence on Sandinista activities for the Contras, and continuing shortages of war materiel persuaded him to start including lethal supplies in the cargo. Soon, weapons and humanitarian supplies were being stacked side by side at the Ilopango airfield in El Salvador that had become a staging post for the operation.

In mid-March 1986 an acrimonious debate on increasing the scale and scope of aid to the Contras ended in a negative Congressional vote: 222-210. Not even a nationwide address by Reagan on 16 March in which he likened his aid request to President Truman's stance against Communist infiltration in Greece at the outset of the Cold War could garner the votes needed. Reagan declared the 20 March vote to be a "dark day for freedom," and White House sources explained away polls that found most Americans opposed Contra aid as the product of liberal propaganda. This political setback also meant that North's covert illegal operations were viewed as even more essential by hardliners within the NSC. Already using the Enterprise company to launder funds provided by foreign nations, North valued the arms negotiations with Iran as potentially offering another clandestine source of funds. Thus, the Iran-Contra affair illustrates two recurring facets of presidential scandal: the first is a conviction that the rules don't apply to the president and the second is a combination of incompetence and stupidity that makes exposure likely. The Reagan team displayed the latter when they failed to consider the character and effectiveness of both the Contra leaders (some of whom were drug traffickers) and their Iranian contracts, notably Ghorbanifar, who were unable to secure hostage releases despite repeated promises and who rarely demonstrated that they had the influence they claimed within the Ayatollah's regime. Like other genuine experts in Middle Eastern matters, George Cave, for instance, who had the clear advantage of speaking fluent Farsi, told CIA Director William Casey in March 1986 that he was unhappy with Ghorbanifar's role. Casey bluntly told him he had to make it work.

Money was the key for North. In the spring 1986 negotiations, the Iranians had added spare parts for HAWK missiles to their previous shopping list of TOW missiles. By inflating the price charged to the Iranians from just over $13.4 million to $15 million, North explained to Poindexter in early April, the deal could generate funds that would bridge the "gap" in support for the Contras caused by the negative Congressional vote. To underline the administration's commitment to the new relations and ensure that the *quid pro quo* of hostages for arms was fully understood, former NSA McFarlane was scheduled to go to Tehran as Reagan's personal envoy. Warning lights started to flash even as the plans gathered pace. Robert Oakley, the State Department's counterterrorism coordinator, took his concerns to the Secretary of State's office outlining that the NSC's activities had "explosive domestic political and foreign policy implications" and that knowledge of these activities was so widespread that a leak was highly likely.

Nevertheless, on 23 May, McFarlane with two aides travelled via Germany to Tel Aviv under assumed names on false Irish passports. They rendezvoused with North and Israeli negotiator Amiram Nir before setting off for Tehran on 25 May. At this point, incompetence intruded again. There were no Iranian officials waiting to meet the American delegation and since this was the period of Ramadan, no meeting could be scheduled until sunset, so they were left to cool their heels in a hotel. The initial Iranian response was to express disappointment that the plane had brought so few of the HAWK components they had ordered rather than to lavish attention on Reagan's special envoy. To Iranian bemusement, McFarlane had brought cake. For his part, McFarlane grew incensed at the successive slights and announced that he would not enter talks with anyone who was not his equivalent in rank. Predictably, the visit did not produce any hostage releases, but instead a belated realization that the Iranians were not directly in control of the groups holding the hostages and that Ghorbanifar and other intermediaries had misrepresented the deal in play to both sides. The Americans also came to appreciate that domestic politics in Iran made any rapprochement with the US a risky move for an Iranian public figure to support. On the flight back, it was evident to the Iran experts among the delegates that this mission had been both misconceived and premature. On his return, on 29 May, McFarlane personally recommended shutting down the initiative to Reagan.

At the same time, the dubious activities of North's associates in Central America were attracting press attention. At the end of May, two US journalists filed a civil lawsuit seeking to expose the arms and drug dealing that had become intertwined. By the summer, North was obliged to appear before the House Intelligence Committee, although his boss John Poindexter wrongly assumed that he would opt to withhold information rather than give false testimony. The pressure on North was growing and his bosses discussed having him transferred, although this was framed in terms of concern for his wellbeing rather than the growing risk of exposure. By September, Costa Rica's President Oscar Arias had grown so frustrated at the continued use of an airstrip in his country to resupply the Contras that he instructed his new minister of security to hold a press conference "naming names." The US ambassador persuaded Arias to hold fire, but after a delay, the conference went ahead although to North's relief it named the personnel working for Secord's Enterprise company only by their aliases. Relief was tempered by the reality that Costa Rican security forces had seized the airstrip. This was by way of a prelude for the disastrous shooting-down of the C-123 cargo plane by a Nicaraguan missile on 5 October 1986. Within forty-eight hours, the sole survivor, Eugene Hasenfus, was paraded before TV cameras in Managua. On October 8, key personnel on the Restricted Interagency Group met to determine how best to maintain the administration's cover story denying all involvement. As part of this, the aircraft and equipment that the Enterprise had secretly mustered at its bases was pushed into an excavated pit, covered with explosives, blown up, then saturated with fuel and cremated.

The Iranian side of the NSC's covert operations was also in trouble. Arms talks had not yielded the promised hostage releases. On the contrary, the threat to the hostages had increased due to other US interventions in the volatile region, such as the bombing of Libya in April which has been linked to the murder of Peter Kilburn, an American University of Beirut librarian, by his captors. The desperate situation had attracted an ugly range of con-artists posing as potential intermediaries with the terrorists, but always demanding payment upfront. A dearth of sound intelligence equally made tentative rescue operations impractical since they had to begin with definitive information on the hostages' location. The embers of the Iranian deal were almost extinguished when the US Army Logistics Command sent out pricing information to a mailing list that still astonishingly included Iranian contacts, thus enabling them to see that Iran had been massively overcharged. North and others had to make the case that the list price was the basic cost of manufacture and should not be taken as a guide to the commercial cost, which inevitably included a wide range of additional expenses. The release of Catholic priest, Lawrence

Jenco, on 26 July, albeit to Syrian forces in rural Lebanon, was attributed by North to the continuing efforts of his Israeli intermediaries. Seeking to reinvigorate support for his scheme, he warned that a US termination of the initiative would be an affront to Israeli friends like Shimon Peres and concluded that the lives of the three remaining US hostages would be sacrificed if the administration did nothing. Throughout the scandal, beneath all the illegality and incompetence, there runs the fact that human lives were at stake.

With new Iranian contacts, the arms negotiations went forward in October with a meeting in Frankfurt. The resulting plan saw multiple American concessions, the chief of which was that 500 TOW missiles would be delivered before a single hostage was released. North also promised to use US influence with Kuwait to secure the release of some, if not all, of the seventeen prisoners linked to bombings in the Emirate, and given earlier complaints about overcharging, the cost of the missiles was cut. North then misrepresented the outcome to Poindexter to secure his approval and, even though the Iranians had complained about the quality of the munitions supplied in the past, he agreed with his Israeli intermediary to palm off to the Iranians 500 missiles that Israel wanted to return to the US as substandard. Thus, even before hardliners in Tehran, working with their Hezbollah allies, exposed the whole initiative, North had damaged it in several ways as a basis for improved US-Iranian relations.

If the deceit and incompetence endemic to the Iran-Contra affair were scandalous, the cover-up was in many respects even more so. Not only was the remainder of the Enterprise's air operation destroyed to prevent further disclosure, but memory loss swept the CIA, Pentagon, and State Department. When Reagan was asked who the crew of the shot-down plane were working for, he replied simply: "Not us." Assistant Secretary of State, Elliott Abrams, gave unqualified denials of official involvement, attributing the supply operation to private sponsors of the Nicaraguan resistance, while insisting that, since it would be illegal for the US government to be involved, no agency had been. He testified to this effect before congressional committees in both House and Senate. Despite being personally involved in soliciting funds from foreign governments for the Contras, Abrams denied any knowledge of such funds or efforts to secure them. In short, he brazenly lied. In early November, when news of

MacFarlane's trip to Tehran broke and the press focus switched, the same pattern of denial continued. Urging the White House to come clean rather than cover up, Secretary of State Shultz was scathing in private comments to his aides at the time. He referred to the public relations exercise as "amateur hour" and confided to a friend that he feared for Vice-President Bush when he saw him on TV declaring that the very idea of selling arms to Iran was "ridiculous." Bush needed to be careful how he played "the loyal lieutenant role" since his presence at the key meetings was documented. He could be caught "in a web of lies." He met with Bush on 10 November 1986 but was unable to convince him to change course. Bush maintained this denial of knowledge throughout his successful 1988 presidential campaign.

President Reagan met his top advisors on 10 November to discuss an agreed response to questions about Iran. Poindexter's summary of the initiative reflected not the reality but what was seen as the most defensible version of events. It stressed developing contacts with Iranian moderates in preparation for the post-Khomeini succession crisis and attributed the first arms delivery in 1985 to the Israelis. When Shultz returned to the State Department, he complained to aides that others were intent on "distorting the record" and risked "taking the President down the drain." Ominously, he said: "It's Watergate all over." Reagan himself expressed his frustration with the continuing press questions in his diary entry for November 12. He complained that the media was "trying to create another Watergate" and he was determined to make a public statement in an attempt to put the matter behind him. Vice-President Bush was haunted by the same analogy. In his diary, he wrote of how he remembered Watergate and "the way things oozed out" and worried that the administration was really "hemorrhaging."

Whatever its intention, Reagan's 13 November speech did not staunch the wound. It alluded to "small amounts of defensive weapons" that could "fit into a single cargo plane." It asserted "full compliance with the law," and insisted that there had been no trading of arms for hostages. Chief of Staff Don Regan and NSA John Poindexter gave eight TV interviews but could not get their story straight. Worse still, when George Shultz appeared on CBS's *Face the Nation*, he was quizzed over whether there were further arms shipments planned and he vacillated; that was not the policy and he would oppose such a move, but he couldn't speak for the entire administration. Shultz assumed he would be fired for breaking ranks, but instead Reagan publicly praised him. Media interest predictably prompted congressional investigation and Poindexter instructed aides to pull together a chronology of events that would exonerate the President. When this circulated to the Justice Department, it made officials there fully aware of arms shipments during 1985 that should have been reported to Congress. Poindexter asked his NSA predecessor Robert McFarlane to review the chronology and on November 19, the latter removed all suggestions that Reagan had pre-authorized the summer 1985 shipments and deleted details of the HAWK missile delivery, replacing it with a vague reference to "other transfers of equipment" between Israel and Iran in the fall. The same day, Reagan held a press conference in a further attempt to quell the growing controversy and instead added further inaccuracies. He insisted that the issue was limited to arms shipments by the US alone that occurred after 17 January 1986, when he gave his authorization. He described the shipment as 1000 TOW missiles (it was actually over 2000) and incredibly still asserted that this had been delivered in a single cargo plane with "plenty of room left over." It had been part of a broader diplomatic initiative and even if in passing, he conceded that subsequently three hostages had been released, it was not an "arms for hostages" deal. Twenty minutes after he finished speaking, the White House press office confirmed that the President had misspoke: it had not been the US acting alone; there had been a third country (Israel) involved.

Wrestling with the reality that there had been shipments well before Reagan's January 1986 finding, NSA Poindexter took the extraordinary step of destroying the December 1985 intelligence finding that Reagan had approved to retrospectively authorize the arms deal. He did so because it spoke narrowly of trading arms for hostages, precisely the accusation dominating the media frenzy. Concluding that this misrepresented Reagan's intentions in a way that would be politically damaging, he tore up the document and threw it in the waste-bin. Poindexter also had a conversation with Oliver North about documents he had related to the HAWK shipment and later admitted that after it, he felt pretty sure that North was about to destroy them. He did not tell him to do so, but nor did he advise against it. While this was happening, Attorney General Meese had begun what he characterized as an informal inquiry. This included phone calls and meetings with Poindexter, McFarlane and others, whom he questioned about the Iranian shipments, but he made no attempt to secure the relevant documents. He also seemed to invite Secretary Shultz to confirm the idea that Reagan had not known about the HAWK shipment in November 1985, even though Shultz's own recollection was that the President did know.

Meese had assigned two senior staff members to look for evidence on the 1985 Iran initiatives from Oliver North. As they sorted through piles of records, they came across a six-page summary entitled "Release of American Hostages in Beirut" dated April 1986. To their alarm, they came across a section on page 5 that emphatically stated that allocation of "residual funds" from the arms deal would include $12 million "to purchase critically needed supplies for the Nicaraguan Democratic Resistance Forces." At lunch with the Attorney General, they alerted him to their discovery. "Oh shit," was Meese's immediate reaction. The fusion of the two controversies into one boosted the threat to the President. Not only was there no formal authorization on record for these covert actions but they had involved the channelling of funds into private hands that should properly have gone to the US Treasury. Meese then decided to interview North himself, although notes on the interview suggest he did so to gather material for Reagan's defense. For instance, "N[orth] **believes** [emphasis in the original] RR [Reagan] authorized it [the Nov 85 missile delivery] himself b/c M[cFarlane] wouldn't go off on own." Meese also disputed North's insistence that Reagan's motivation had always been getting the hostages out rather than building a new strategic relationship with Iranian moderates. North offered to check his records to see if there was a presidential authorization for the diversion of funds and blithely told the Attorney General that someone should "step up" and say the HAWK missile sale was authorized in November 1985. In other words, they should lie to protect Reagan.

Meese evidently did not see his role as the nation's chief law enforcement official as requiring him to uphold the law rather than protect the President. This is demonstrated by his failure to secure the written records that might prove guilt. After his interview, North spent a five-hour period reviewing and shredding documents. He later testified that in fact, he had been destroying documents ever since the news broke of the shot-down plane. His assistant, Fawn Hall, confirmed that there had been a "shredding party" over the weekend prior to North's interview with Meese. At a meeting of senior intelligence staff on 24 November, Meese laid out a version of the Iranian talks that portrayed Reagan as unaware that an illegal action was planned, and no one objected even though several people present knew that this was untrue. This became the first stage in crafting the broader cover story that there had been a "rogue operation" within the NSC, pursuing missions without proper authorization, including the diversion of funds to the Contras. And further, that as soon as Reagan was informed, he acted to stop it. On 25 November, Reagan accepted Poindexter's resignation and Shultz, Meese and CIA director Casey briefed congressional leaders along the lines agreed.

Amplifying this trend to protect the President, Republicans in Congress had lasting memories of the damage done to their party by Watergate, and so, they, too, were happy to pin misconduct onto a small group in the NSC and to accuse Democrats of partisan point-scoring over an incident that the popular Reagan also deplored. Wary that such a PR strategy might work, Democrats made concessions, setting a tight schedule for committee hearings and promising a final report by November 1987, a full year before the next presidential election. The senior Democrats chosen to serve on the investigative committees were generally moderates, but the House Republicans selected were often figures seen as loyal defenders of the President. As a result, the House Committee investigation was overtly partisan from its inception culminating in a minority report by Republican dissidents, rejecting the investigation's findings. The investigative process itself was hampered by the unwillingness of the intelligence community to allow access to its documents. Despite the already available secure facilities on Capitol Hill used by the established intelligence committees, the agencies sometimes refused to allow documents to be sent across or copied, and when members were given access, they were sometimes forbidden to take written notes. While this was a cause of delay, it also made it easier to accept the cover story than to establish the facts.

The shadow of Watergate was tangible for the investigators. Not only did the chief legal counsels to the committee feel constrained by the very high standard of proof that would be needed to secure the super-majority required for a successful impeachment, but they were also haunted by their memory of the damage that the earlier episode had done to public faith in America's political institutions and to its international standing. Chairman of the Senate Committee, Democrat Daniel Inouye, feared that perceived US weakness domestically might spur Soviet aggression with further proxy wars, like those in southern Africa in the 1970s that he linked to Watergate. Others feared that a deepening presidential crisis would make Soviet concessions on arms less likely in the ongoing negotiations. With eyes already drawn to the 1988 presidential race, and anticipating Republican reasoning during Trump's second impeachment, Democrats weighed the wisdom of taking the impeachment route against a president who would be leaving office in any case at the end of his second term. After all, the punishment for impeachment was removal from office and non-eligibility for public office, and by January 1989, neither would be relevant to Ronald Reagan. Senator Daniel Moynihan of New York summed up the thinking: "This nation does not want and does not need another destroyed presidency." Only the most compelling evidence would force Congress to impeach Reagan. The scandal of negligence would be insufficient.

The President's own Special Review Board, usually referred to as the Tower Commission after its chair John Tower, released its report on 26 February 1987, before congressional hearings began, and provided the escape route for Reagan and Congress that both in a sense preferred. Despite efforts by Poindexter to delete incriminating emails, the FBI provided the Commission with copies found on back-up drives. The Commission's report not only ensured that Poindexter would face intense congressional questioning but pointed the finger emphatically at the President's Chief of Staff Donald Regan who had allowed the "flawed process" to develop and in their view bore primary responsibility for the chaos that reigned in the White House. Reagan himself did not escape criticism, however. The Tower Commission condemned his failure to insist on proper accountability and rigorous policy and performance review; his management style allowed the damaging episode to occur. Such severe criticism enabled Reagan to evade closer scrutiny, developing a sympathetic narrative that the genial President had been let down by overzealous subordinates. Even the blame attributed to Reagan was shared among his senior Cabinet members, such as Secretary of State Shultz and Defense Secretary Weinberger, who were rebuked for their refusal to challenge what they knew to be a dangerous series of initiatives. They had been content to stay clear personally, and this stance, the Commission concluded, had not served the administration well.

Bubbling along in the background for the Tower Commission was an issue that would subsequently stymy the Special Prosecutor's investigation of Reagan: namely, the President's mental health. On the most human level, the early signs of what was later diagnosed as Alzheimer's Disease was a tragedy, but in the context of presidential power, the significance of his diminished competence may be seen as scandalous. The Twenty-Fifth Amendment ratified in 1967 had addressed the issue of what to do if a president was unable to discharge his duties. It offered two mechanisms. The first allowed the president to notify Congress that he was temporarily delegating his powers to the vice-president due to incapacity and Reagan had used this process for a very short period in July 1985 when he underwent surgery. Some have claimed that he took back his powers prematurely and while his faculties were still impaired, he gave McFarlane the go-ahead for the next phase of the Iranian arms deals. The second mechanism allows for the vice-president and a majority of the principal Cabinet officers to declare that the president is no longer able to govern and thus ask for congressional approval of the vice-president's accession to the president's role. It also allows for the president to challenge this claim and if it is reasserted by the vice-president and Cabinet, then Congress must adjudicate. At various points, especially in the torrid political aftermath of the 2020 election, the second route was discussed in relation to Donald Trump, who continued to insist that Joe Biden's victory was the product of electoral fraud, even as multiple legal challenges failed for lack of evidence.

There were private discussions in the White House in early 1987 stemming from personal encounters with the President in which his confused memory was evident. NSA Poindexter felt that by this stage, Reagan's Alzheimer's was clearly a factor, but that its full extent was not seen because Reagan chose to remain largely silent during private staff discussions and remained a skilled performer when delivering prepared remarks to a public audience. Incoming Chief of Staff Howard Baker received a memo from James Cannon, who had been asked to assess the situation, and was shocked to learn that invoking the Twenty-Fifth Amendment was a genuine possibility. But Baker and other members of the team assembled to enable the administration to continue working while the Iran-Contra scandal raged, concluded that Reagan was not incapacitated sufficiently to warrant such a drastic step. At the same time, members of the Tower Commission had been astonished by the inept way Reagan had responded to some of their probing questions; saying that he didn't remember, but his advisors had told him to say this and then reading from a prepared script.

If Reagan's subsequent Alzheimer's diagnosis provides the basis for claiming that his conscious involvement in the substance of the scandal remains in doubt, the failure of the congressional and Independent Counsel investigations to ensure that Iran-Contra's most active players – Poindexter and North, most notably – were held fully accountable was due to their adverse effect on each other. The Tower Commission had already shown that the two men's evidence would be central to understanding the affair. But whereas the congressional hearings sought to ensure that they divulged their activities in publicly televised hearings (in order to develop political momentum for any challenge to Reagan or his likely successor Bush), Independent Counsel Lawrence Walsh recognised that his investigation's hopes of a successful prosecution would be greatly diminished by televised testimony. This was because the defendants could reasonably argue that their Fifth Amendment protection against giving self-incriminating evidence had been denied in a way that prejudiced all likely jurors. So essential did Congress deem North and Poindexter's testimony that both were granted immunity in order to ensure that their appearance was not reduced to a repeated invocation of the Fifth.

Steered partly by the Tower Commission's report, the legal counsels for the congressional investigation concluded early on that at the heart of the Iran-Contra scandal was a mindset that assumed that Congress and even some parts of the executive branch, notably the State Department, stood in the way of achieving key foreign policy objectives. This made it appear both logical and appropriate to act outside the established system, using the NSC and an elaborate private apparatus to do what the foreign policy "establishment" would otherwise obstruct. As a result, Iran-Contra's creators saw circumventing the checks and balances of the Constitution through covert actions and lies to Congress as patriotic. What the reaction to televised hearings also eventually demonstrated was that a significant proportion of Reagan's ardent supporters would share this mindset and rally behind North as an American hero. Both the belief that there is a "deep state" blocking the keeping of campaign promises and that partisan investigations target patriots would be features of the Trump presidency.

Among earlier witnesses who set the stage before North's appearance was former NSA Robert McFarlane. Testifying just weeks after a suicide attempt, his evidence had to be extracted with some care. Nevertheless, it did establish that President Reagan had given personal approval for the arms deals and had been largely focused on releasing the hostages. McFarlane also told the committee that he had told staff that the NSC was governed by the terms of the Boland Amendment regarding Contra aid, a stance that contradicted others such as North who insisted the opposite. Other witnesses included North's deputy in Central America, Robert Owen. He readily admitted that the CIA had assisted in the delivery of military as well as humanitarian aid to the Contras, and that this had been done covertly for political reasons. At the same time, he expressed his own deep admiration for North, verging on adulation. Owen's final statement to the committee included a poetical tribute to his superior officer whose very existence on "this troubled earth," along with faith in God and the support of his family was what sustained Owen in the "darkest hours." Seeking to challenge this glowing portrait, the committee spent time interrogating witnesses who could show that North had personally benefitted, even if on a far smaller scale than others, like Richard Secord. It also interrogated North's secretary, Fawn Hall, about the shredding, removal and alteration of classified records in November 1986. She justified her actions partly by affirming her trust in North but also by declaring that "sometimes you have to go above the written law." Assistant Attorney General Charles Cooper conversely tried to mitigate the Justice Department's failure to enforce the law by stressing the misleading information offered by both Bill Casey of the CIA and North himself. He declared that he would be sceptical of anything North told him, even under oath.

In the meantime, North's lawyers secured major concessions for their client. North was not required to submit to a private deposition in advance and was scheduled to appear for three days of hearings (each comprising a maximum of ten hours), but with no possibility of recalling him. North was required to present records for a designated time frame (1 January 1984, to 26 November 1986), but the deadline for submission was just three days prior to his appearance. This gave committee staff seventy-two hours to process thousands of pages, an impossible task which meant that they could not fine-tune their questioning. At the same time, as already mentioned, the grant of immunity would stymy subsequent efforts by the Independent Counsel to prosecute North for his illegal actions. Once the hearings began, the failure of the committee to consider the "optics" of the televised hearings worked significantly to North's advantage.

The joint committee's sheer size was partly responsible since it required the construction of a large, raised platform for the questioners. The television cameras in the room thus captured them in what was known in Hollywood as the "villain's angle." Conversely, the same cameras directed to capture the witnesses' responses, caught them looking upward with the "hero's angle," and no one exploited this cinematic effect better than North. Clad in his dress marine uniform, displaying his combat service decorations, he seemed to embody the patriotism at the heart of his defense. In contrast, even though its chairman, Daniel Inouye, had lost an arm fighting for his country, the committee's suit-clad civilians inspired far less popular sympathy. With the justification of patriotism, North readily admitted key aspects of his work: setting up the Enterprise to funnel funds and supplies clandestinely, diverting profits from the Iranian arms deal to benefit the Contras, lying to Congress about his activities, and falsifying and destroying documents. He did so without embarrassment or remorse. "I did a lot of things, and I want to stand up and say that I am proud of them," he declared. Obeying the orders of his President was in keeping with his military code of honour. He had shown his loyalty.

Eventually, his dramatic account of all that he had done in the service of his commander-in-chief was challenged not unreasonably with the question: if all this was so in line with the President's wishes, why had Reagan fired him, along with Poindexter, from the NSC? North wrapped himself firmly in the flag, declaring:

> *This lieutenant colonel is not going to challenge a decision of the Commander in Chief for whom I still work, and I am proud to work for that Commander in Chief, and if the Commander in Chief tells this lieutenant colonel to go stand in the corner and sit on his head, I will do so.*

When Chairman Inouye understandably felt compelled to place on record that soldiers were not required to obey illegal orders, as the Nuremburg war trials vividly demonstrated, North's legal counsel angrily objected to this impugning of his client's character. Yet, likening North to German soldiers and other officials who implemented Hitler's "final solution" was making the most telling comparison in the case of an officer who insisted that he only did what he was ordered to do and was proud of his unfailing obedience.

No matter how disturbing the analogy might be, the media coverage made clear that there was a considerable portion of the public that admired Oliver North's stance and most of them were Republican leaning voters. At the very least, Democrats had to realize that going after North was likely to galvanize Republican turnout in the 1988 elections. One Senate investigator summed up why, after North's testimony, the committee was keen to wrap up the hearings as quickly as possible. He declared: "We were not about to look for trouble." Fortunately, the testimony of NSA John Poindexter gave an obvious point of closure. He testified that he had not told the President about the diversion of funds and unlike North, who had pointed to his superiors as the decision makers, Poindexter offered himself as the scapegoat by insisting that the buck stopped with him. Whatever the circumstantial evidence, most of the committee concluded at that point that they would not be able to prove Reagan's guilt in a way that would justify impeachment.

The remaining witnesses testified in ways that under normal circumstances might well have been scandalous. Secretary of State Shultz stressed his opposition to the arms for hostages deals and the efforts to circumvent the Boland Amendment but did not disclose the documentary record made by his close aides, which, when revealed to the Independent Counsel in 1992, showed that he knew more than he admitted. Defense Secretary Weinberger similarly stressed that he had opposed the initiatives and complained about Poindexter and others keeping him from the President because of his stance. The Independent Counsel eventually found that Weinberger had also kept his own notes of meetings, a fact that he flagrantly denied in sworn testimony to Congress, which led to his subsequent indictment. Despite some hostile questioning, Attorney General Meese seemed entirely comfortable with the "informal" approach he had taken to investigating the Iran-Contra controversy when it became clear that it might entail serious wrongdoing. Former Chief of Staff Don Regan, who had been blisteringly criticized by the Tower Commission report for not ensuring that the President was properly informed, confirmed that he and Reagan had known about the November 1985 HAWK shipment to Iran including the proposed cover story that its cargo was drilling equipment; testimony which directly contradicted Reagan's to the Tower Commission. He also disclosed that he and the President had discussed pardoning both Poindexter and North and had not done so because such pardons would imply guilt, and Reagan did not feel they had done anything wrong. Collectively, this was quite a list of governmental failures.

Another way in which Iran-Contra foreshadowed the pattern of future presidential scandals was that the Congressional investigations produced widely differing, partisan versions of the same facts. Already what would prompt the Clintons to complain of a right-wing conspiracy and the Trump team to speak of witch hunts and fake news was taking shape. The majority report, written by Democrats, was deeply critical of the administration and spoke of its "secrecy, deception, and disdain for the law." Whenever the goals set by President Reagan ran up against the law, Iran-Contra showed, it was the law that had to give way. Congress, the report concluded, "cannot legislate good judgment, honesty, or fidelity to the law." Eight Republican committee members chose not to sign off this report, but instead to submit a minority report of their own.

While the minority report conceded that the administration had made mistakes, it insisted that these were no more than "errors of judgment" such as any administration might make. Far more scandalous in its view was the Democratic majority's effort to whip up hysteria by claiming a constitutional crisis where none existed. The report rejected claims of a systemic disregard for the law, or of a cover-up. Instead, it found the root cause of the controversy to be the Boland Amendment, which it characterized as a reckless intrusion by Congress on the foreign policy-making prerogative of the Executive branch. As a sign of the direction of the Republican Party, the report even went so far as to criticize President Reagan for signing rather than vetoing the Boland Amendment and for cooperating with Congressional investigators rather than invoking executive privilege. In contrast to the majority report, which included recommendations to tighten executive procedures in order to ensure legal compliance, the minority report's recommendations set limits to congressional oversight, proposed new penalties for lawmakers' disclosure of government secrets, and expanded the scope for presidential discretion or flexibility when faced with legal restrictions. According to opinion polls, most US citizens sided with the majority report's judgment that "ultimate responsibility" rested with President Reagan. He had set the policy that North and Poindexter loyally followed. He had approved selling arms secretly to Iran and had declared that ways must be found to maintain the Contras "body and soul." However, unlike the popular majority that felt strongly in 1974 that Nixon had to go, a far smaller proportion of Americans in 1987 felt sufficiently scandalized to want Reagan ousted before his term ended in January 1989. Watergate had proved a national nightmare, people remembered; why go there again?

The conclusion of the congressional investigation still left the Independent Counsel at work. Lawrence Walsh's probe had no time limit and eventually stretched to seven years with a final report published during the first summer of Bill Clinton's presidency. He oversaw the prosecution of several participants in the Iran-Contra affair, even though some of the convictions were overturned on appeal. His staff uncovered evidence that suggested the culpability of senior officials and did so amidst such difficulty that it was reasonable to infer that the proof had been concealed to obstruct justice. However, where the Watergate cover-up deepened public outrage, the Walsh inquiry served to sharpen partisan feeling, and a sense among Republican loyalists that it was being used as a weapon. Walsh himself, a sprightly 74-year-old when he took up his role, had begun as an Eisenhower Republican and his appointment had initially only raised doubts about impartiality from the Democratic side. But the Republican Party under Reagan was changing, and its base was already unhappy with middle-of-road, consensus politics. Anything that helped the Democrats was the work of an enemy; hell, maybe, even of the Devil himself!

On 16 March 1988, the Office of Independent Counsel (OIC) filed conspiracy charges against Poindexter, North, Richard Secord, and arms intermediary Albert Hakim. Since the Boland Amendment did not identify criminal penalties, the prosecution was based on the idea that the Iran-Contra affair involved using US funds for illicit purposes; funds, particularly in the case of the profits from the arms sales, that should have remained under the control of the US Treasury. Apart from Secord who declined immunity, all defendants had secured a guarantee of immunity from congressional investigators, and on this basis not only their own testimony but that of their co-defendants could not be used as evidence in any trial. Their claim that such use would jeopardize their right to a fair trial was upheld in June 1988. At the same time, Reagan's Justice Department, along with the intelligence community, refused on national security grounds to release documents requested by the OIC, making other charges against North and others unsustainable. As preparations for North's trial proceeded, the Department also took the highly unusual step of filing a supportive brief endorsing a defense motion for the conspiracy and theft charges to be dropped. Building on the minority report from the congressional investigation, the brief asserted that the Boland Amendment "invaded" the sphere of foreign policy-making that the Constitution had delegated exclusively to the president since his authority in this context extended to covert diplomacy. The federal court disagreed, and the charges remained.

In a further sign that the OIC was being portrayed as a partisan operation by Republicans, Senator Robert Dole joined a growing chorus of conservative commentators who declared that the prosecutions criminalized policy differences. This allowed the OIC's targets to portray themselves as victims and the investigators as villains. Assistant Secretary of State Elliott Abrams who had lied to Congress about the Contra operations now called Walsh worse than either Iraq's Saddam Hussein or Libya's Muammar Qaddafi. NSC consultant Michael Ledeen, who had been instrumental in the Israeli-brokered arms deals with Iran likened the OIC to the Spanish Inquisition. Dropping its conspiracy and theft charges against North, the OIC proceeded with lesser charges in January 1989. It was during this trial that North was compelled to hand over 2617 pages of handwritten notes detailing high-level meetings and other discussions revealing the full extent of the scandal, notably that the solicitation of funds from foreign powers had been done via *quid pro quo* arrangements that entailed concessions to nations as disparate as Saudi Arabia, South Korea, and Panama.

When decades later Donald Trump complained about the uproar over his telephone conversation with Ukrainian President Zelensky, in which Trump indicated that US aid to Ukraine was contingent on Zelensky doing him a favour (by conspicuously launching a probe into the activities of Hunter Biden, son of the putative Democratic nominee, Joe Biden), he was following what he saw as normal practice. The anticlimactic outcome of North's trial certainly offered little deterrent for future wrongdoing. He was found guilty of two counts of altering or destroying documents and one count of accepting an illegal gratuity in the form of a security gate to his home. Placed on probation for two years and fined a total of $150,000, he was also ordered to do 1200 hours of community service, which he had to fit into his now busy schedule as a sought-after conservative speaker and pundit. Scandal did not end North's career, instead it launched his new one. Moreover, in July 1990, the Court of Appeals vacated his convictions as prosecution witnesses may well have given evidence influenced by the public congressional hearings against which North had been granted immunity. The scandal of Iran-Contra was not just what was done, but the many ways it eroded accountability under the law. The erosion has continued into the Trump era.

John Poindexter's case did not come to trial until March 1990 and while the judge conceded that the new President George Bush would not have to testify, he did allow Reagan to be called. However, when the private deposition took place, it simply showed the former President's memory loss. He replied "I don't recall" or "I can't remember" on eighty-eight separate occasions. The charges against Poindexter included giving false statements to Congress and destroying or removing documents. The jury found him guilty on all counts on April 7, and the judge sentenced him to six months' imprisonment for each charge, although these were to run concurrently. Once again, the verdict was overturned on appeal due to the likelihood that immunized congressional testimony had influenced the outcome.

Amidst these setbacks, the OIC discovered some new sources of evidence in the summer of 1990. Much of this came from notes obtained from the State Department, but in October the investigators found a reference to note-taking by Defense Secretary Weinberger who had testified that he did not take notes. It took a year, but some 7000 pages of handwritten notes were found among the papers he had deposited at the Library of Congress. On 16 June 1992, the OIC indicted Weinberger on five charges of obstruction, perjury, and false statements. When one obstruction count was dismissed by the presiding judge on a technicality, the OIC filed a new charge on October 30, a move that cemented its pariah status with Republicans as it came just four days before voters would decide whether President Bush should have a second term. As part of their court action, Walsh's team released extracts from Weinberger's notes that showed that Bush had known more about the Iranian arms deals that he had admitted. Even some Democrats were startled that the team would take such a step so close to election day; it thus foreshadowed the later controversy over FBI Director, James Comey's decision to announce fresh probes into the Hillary Clinton email scandal in the run-up to the 2016 election. In both cases, the elections did not go well for the candidate concerned.

However, whereas the Clinton email scandal simply spluttered on after her defeat by Donald Trump, the potential threat posed to Bush by the Weinberger trial prompted the lame-duck President to issue a Christmas Eve pardon to Weinberger and five other Iran-Contra figures under investigation. This effectively shut down Walsh's probe and unsurprisingly, he denounced it as "the last card in the cover-up." Bush himself alluded to Watergate obliquely in a statement that accompanied the pardons. Just as President Gerald Ford had pardoned Nixon to put "the long nightmare behind us" and to enable the nation "to heal," so Bush declared that his actions followed the "healing tradition" of past Presidents. He also invoked the reasoning of the Republican minority report by insisting that the prosecutions were criminalizing policy differences that should be settled "in the voting booth, not the courtroom." In the partisan charged aftermath of Bush's defeat, the pardons seemed a tit-for-tat exchange for the OIC's pre-election document release.

By the time, Walsh's report was finally submitted in 1993, there were few Republicans willing to see it as the product of a truly independent investigation. Instead, his protracted investigation had generated support within the GOP for allowing the Independent Counsel law to lapse under its "sunset clause." The fact that President Bill Clinton had favoured its renewal as a candidate in 1992 proved ironically consequential since it eventually allowed Kenneth Starr's appointment. Starr's controversial investigation can itself be linked to the conviction among some Republicans that Iran-Contra showed the lengths Democrats were prepared to go when they had control of Congress, although it stemmed more clearly from the GOP conviction that "slick Willy" (as Clinton was sometimes known) and his wife were corrupt con-artists. The incivility that grew during Iran-Contra was boosted further by the investigations of the multiple Clinton scandals.

But it is worthwhile asking what the Iran-Contra episode suggests about the American public's capacity to be scandalized. Although Nixon and some of his contemporaries felt that the uproar over Watergate was unjust, given that many of the tactics of harassment within it had precedents in Democratic presidential actions, there is little doubt that most Americans, including those who had voted for Nixon in 1972, were shocked by what investigators found behind the bungled burglary. Much of it exposed the arrogance of power, the sense that whatever the president decided to do was by definition "right." Fundamentally, that same arrogance and disdain for their opponents was endemic in Reagan's inner circle, especially among those who instigated the two clandestine missions. Limiting aid to the Contras was not an act that reflected an honest assessment of the benefits of regional stability to the United States; it grew instead, Reaganites felt, from a mix of cowardice and soft-hearted sentimentality that refused to see the Communist threat. Similarly, for many people, perhaps, the only fault with the Iranian arms dealing was its failure to get the hostages out. Success, as President Kennedy put it, has a thousand friends, but defeat is yours alone. Whether most Americans really considered the longer-term geopolitical merits of cultivating Iranian moderates is doubtful.

Arguably, the most scandalous aspect of the Iranian side of the scandal was deep-seated incompetence, rooted in a failure to scrutinize claims that "moderates" within the Iranian regime would be in a position to shape the action of revolutionary jihadists in Lebanon. Surely, those most directly in control of the patronage given to these groups would be more likely to be hard-line figures eager to secure the military resources needed to enable the new Islamic republic to triumph over its more secular adversary, Saddam Hussein's Iraq. To believe the contrary was as far-fetched as believing that moderate Democrats in Congress might influence the behaviour of Nicaragua's right-wing resistance. Yet the NSC had blindly accepted such thinking and had been scarcely more diligent in evaluating either the motives of Israeli intermediaries in the arms sales or the actions of the Contra leaders backed by the secret slush fund. Many of these figures might fairly be seen as profiting from American incompetence.

As a milestone in the history of presidential scandals, Iran-Contra also signalled that the revelation that officials had lied and deceived those empowered to hold them accountable was simply not scandalous enough. Even the fact that they had destroyed documents and concocted cover stories, was insufficient to spark outrage across the country on a scale that demanded action. While it is true that by the end of Oliver North's testimony, most Americans polled felt that Iran-Contra had been a mistake and that the administration had reason to feel guilty, most Republicans were certainly not ready to insist that those involved in the cover-up should be punished. The small faction that had felt that those punished over Watergate had been scapegoats was far larger by the time of Iran-Contra as demonstrated by what was termed "Ollie-mania."

Chapter 3

Do You Trust the President? Clinton and the Character Question

Among recent presidents, Bill Clinton and Donald Trump are the most readily associated with scandal. The Clinton years were so scandal-ridden that when Trump ran against Hillary Clinton in 2016, he felt able to defend himself by invoking the scandals that still tainted her husband. The two men were also connected in other ways. The Clinton presidency set the stage for Trump's because it was made possible by the way in which American expectations about their president's personal character had evolved, and how public mistrust had grown as partisanship intensified. What particularly enraged their opponents was that somehow the Clintons always seemed to escape. Neither the Starr Report nor the impeachment trial managed to remove Bill from power, nor did they dent his largely positive, public approval ratings. On the contrary, Clinton's approval rating as president rose 5.6 percentage points during the three months when the Lewinsky scandal broke. He finished his term with a Gallop poll average approval of 55 percent; well above Trump's 41 percent. He always seemed able to spin his way out of situations through smooth talking and legal manoeuvres. A sizeable chunk of the nation proved ready to excuse his character flaws because of his overall competence. They didn't necessarily like or trust Bill Clinton, or the First Lady, but the economy was humming along. In this sense, too, Clinton paved the way for Trump by sharpening the question: *can presidential misconduct truly scandalize Americans anymore?* Scandals that had been fatal for past presidential candidates would not prevent Donald Trump from winning in 2016. Instead, his supporters seemed willing to shrug and say that it was just Trump being Trump. He himself boasted that he could shoot someone on Fifth Avenue and his supporters would back him. They liked his authenticity: "hey," they'd say, "he's a character."

The gap between a politician's public persona and his private personality is nothing new. What you get is usually not full disclosure. The gulf between the man (we have yet to have a woman president) and the image often grows out of efforts to portray presidential hopefuls according to certain stereotypes. Veterans, for example, have been able to trade on their military past as proof of their patriotism and bravery. No one doubted that George Washington or Dwight Eisenhower would make a competent commander-in-chief. As recently as 1960 both Kennedy and Nixon presented themselves as World War II naval veterans, although Kennedy's heroic saving of his crew after their torpedo-boat was sunk gave him a definite edge over Nixon; the legacy of the latter's naval career was mainly improved, poker-playing skills (his winnings were enough to pay for law school). Ever since the Vietnam War divided Americans, the character issue has become about who evaded military service. George Bush Senior's World War II pilot experience spoke for itself, but his son G.W.'s time in the air wing of the Texas National Guard seemed just a devious way to avoid Vietnam. Ironically, in 2004, when G.W. faced Democrat John Kerry, a genuine Vietnam vet, it was the latter's valour, despite the medals he was awarded, that was challenged. Kerry's anti-Vietnam War activism in 1970-71, which had included the symbolic throwing away of these medals, certainly made it more difficult for him to rally his fellow veterans.

The so-called "Swift Boat" scandal involved hostile Bush-supporting veterans alleging that Kerry did not deserve the medals awarded; an investigation refuted their claims, but Kerry's campaign was damaged. The successful smear showed the divisive potential of the memory of Vietnam nearly three decades after the war's end, and how the heightened level of partisanship generated claims without a factual basis, but it was unusual since earlier campaigns had been all about the failure to serve one's country. Vietnam was among the many issues that raised questions about Bill Clinton's character in 1992, both in terms of evading the draft and of protesting against the war while studying in England. More recently, in the 2016 election, voters learned that when the Vietnam draft threatened the young Donald Trump, a physician and family friend conveniently discovered, in timely fashion, that he had a foot condition (heel spurs) that secured his fifth deferment of enlistment. As a test of character, being a war hero is just not what it was.

The tendency for presidential contenders to manipulate their public image leaves them open to scandal since both their rivals and the media know that exposing a hidden secret can peel away supporters and grab an audience. Contemporary media can sometimes seem little more than a scandal factory. The murky scandals of the Clinton presidency cannot be understood outside of this changing media landscape in which the distinction between news and gossip was blurring. Back in Kennedy's time, the sexual escapades of the president were not the kind of things a news anchor like Walter Cronkite would talk about, and even the gossip magazines focused more on Hollywood than Washington. During the 1960 campaign Kennedy was less worried that the press would expose his adulteries than that they would expose his health issues or exploit public fears that he might be too devout a Catholic. The narrow margin of Kennedy's victory was partly down to the fact that so many Americans believed that Catholics were required to take orders from the Pope. In office, Kennedy carefully avoided any hint of such deference, and after the televised requiem mass at the tear-stained end of his presidency, the vehemence of American anti-Catholicism seemed to go into sharp decline.

At the same time, the importance of evangelical Protestantism particularly in the resurgent Republican coalition from 1980 onwards ensured that personal morality, and therefore scandal, remained a live issue. This was particularly true for Bill Clinton, as this chapter will show. Questions were raised about his character during the campaign and doubts about his personal integrity and sexual morality dogged his presidency. The furore over Clinton has made the widespread support for Donald Trump among white evangelicals a puzzle to some. But their spokesmen have explained this in theological terms; apparently, God can make use of unexpected instruments, and Trump was prepared to deliver a conservative Supreme Court, which in turn has revoked the constitutional protection for abortion which so enraged most evangelicals. As further proof of religion's continuing influence, senior members of the Catholic church have denounced President Joe Biden for his failure to uphold an anti-abortion stance. Thus, the important role of religion in American public life continues to shape the dynamics of presidential scandals.

Clinton's impeachment in 1999 was in some respects foreshadowed by the scandals that damaged the candidacies of earlier Democratic hopefuls.

At the end of the 1960s, despite the widely reported sexual revolution, the belief remained that presidents should be morally upright, family men. It was this assumption that made the Chappaquiddick incident so deeply damaging to the chances of Ted Kennedy, the third Kennedy brother to aspire to the presidency. On 18 July 1969, the Massachusetts Senator was hosting a party for key staff from his brother Robert's presidential bid which had ended so brutally in Bobby's assassination just over a year earlier. The party was at a cottage on Chappaquiddick Island at the eastern end of Martha's Vineyard, and senior staffer Mary Jo Kopechne was among the guests. Sometime around midnight she accepted a lift from Ted Kennedy, but on the drive back to the mainland, his car overturned on a small bridge and landed upside down in the water. Kennedy escaped the vehicle and survived; Kopechne drowned. More damning to his character, ten hours elapsed before the accident was reported. Kennedy pleaded guilty to leaving the scene of an accident and received a suspended two months' jail sentence. But the character questions lingered.

The headline-grabbing moon-landing, which happened on the evening of the next day, 19 July 1969, slowed news coverage of the tragedy. But once that fascination faded, press speculation escalated. The 28-year-old Kopechne was sometimes referred to as just a "young blonde," and there was innuendo: what was she doing alone at night in a car in an isolated spot with a married US Senator? Kennedy gave a televised comment about what happened. Miss Kopechne had felt unwell, and he had offered to drive her back to her hotel, but unfamiliar with the island, he had taken a wrong turn on the unlit rural road. He had not been drinking but in the accident, he suffered concussion. He claimed to have made repeated attempts to reach the submerged vehicle and release Kopechne but was unable to do so due to poor visibility and cold currents. Eventually, he walked back to the cottage and alerted his cousin Joseph Gargan and another campaign aide, Paul Markham. Together they returned to the scene and made further futile rescue attempts. They then drove back to their Edgartown hotel where the shocked and concussed Kennedy tried to rest. He attributed the delay in contacting the police to his mental confusion. Officers recovered the car and Kopechne's body the next morning.

Ted Kennedy always insisted that speculation about the nature of his relationship with Miss Kopechne was shameful. But the incident clearly had suspicious aspects. Why didn't he call the police immediately? The delay was long enough, cynics scoffed, to allow him to sober up. If he was driving Kopechne back to her hotel, why did she leave her key behind at the cottage? There were certainly enough unanswered questions to ensure that when Nixon pondered the possibility of a Kennedy challenge in 1972, he pressed aides to stir the pot over Chappaquiddick, and that included uncovering what Kennedy staffers had done to minimize the damage. In 1980, Ted Kennedy launched an unsuccessful challenge to President Carter. If he had secured the nomination, Republicans were already planning to use Chappaquiddick. They were confident that the unanswered questions would make voters doubt Kennedy's character. By this time, as a sign of how public morality was changing in other respects, Ronald Reagan was able to benefit from a more relaxed attitude to divorce. The taint of scandal attached to divorce had still been sufficient to hamper Democrat nominee Adlai Stevenson in the 1950s, and to dampen Republican Nelson Rockefeller's hopes of securing his party's nomination in 1964. But by 1980, Reagan's 1949 divorce was a distant memory compared to his twenty-eight years of marriage to his second wife, Nancy, thus enabling him to become America's first divorced president. Melania Trump, of course, became First Lady in 2017 as Donald's third wife, and the tabloid headlines that documented Trump's various pairings and divorces no longer seemed politically damaging. For that, Trump had Clinton partly to thank since it had not always been that way.

In 1984, Vice-President Walter Mondale faced a serious, though ultimately unsuccessful, challenge for the Democratic nomination from Colorado Senator Gary Hart. After Mondale went down to a landslide defeat to President Reagan, pundits quickly labelled Hart the favourite for the 1988 nomination. He announced his candidacy early in 1987, hoping to secure donations that would enable him to avoid adding to the $1.4 million debt that his 1984 bid had accrued. However, newspapers quickly depicted him as a reckless womanizer, whose adulterous affairs raised serious questions about his character. Photos emerged of Hart on a Florida quayside, waiting to board a yacht for the vacation island of Bimini. In his lap was an attractive fellow passenger, Donna Rice, and in a gift to caption and headline writers, Hart was sporting a t-shirt with the yacht's name: "Monkey Business." The *Miami Herald* was then tipped off that Miss Rice was spending another weekend with Hart at his Washington townhouse and other papers took up the story. Just as his campaign team was trying to switch the story to the evils of tabloid sensationalism and its invasion of personal privacy, the *Washington Post* privately presented them with its own evidence that Hart enjoyed a long-term relationship with yet another woman living in DC, and the likely impact of that story, (especially on campaign donors), breaking so soon after the first scandal, was enough to induce Hart to end his presidential candidacy on May 8.

Lee Atwater, Bush's 1988 campaign manager, subsequently confessed that he had set Hart up. He had even arranged for the yacht used for the trip to Bimini to be switched to one with the more suggestive name. Polls indicated that public regard for Hart had plummeted with far fewer positive assessments than pollsters had found a year earlier. Just as importantly, while some Hart supporters defended their candidate and insisted that the race should be about policies, the sex scandal weakened Hart's hold on undecided Democrats and boosted hostile sentiment among Republican voters. An effective election tactic, the scandal worked to polarize opinion giving Republicans another reason for voting for Bush while supplying an excuse for Democrats to stay at home. Atwater and other Bush campaign supporters used negative campaigning effectively against the eventual Democratic nominee Michael Dukakis so it seems likely that if Hart had stayed in the race, his love life would have been scrutinized again in the final election contest. Thus, in 1988 scandal both helped to win the election, and to bury another scandal. If Americans had felt able to set Hart's lapses aside and make him their president, Bush would not have been able to pardon the key players in the Iran-Contra affair, which, as we have seen, was a far graver scandal than any monkey business Gary Hart managed in 1987. President Bush's pardons essentially ended the Iran-Contra investigation, which might otherwise have raised questions about Bush's own involvement. Instead, that scandal faded away.

Harry Truman's declaration – "the buck stops here" – is often taken as a sign that the president is responsible for what happens in his administration. Sometimes this means that the actions of others can create scandals that taint the president indirectly. Ronald Reagan is seen as an exception since he retained popularity, even in the face of the Iran-Contra scandal. His administration, on the other hand, retains a dubious reputation with corruption charges levelled against the Defense Department, particularly the Navy, against Housing and Urban Development officials in relation to bribes from contractors, against the Environmental Protection Agency for its too cosy relationship with business, and against his Attorney-General Ed Meese. More generally, the 1980s as a decade seems indelibly stained by the movie *Wall Street*'s mantra "Greed is Good." The collapse of Savings and Loan Associations within the real estate market and the prevalence of junk bonds and asset stripping takeovers in the financial markets during this decade, all left ordinary Americans feeling worried and as losses grew, angry. Although overall, Bush benefitted from the Reagan legacy as a candidate in 1988, he seemed out of touch with ordinary Americans worried about their savings and the cost of living, and he also faced closer scrutiny with the growth of cable TV news. With hindsight, the scandals caused by looser regulation of financial institutions and the drift of news outlets towards gossip, both in terms of the coverage of the private lives of public people and in terms of a greater willingness to run a story, even when it was still little more than a rumour, set the stage for the scandals that rocked the Clinton presidency.

The mainstream media's eagerness to pursue sex scandals was also demonstrated in the unlikely setting of a US Supreme Court Justice confirmation hearing in 1991. The retirement of Thurgood Marshall, the first African American to serve on the Court, offered President Bush a chance to nominate a new associate justice. Since justices are appointed for life, and the Court determines how the Constitution should be interpreted, successful nominees have a lasting effect on US politics, and so Bush knew he had to nominate a conservative. At the same time, there was a consensus that replacing Marshall with a white justice would be a retrograde step. Accordingly, Bush nominated Clarence Thomas, a relatively inexperienced, African American judge whose conservative views on affirmative action had earlier made him Reagan's choice to head the Equal Employment Opportunities Commission (EEOC) in 1982. Civil rights groups were not appeased since Thomas's views were antithetical to Justice Marshall's lifelong efforts to interpret the law to advance racial equality. Nevertheless, Thomas's confirmation seemed on course until an African American, former EEOC lawyer, Anita Hill, charged publicly that while she was working for Thomas, he had sexually harassed her. Since the formal Senate vote was still pending, the televised confirmation hearings were reopened.

Hill testified that Thomas had initially asked her for a date, which she declined, telling him that she did not think it advisable as it might jeopardize their working relationship. Thomas persisted. Subsequently, despite Hill's manifest distaste, he used their conversation in the workplace to regale her with lurid accounts of the pornographic movies he enjoyed. He would boast about his own sexual prowess, both in terms of his hefty penis and the pleasure he gave women through oral stimulation. Distressed by these unwanted confidences and sensing that her indifference angered her boss, Hill had felt compelled to seek work elsewhere. Her televised account in 1991 sparked intense media coverage. Invited to respond, Thomas denied every aspect of Hill's testimony and angrily denounced the televised hearing. It was not just a "national disgrace," he declared. As an African American, he regarded it as a "high-tech lynching for uppity blacks." Republican Senators on the Judiciary Committee questioned Hill intently, seeking to disprove her allegations and malign her intentions. Senior Democrats, including Ted Kennedy and committee chair Joe Biden, did little to protect Hill from this barrage of hostile questions; so much so, that the hearings have gone down in history as the moment when an all-white and all-male Senate committee dismissed harassment allegations in a way that exposed their own racial and gender biases. Thomas was duly confirmed, and now forms part of the majority, conservative faction on the Court. Revelations about his acceptance of gifts from millionaires and his wife's involvement in efforts to overturn the 2020 election result have further tarnished his reputation. But Hill's testimony proved a watershed moment which highlighted the scandal of sexual harassment in the workplace and foreshadowed not just Bill Clinton's problems in the Paula Jones case, but the later hearings that controversially confirmed Trump nominee, Brett Kavanaugh, despite accusations of past sexual misconduct. The Anita Hill scandal that dominated the headlines at the end of the Bush presidency thus set the tone for the media obsessions of the Clinton years.

Sources close to President Clinton, to use a phrase that would become ubiquitous on cable newscasts, have confided that he shelved a possible presidential bid in 1988 after seeing the fate of Gary Hart. A member of Governor Clinton's security detail, Roger Perry, recalled teasing the

Governor over his ruse of going jogging when he was really visiting one of his girlfriends. "Governor, you're gonna make Gary Hart look like a saint," Perry said. "Yeah, I do, don't I?" Clinton laughingly replied. Four years later, he felt able to run for president, building on his established profile not just as a four-term Governor of Arkansas, but as chair of the Democratic Leadership Conference, a group that advocated pragmatic, centrist policies on welfare reform and the economy in order to woo back those Democrats who had started to vote Republican with Ronald Reagan. Having seen the negative campaigning used by the Bush team in 1988, Clinton had to know that attacks would be made on his character, and scandalous accusations were quick to emerge. When asked about recreational drug use during the primary campaigns, Clinton admitted that he had tried marijuana during his time in England as a Rhodes Scholar at Oxford, but added he didn't like it and didn't inhale (a comment that became a punchline for comedians at the time). It also set a pattern. Unable to deny the charge entirely, Clinton responded in a way that seemed smart and calculating rather than open and candid. He would eventually acquire many nicknames; one of the more enduring was "Slick Willie."

His pot-smoking admission was another sign that the standards expected of a future president were softening. Clinton also faced hostile questions about his participation in anti-Vietnam War demonstrations while in England, which opponents portrayed as a betrayal of his countrymen who were fighting and dying in that war. It has subsequently emerged that the Bush administration asked the British government to check whether Clinton had applied for UK citizenship in an effort to avoid the draft in the late 1960s. Some have seen this as a precedent for Donald Trump's efforts to secure another country's (Ukraine's) assistance to win an election. It was also reported that during this turbulent, Cold War period, Clinton had visited the Soviet Union; a decision presented by Republicans as further proof of his lack of patriotism. There were even wild rumours that he was recruited by the KGB.

As a young, well-educated, and articulate Democratic candidate, Clinton drew comparison with John F. Kennedy. Aged 16, Clinton had met President Kennedy at a youth event in Washington and the photograph of the two shaking hands was used by the Clinton campaign to suggest that the torch of leadership had been passed to a new generation. However, by

1992 posthumous revelations about Kennedy's womanizing meant that the parallel fed suspicion that Clinton had his hero's overactive libido as well. The first serious accusation of adultery materialized in January 1992 in the far from bashful form of Gennifer Flowers. She claimed to have had a twelve-year long affair with the Arkansas governor and had supplied the gossip magazine *Star* with taped phone conversations to corroborate her story. Seeking to contain the damage, Clinton agreed to be interviewed with his wife on the CBS primetime news program, *60 Minutes*. The show aired immediately after the Superbowl, and the audience was estimated at over fifty million viewers. Hillary Clinton was strongly defensive of her husband in the interview. While insisting that she was not fulfilling the stereotypical role of the loyal wife "standing by her man," she did just that, declaring that she was there because she loved and respected Bill, and honoured what they had been through together. In short, she was standing by her life choices.

In the perennial gender politics of public life, Hillary (not for the last time) was in a "no-win" situation since the campaign's political consultants were already reporting that her career as a lawyer, and her comment that she was not the kind of woman to "stay home and bake cookies," had alienated conservative female voters. Backing her adulterous husband publicly now risked offending more progressive, feminist ones. The mixed reputation of Hillary Clinton as First Lady was thus taking shape even before the 1992 election. Eventually, the Clinton scandals would mark a watershed in the media's treatment of the First Lady since Hillary was targeted more than her predecessors because she presented herself as an active political advocate. Part of the Clintons' campaign image was that the couple were a team in almost the same way as the traditional president/vice-president ticket. As we shall see, the major scandals faced in the Clinton presidency – the Whitewater financial scandals, the Vince Foster suicide, and even the Paula Jones and Monica Lewinsky sex scandals seemed as much about public feeling towards Hillary as toward Bill.

In the first instance, it emerged that Hillary was the one who made the investment decisions and whose legal work linked the couple most closely to the suspect financial chicanery that surrounded the speculative Whitewater real-estate project. Deputy White House counsel, Vince Foster's death stirred ugly rumours, some of which claimed that it was the outcome of a failed affair with Hillary. More insidiously, although the Lewinsky affair was clearly rooted in her husband's behaviour, it deepened questions about Hillary and her intense ambition. Conservative critics even saw the tawdry details as underlining how a career-focused wife like Hillary, heightened the danger that a husband might stray. To critics on the Left, on the other hand, both Hillary and Bill came to epitomize a Democratic political establishment that won elections with promises to the disadvantaged but governed in the interest of the advantaged, especially when the latter could prove useful to them as donors and patrons. This explained their readiness to back corporate deregulation while in power, to sign off welfare cuts and brutal penal reforms, and to accept financial support from dubious sources both for the 1996 campaign and for their post-presidential Clinton Foundation. The Clintons might boast that they were a "new kind of Democrat," but to progressive critics, they seemed an old kind of politician. When Bill Clinton became only the second president to be impeached in the Senate, some reporters pointed delightedly to the irony that, as a young lawyer, Hillary had helped prepare articles of impeachment against Richard Nixon over Watergate. Bill was certainly seen as a master of "spin", but Hillary too was seen as adept at legal subterfuge. Both seemed tricky customers, and if Nixon was famously disbelieved when he declared that he was not a crook, Hillary could never shake off the label "Crooked Hillary" that Trump pinned on her in 2016.

The lurid nature of the Lewinsky scandal obscures the beginnings of the Clintons' problems in the White House. Like Jimmy Carter's Georgian team, they stirred controversy inadvertently as newcomers to Washington. For instance, there was a Congressional investigation into their decision to fire staff in the White House travel office. The new administration had received an independent auditor's report that highlighted chaotic financial record-keeping and dubious practices suggestive of kickbacks and other corrupt practices. As an attorney, Hillary was keen to address the situation promptly. She urged Vince Foster (with whom she had worked in Little Rock) to act. However, the summary firing of the Travel Office staff in May 1993, followed by the hiring of World-Wide Travel, a well-established agency, immediately aroused media suspicion since the latter was Arkansas-based and even had ties to the Clinton family. "Travel-Gate" eventually triggered a self-critical White House investigation; an FBI investigation; a report from the General Accounting Office; a partisan probe by the House Government Reform and Oversight Committee; and finally, it became tangentially involved in the Independent Counsel investigations.

Ultimately giving rise to no clear allegations against the Clintons, the scandal revealed how the new environment of 24-hour cable news fuelled the hunt for headlines. Hostile coverage also stemmed from the comfortable treatment the old Travel Office staff had given to the White House press corps whose travel arrangements and personal preferences they had indulged. In short, reporters were angry that they had lost some key perks of the job. In other respects, too, the Clinton era marked an important transition as the changing media practices sped the flow of scandal. Newspapers and TV news were confronting the reality that the Internet gave the public new, seemingly free, and immediate sources of information. Crucially, online sites, such as the *Drudge Report*, did not see the need to corroborate their stories by checking reliability across multiple sources. They felt free to share rumour and speculation, and in the market-driven frenzy to keep up with a developing story, cable news, network news and the press steadily loosened their own rules on source-checking. In the process, some news became little more than gossip, and ultimately, some became fake, with Donald Trump in key respects, the unlikely beneficiary.

Whitewater, a far bigger scandal for the Clintons than Travel-Gate, was a legacy of their Arkansas days when Bill was an aspiring politician and Hillary, a bright young lawyer. Politics had brought Bill into contact with real estate developer, Jim McDougal, and Hillary had gone to work at the well-regarded, Rose Legal Firm in Little Rock. By 1979, she had become its first-ever female partner and had developed a national profile for her *pro bono* child welfare advocacy. Bill had been elected governor a year earlier, but since Hillary generated most of their income, she led on investment decisions. When *New York Times* reporter, Jeff Gerth, probed the couple's finances during the 1992 campaign, he noticed that unlike the candidate, Bill Clinton, Hillary was not expected to disclose her income, and she refused to take questions on the subject. It was Gerth, who discovered the Clintons' involvement in the Whitewater project.

He had always thought that the full scandal of the Savings and Loans (S&L) collapse in the 1980s had never been properly exposed. The crisis in this sector of the credit market had begun when the Federal Reserve raised interest rates at a time when many S&L companies were committed to long-term fixed-rate loans and so needed to generate income through speculative schemes. This was compounded by lax regulation at a time when companies were starting to offer a wider range of products. In many ways, the S&L crisis prefigured the larger 2008 financial crash. Gerth had already revealed that President Bush's son Jeb had been involved in a collapsed Florida S&L, so when he learned that Clinton's business associate, Jim McDougal, had run another failed S&L, Madison Guaranty, he was keen to check on the Democratic challenger's involvement. He learned from McDougal himself how the latter had made payments into the Whitewater project on behalf of the Clintons when faltering sales did not cover scheduled loan repayments. Gerth wondered why McDougal would do such a thing; what was in it for him? Seeking access to more capital, McDougal had also acquired Madison Guaranty, which was regulated by an Arkansas state agency for which as Governor, Clinton was technically responsible. Deepening Gerth's suspicions, he learned Clinton had asked McDougal to retain the Rose Legal Firm, and specifically Hillary Clinton, as the Madison Guaranty's legal counsel in proceedings before this agency and had subsequently received favourable assessments from the state regulator.

Gerth smelt a scandal. The Clinton campaign referred him to a New York-based attorney, Susan Thomases, who had agreed to act as Hillary's lawyer. "I don't want everyone digging into our personal records," Hillary had told Thomases in a tone that reflected her Trump-like conviction that one's finances were nobody else's business, even if your husband was running for president. She reiterated this position when the *Washington Post* pressed her for further disclosure in August 1992. To help Thomases handle enquiries, Hillary's colleagues, Webb Hubbell and Vince Foster, gathered Whitewater-related materials from the Rose Legal Firm's files and handed them over to the campaign. Thomases met with Gerth and sought to mollify him by explaining the Clintons' limited involvement in this unsuccessful real estate development, but Gerth still felt he was onto something. During the primary season, however, Whitewater, a complex financial matter with many disparate parts, failed to capture public interest, and given his own family's vulnerability regarding the S&L debacle, the Bush campaign did not make it an issue. When the Clinton team released a report in late March 1992 highlighting that the Clintons lost $68,900 in the venture, and that the available records indicated that the McDougals (Jim and his wife Susan) "exercised total control" over the Whitewater company's activities, the story lost momentum.

One force keeping the story alive as the 1992 election neared was L. Jean Lewis, a federal investigator for the Resolution Trust Corporation (RTC), the federal agency established to probe the actions of bankrupt S&Ls. Lewis, a churchgoing patriotic Republican, was no Bill Clinton fan. Going through McDougal's Madison Guaranty records, she noticed checks made out to the Bill Clinton Political Committee, as well as checks from Whitewater that drew funds from other McDougal-controlled entities in the recognizable pattern of a pyramid scheme. By enabling Whitewater to stay afloat by swapping funds across different accounts, the McDougals, and indirectly the Clintons, had benefited from fraudulent actions. Lewis's referral of the matter placed the U.S. Attorney's office in Little Rock in a tricky position. By this stage, Jim McDougal had been acquitted in Arkansas' state courts, and was suffering multiple health problems, including manic depression, alcoholism, and heart disease. If the office pursued fresh allegations in federal court and expanded the investigation to include the Clintons, it might look like a political manoeuvre, orchestrated from the White House just as the election neared. On reaching Washington, the Madison referral went to Robert Mueller, now famous as Trump's Special Prosecutor, but then working as an Assistant Attorney-General in the criminal division. In a further coincidence, Lewis's report was also sent to the then Attorney-General William Barr; despite its being marked urgent, he failed to respond. Mueller, on the other hand, advised the FBI to investigate and the Bureau, in turn, recommended a "limited investigation." Fearing political repercussion in Arkansas, Little Rock's U.S. Attorney's office refused to participate in this probe. Local FBI agents similarly reported that they saw little value in further action and wondered why Madison Guaranty warranted a second look whereas two other, local, failed S&Ls, with far greater losses, were not to be investigated. Once again, Whitewater was proving a scandal that did not bloom.

During the presidential transition in December 1992, Little Rock businessman and campaign adviser, Jim Blair, urged Clinton to sever any remaining ties to the Whitewater venture before his inauguration.

Accordingly, Vince Foster presented Jim McDougal with an agreement whereby McDougal would buy the Clintons' interest in the company for $1000 thereby releasing them from all future liabilities and would file any overdue corporate tax returns. In an ill-tempered meeting, McDougal pushed back. Foster agreed that the returns should be prepared and filed by the Clintons within ninety days. Although the signed agreement spoke of $1000 being received, McDougal apparently paid nothing. Nonetheless, as Christmas approached, it appeared that Whitewater was no longer a Clinton concern.

A far greater priority for the Clintons in December 1992 was filling the many posts in the new administration. New York-based attorney Bernard Nussbaum was one appointee. He had mentored the young Hillary Rodham during the Watergate investigation and recalled being bemused when she had insisted that he meet her boyfriend, Bill Clinton. Back then, his mockery of her conviction that Bill would be president one day had so infuriated Hillary that he recalled that she had slammed the door of his office and left. Years later, Nussbaum was happy to consider becoming White House Counsel, the same role that John Dean had had during Watergate. Before taking the job, he told the President-elect that virtually every president since Nixon had faced a legal problem that quickly became a political problem, so the position of White House Counsel was strategically important. Few of the post-World War II presidents, he declared, would have survived the intense media scrutiny of their lives that was now the norm. The Clintons had to realize that there would always be people actively seeking dirt on them for commercial and/or political reasons; hence, they would need considerable legal protection. Nussbaum's formulation captured key aspects of why scandal was a recurrent phenomenon in the Clinton presidency. They would be locked in legal and PR battles over allegations that took details from their lives to feed every rumour of scandal.

Having agreed to be the president's lawyer, Nussbaum was introduced to his deputy, Vince Foster. Foster saw himself primarily as Hillary's lawyer, which made for a convenient division of labour. As well as Foster, Hillary had brought another former colleague from Little Rock into the administration. Webster Hubbell was nominated Associate Attorney-General with responsibility for its civil law divisions. At the same time, the Clintons were struggling to achieve their goal of appointing the first

1. Richard Nixon. A gift for cartoonists, Nixon's features also nurtured mistrust as suspicions grew.

2. Watergate bag. Expecting burglars' tools, detectives also found state-of-the-art bugging devices.

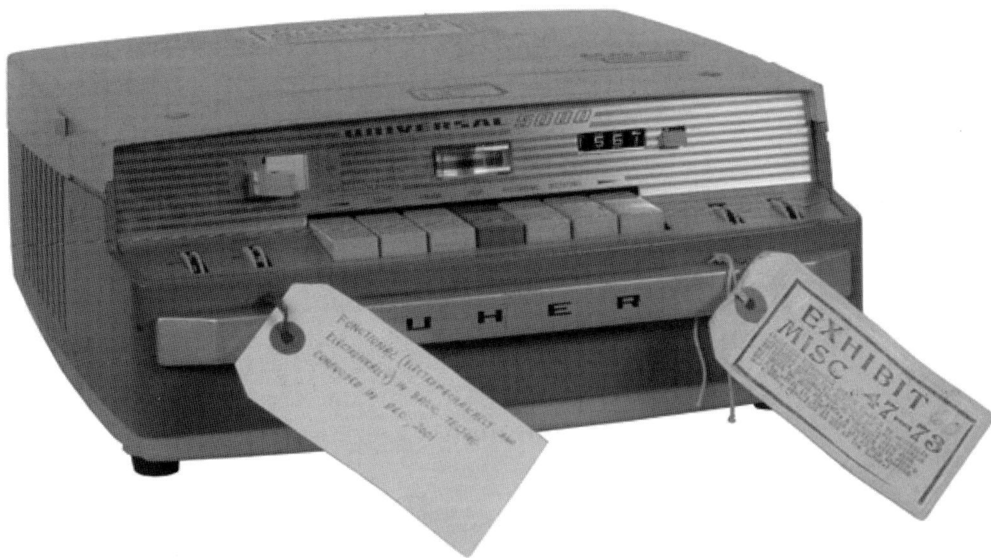

3. Tape Machine. Nixon's secretary, Rosemary Wood, 'accidentally' deleted 18 minutes, 30 seconds of recording in a way that experts were never able to replicate. It deepened doubts.

4. Gerald Ford. Seen initially as a man Americans could trust, Ford lost his reputation when he gave Nixon a full pardon for all crimes.

5. Ronald Reagan. Good looks and geniality were key assets in Reagan's political career. He became known as the 'Teflon President' – nothing stuck to him.

6. Hawk Missiles. Iran desperately wanted US missiles in its fight against Iraq. Supplying them broke both federal law and official policies, and so was done secretly.

7. Reagan made repeated attempts to reassure the public. Attorney General Ed Meese and Chief of Staff Don Regan were supportive of his efforts; Secretary Shultz and Secretary Weinberger, more skeptical.

8. Tower Commission. An independent panel to investigate Iran-Contra, its report criticized Reagan's management style but placed more blame on others. Other probes continued.

9. Oliver North. Testifying before Congress, North successfully presented himself as a loyal soldier obeying orders from his commander-in-chief, the President.

10. Hillary Clinton explains her financials dealings in 1994. In key ways, the Whitewater scandal made the First Lady the initial focus for investigators, both official and journalistic.

11. Clinton's Women Problems: Paula Jones, Monica Lewinsky, Gennifer Flowers. Jones sued Clinton and her case eventually disclosed his relationship with Lewinsky. Flowers drew headlines in 1992 by claiming to be his lover.

12. Independent Counsel Kenneth Starr testifying to the House Judiciary Committee. An ardent Republican and devout Christian, Starr's team was criticized for its tactics in the Lewinsky scandal.

13. Bill and Hillary Clinton and Buddy the Dog. Despite the intense media scrutiny, the First Family continued to project a positive image of their life together.

14. Clinton delivers the 1999 State of the Union Address in the context of his impeachment in the Senate.

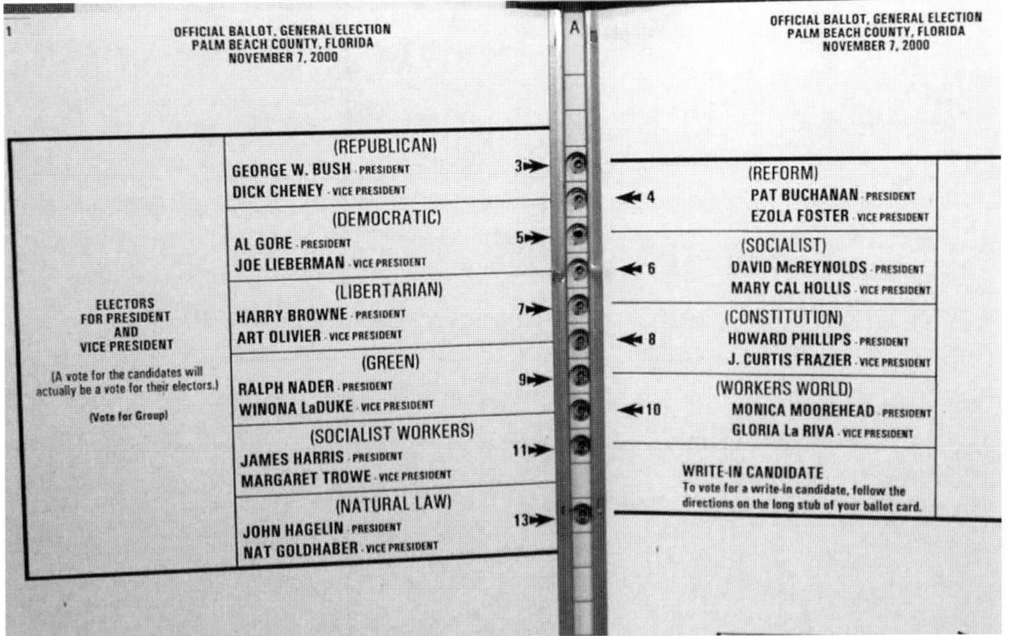

15. The butterfly ballot used in Palm Beach, Florida may have caused Gore supporters to vote for the wrong candidate.

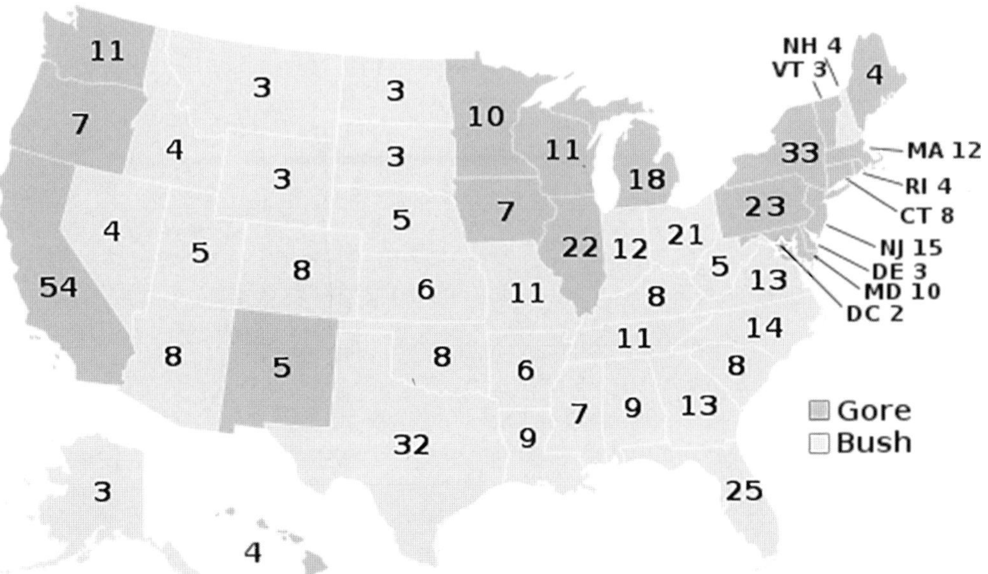

16. Electoral College Map showing state allocation to Bush and to Gore. Despite the close result in one state, the US Supreme Court ruled that no further recounts should occur in Florida.

17. Examining a disputed ballot in Florida. Sometimes, the punch-hole on a ballot could not be determined by the machine and it had to be manually inspected.

18. Vladimir Putin and Donald Trump at the 2019 G20 Summit in Osaka, Japan. Amid concerns about Russian interference in the 2016 election, Trump always spoke positively about Putin.

19. Special Prosecutor Robert Mueller. Former FBI Chief Mueller was advised he could not charge a sitting president, but his report confirmed Russian interference and did NOT exonerate Trump.

20. Donald Trump Jr. The Trump campaign was a family affair. His son Donald was central to the Trump Tower meeting with Russian operatives and was a loud champion of his father at rallies.

21. Ivanka and Jared Kushner at the dedication of the US Embassy in Jerusalem. The most influential family members in the Trump administration, Kushner played an important role in Middle East policy despite some perceived conflicts of interest.

22. President Trump at Honeywell's factory for N95 masks in Arizona in 2020. Despite expert advice, Trump refused to wear a mask during the pandemic, even in a mask making facility that required it.

23. Trump hosts a rally in Nevada September 13, 2020. Trump's election rallies defied health regulations in several states including Nevada, thereby endangering the lives of his own supporters.

24. Trump supporters march on the US Capitol, 6 January, 2021. The culmination of Trump's refusal to allow a peaceful transfer of power to Joe Biden was a rally at which he urged his followers to fight like hell. They took him at his word.

25. Rudy Giuliani. Among the most outspoken of Trump loyalists in the fight to overturn the 2020 election result, Giuliani has consequently faced disbarment as a lawyer in several states and now criminal indictments.

female US Attorney-General. Two successive nominees had withdrawn after press revelations that they had employed undocumented migrants as domestic workers. Hubbell too faced a challenge to his confirmation before the Senate Judiciary Committee. Not only did it seem that his main qualification was his longstanding friendship with the President and First Lady, but he was a member of the Little Rock Country Club, which, despite the outlawing of racial exclusion in 1964, still had no African American members. He was eventually confirmed by the Senate in April 1993 by which time he had resigned from the Club, which happily had recruited its first black member. This illustrated how media coverage of past ties would drag the White House into a steady stream of fresh scandals.

When they followed the Clintons to Washington, Foster and Hubbell felt it prudent to gather any remaining Clinton-related papers at the Rose firm, including those dealing with Whitewater, and file them in the Deputy White House Counsel's office. Foster had the job of ensuring that the sale of Whitewater to McDougal did not excite interest when it appeared on the presidential couple's 1992 tax return, whether as a tax-reducing loss item or as a capital gain. Foster knew that the return should ideally corroborate the campaign's story that Whitewater had lost the Clintons money. But fearing an IRS audit, and unable to disentangle the company's erratic records, he eventually decided in April 1993 to record the sale as a small gain. Meanwhile, a fresh scandal was brewing for Hubbell, arising from his dubious actions while working at the Rose Legal Firm. Foster received a visit from a former colleague on 12 May and it was probably then that he learned that Hubbell was accused of over-billing and cheating on his expenses. This was while the *Wall Street Journal* was targeting Hubbell as part of an ongoing campaign against what it saw as the new administration's lacklustre performance, and while the "Travelgate" episode was generating wider, negative press coverage. Once again, Hillary urged Foster to deal with it.

On 17 June 1993, the *Wall Street Journal* switched its attention to Foster. He, among others, was facing internal scrutiny for his handling of the Travel Bureau episode and drawing fire for defending the secrecy surrounding Hillary Clinton's pending healthcare reform proposals. Adding to the pressure, in late June Jim McDougal started complaining that he still had not received the Whitewater documents, promised when he agreed to "buy" the Clintons out of the venture in December. Given McDougal's increasingly volatile state of mind, Foster may well have been reluctant to hand over materials that McDougal might potentially use to embarrass the First Lady. Colleagues at this point began to notice that Foster was not himself. His wife recalled he lost his appetite, showed a reluctance to socialize, and had difficulty sleeping. By mid-July he was experiencing panic attacks, and he confided to her that he was desperate to escape his new job. On 20 July, Linda Tripp, later famed as Monica Lewinsky's ill-chosen confidante, was working as an executive assistant in the White House. She saw Foster leave his office around 1 p.m. He drove to Fort Marcy Park, a National Parks Service facility, where he found a secluded spot, placed a .38 revolver in his mouth and pulled the trigger. He was the first of several casualties in the Clinton scandals.

Foster's death fanned a phenomenon that had been growing in American culture for decades: the public appetite for conspiracy theories. The sad truth that a shy, fragile man was broken by work pressures, and his own belief that he was letting people down, was buried in torrid speculation. On 22 July, an uncontrite *Wall Street Journal* called for an investigation, even though the police had ruled the death a suicide. On radio talk shows and in tabloids, no speculation was too bizarre. There were stories of drug-smuggling and hidden bank accounts, of Foster's secret love life, with Hillary as the *femme fatale* in some versions and gay lovers triggering his shame in others. Some insisted that the death was not suicide, but a White House-orchestrated assassination. Every detail from the position of the body and the gun to the small quantity of blood at the scene and the disposition of documents from Foster's office was scrutinized to turn his death into a mystery tale.

The energetic efforts of anti-Clinton activists fed this speculation in their quest for any destructive scandal. Future Trump supporter, David Bossie, was communications director for one such group, Citizens United. In the summer of 1993, he was contacted by retired Arkansas Supreme Court Justice Jim Johnson, who was already feeding information to *Clintonwatch: Proving Character Does Count in a President*, a monthly newsletter published by Citizens United's founder, Floyd Brown. Brown's own right-wing credentials included the creation of the notorious "Willie Horton" ad, used to taint Michael Dukakis's 1988 presidential bid. Johnson's hostility to Clinton was well captured when he remarked that the decent people of Arkansas had best apologize to the world for spawning as president, this "queer-mongering, whore-hopping adulterer; a baby-killing, draft-dodging, dope-tolerating, lying, two-faced, treasonist [sic] activist." Now Johnson urged Bossie to contact a man named David Hale, whose Capital Management Services company was under investigation for the misuse of federal small business loans. On 20 July, the day of Foster's suicide, the FBI had obtained a warrant to search and seize Hale's business records.

From Hale, Bossie learned that the questionable loans Hale had made, and for which he had fraudulently secured matching funds from the federal Small Business Administration (SBA), had rarely gone to ventures that met the prescribed approval criteria, such as those for minority entrepreneurs, whose economic opportunities might be limited by institutional barriers in the finance market. Instead, they had gone to what Hale termed the extended Democratic "political family" in Arkansas, including the McDougals and Clinton's successor as governor, Jim Guy Tucker. Hale alleged that in 1985 Governor Clinton had met him and Jim McDougal at the latter's Castle Grande development office in Little Rock to discuss a loan that would illicitly tap SBA funds by having them funnelled through McDougal's wife Susan's company, Master Marketing, (female entrepreneurs being seen as disadvantaged in the finance market). Clinton's involvement seemed linked to his Whitewater investment, so Hale's nefarious dealings might make the latter into a genuine scandal worthy of further investigation. While seeking immunity from prosecution if his client implicated others, Hale's attorney, Randy Coleman, contacted journalist, Jeff Gerth.

In the light of the Hale revelations, federal investigators were considering reactivating the Madison Guaranty investigation, and in September 1993, Clinton officials learned that this might involve the President and First Lady as "more than simply potential witnesses." Soon, both the *Washington Post* and *New York Times* were in hot pursuit of the story in a pattern that would feed the scandal for years to come. The Hale story broke on the *Post*'s front page on 31 October with the *Wall Street Journal* extending coverage into the following week and Gerth at the *New York Times* expanding it. Mike Isikoff and Susan Schmidt at the *Post* played up the connections to Whitewater by stressing that the loan to Susan McDougal had been used to buy further land for commercial development that offset the losses from the slow sale of plots in the original scheme in which the Clintons had invested. Amid active speculation that, as governor, Clinton had profited from the sale of political influence, Bossie and other conservatives made sure that Hale had a chance to present his claims. NBC featured him on a *Nightly News* segment on 11 November and his was the lead story for Brown's 15,000 *Clintonwatch* subscribers. Deepening the intrigue, several reports insinuated that immediately prior to his violent death, Vince Foster had been desperately managing this very scandal, although NBC conceded that there was no evidence that Foster was aware of the impending FBI raid on Hale's offices.

With the sensationalism of Foster's death adding human interest to a dry financial scandal, other media outlets took up the tale in the hope that they might break an even bigger, story by questioning people in Little Rock. Some journalists flew to Arkansas openly to get Clinton. David Brock, for example, worked for both the Republican-leaning *Washington Times* and the *American Spectator*, the magazine of choice for right-wing, talk-show host Rush Limbaugh's listeners. Already notorious for his attack pamphlet on Clarence Thomas's accuser, entitled *The Real Anita Hill*, in which he alleged that she was "a bit nutty and a bit slutty," Brock was drawn predictably to the still widespread rumours that Gennifer Flowers was by no means the only Arkansas woman with a story to tell about Bill Clinton. Two *Los Angeles Times* reporters also arrived in town chasing rumours that pressure was being applied to silence members of Clinton's former gubernatorial security detail. Some of these state troopers recounted multiple adulterous assignations in what became known as "Troopergate." Based on the troopers' stories, Brock's *American Spectator* article, "His Cheatin' Heart," included a description of Clinton's encounter with a woman called "Paula," and this media exposure prompted Paula Corbin Jones's lawsuit against the President.

To assist the media, Brown and Bossie had opened a Little Rock office, where journalists could read a library of original documents about Whitewater. Helped by their efforts to keep the story alive, a relentless flow of accusations fuelled calls for a more formal investigation with Congressional figures suggesting the appointment of an independent counsel. Ironically, the law establishing this post in the aftermath of Watergate was set to expire, and in the wake of Iran-Contra, many Congressional Republicans were reluctant to see it renewed. Prominent Republican attorney Kenneth Starr had already spoken against renewing the measure. White House counsel Bernard Nussbaum, despite his prior involvement in the Watergate investigations, shared the growing misgivings. The Independent Counsel had proved to be, in his words, "an evil institution." Supposedly independent, it had proved a highly politicized instrument with an inherent tendency to expand its role as it strove to find suspect activity that would justify its time and cost. In doing so, it became a politically motivated "roving searchlight" that could easily load associates of the Clintons with heavy, personal legal costs as they faced FBI investigators and subpoenas for sworn grand jury testimony. It could also quickly become a major drain on the energies of the presidency. A scandal, with or without substance, could damage individuals and harm the processes of governing.

Other White House aides did not share Nussbaum's apprehension. They argued that appointing an independent counsel would confirm that the Clintons had nothing to hide and staunch the unending flow of hostile stories. Managing the news cycle was supposed to be at the heart of the Clintons' media spinning operation. Before the Act was renewed, Attorney General Janet Reno should appoint an independent counsel voluntarily. When directed to do so in January 1994, she declared publicly that she wanted someone "ruggedly independent," which effectively meant a Republican appointee. Experienced prosecutor, Robert Fiske, seemed to fit the bill. Appointed by Gerald Ford as US Attorney in New York, his reputation as a Republican moderate had grown during his time as head of the Bar Association's screening panel where he had opposed ideologically motivated, but underqualified, judicial nominations from the Reagan administration. The objective agreed for his investigation was to identify any federal law violations in relation to Whitewater, especially any that revealed obstruction of justice. But Fiske was also free to investigate all other violations that might come to his attention, inviting the "roving searchlight" that alarmed Nussbaum. Once the investigation was fully under way, it seemed that almost half the population of the Ozarks town of Flippin, Arkansas, where Whitewater was based, had to hire a lawyer to prepare them to testify before the grand jury, lest they inadvertently incriminate themselves. Local pride in Clinton's presidency swiftly dissipated. One of gossip's few saving graces is that it often disappears quickly, but legal investigations counter this tendency. The stench of scandal sticks around as subpoenas freeze talk into sworn testimony.

Fiske's team seemed committed to completing its investigation promptly, however. They would certainly check out David Hale's allegations that Clinton was directly involved in Jim McDougal's shady business deals, and this was likely to lead to fresh charges against McDougal, his wife Susan, and even Governor Tucker. Given the endless rumours, the Foster suicide would also have to be re-examined, even though Fiske expected to conclude relatively quickly that the initial findings were correct. But it was not easy to keep the investigation limited as new scandals emerged. In March 1994, Webster Hubbell resigned as an Associate Attorney General amidst charges of embezzling funds in his past role at the Rose Legal Firm where he and Hillary had worked. Almost simultaneously, Bernard Nussbaum resigned as White House Counsel in the face of repeated media allegations that by preventing law enforcement from searching and seizing documents in the Counsel's office, he had interfered in the initial investigation of the Foster suicide. The forced resignations deepened suspicion of the Clinton White House, and Fiske's team subpoenaed Hubbell's papers. This tough line of leaving no rock unturned went unchallenged partly because it protected Reno's Justice Department, which was facing its own scandal after the 1993 assault on the Branch Davidian compound in Waco, Texas. That incident had left seventy-six dead, including twenty-five children, and had helped to fuel the right-wing anger and paranoid mistrust of government that would inspire the 1995 Oklahoma City bombing.

The work of the independent counsel, while rooted in the ideal of objectivity, simply could not escape political partisanship. Fiske alienated already sceptical, conservative Republicans by seeming to cooperate with the White House via his quiet deposition of the President and First Lady on 12 June 1994, and he lost more GOP support when he urged the suspension of Congressional hearings related to Whitewater until his own report had been presented. Fiske's misgivings stemmed from his knowledge of Watergate when the televised Senate hearings had threatened to jeopardize the prosecution of John Dean and other defendants; a risk confirmed by the more recent Iran-Contra mistrials. Dismay at Fiske ironically ended Republican opposition to the reauthorization of the independent counsel law. Mistakenly advised by his new White House Counsel, Lloyd Cutler, that there was little chance that Fiske would be removed, Clinton signed the renewal measure on 30 June 1994. Attorney-General Reno applied to the designated three-judge panel to request Fiske's reappointment, and it came as a shock when the panel dismissed Fiske and replaced him with the more conservative and blatantly partisan Kenneth Starr, who accepted the post he had previously sought to abolish.

Concurrently, the "Trooper-gate" scandal, heavily promoted by conservative activists, had continued to stir things up. David Brock's article in the *American Spectator* had included salacious claims that Arkansas troopers had witnessed open-mouth kissing and breast-fondling between Hillary and Vince Foster, and that the future President had explained to his security detail that Bible study had proved to him that oral sex was not adultery. While Brock did not pay for these revelations, others had raised nearly $14,000 to be shared by the two main informants. By accident rather than design, the magazine's editors neglected to remove the name "Paula" from a passage that described a 1991 incident that occurred at Little Rock's Excelsior Hotel. At Clinton's behest, a trooper had brought Paula to the Governor's private suite, and then stood guard outside for an hour. The article alleged that when she re-emerged, Paula had told him that she was willing to be the Governor's regular girlfriend, if he so desired.

By 1994, Paula Corbin Jones had been married to her aspiring actor-husband Stephen Jones for just over two years; more importantly, she had been engaged to him in 1991. When relatives and friends brought the *Spectator* article to the couple's attention, her husband's anger at her alleged infidelity amplified Paula's own shock and dismay; jointly they decided to take legal advice. Although her motives have been debated, Jones has always insisted that she was not interested in money or celebrity, but in the restitution of her good name; she wanted the world to know that "I'm not a girl that does that kind of thing." In a sworn deposition she related how she was working the registration desk for an event organized by her employer, the Arkansas Industrial Development Commission. She admitted talking to a Clinton bodyguard, whom, she alleged, relayed Clinton's comment that "you make my knees knock." Later the same bodyguard handed her a note indicating that the Governor wanted to meet her. While a colleague offered to cover the desk for her, Jones followed the trooper into the elevator, and he showed her to a room whose door was ajar. Clinton ushered her inside and Jones recounted, he immediately acted "like he had known me for years." When she revealed that she was newly hired by the Development Commission, Clinton mentioned that her boss, who was a good friend, was his appointee, and seemed to imply that he might be able to help Jones, too. As she moved over to the window, Clinton had grabbed her and tried to kiss her.

Shocked, she claimed that she tried to stem his advances by switching the conversation to his wife and her good work for children. But Clinton ignored this and tried to kiss her again. To collect her thoughts and believing that the armed trooper outside the door prevented her departure, Paula then sat on the couch, and there Clinton made his most shocking move. According to her testimony, he pulled his pants down, exposed his penis, and asked: "Would you kiss it for me?" Disgusted, Jones had insisted she was not that kind of girl, adding that she needed to get back to the registration desk. She felt Clinton was embarrassed by her refusal since he looked "flushed." Pulling up his pants, he had called to her that if she got into any trouble, she should have her boss call him immediately. The entire incident, according to Jones, lasted scarcely fifteen minutes and not the hour alleged in the article. This brief encounter, however, would prove pivotal.

Back in 1994, Corbin Jones's lurid claim that Clinton had solicited oral sex fed the rumour mills that were already fuelled by fresh claims about Foster's death and the misdeeds of eccentric Arkansas developers. The case that Corbin Jones eventually brought was actually the work of many sophisticated, legal minds. Little Rock attorney Daniel Traylor set the ball rolling, but quickly welcomed the opportunity to pass his client onto Gil Davis and Joe Cammarata, two Virginia-based lawyers, who were far more politically savvy and better connected. Professionally, Davis knew Bob Bennett, a high-powered, criminal defence lawyer hired by Clinton to represent him in the Jones case. The hiring of such a big shot was a key reason why Davis concluded that Paula must have a case. To ensure that the suit was filed in federal rather than state court, her attorneys tied Jones's complaint to anti-discrimination and employment legislation; this was a stretch but recast the case as one of sexual harassment in the workplace. Other women with whom Clinton had worked might therefore give relevant testimony. Ensuring extensive media coverage, the lawyers indicated in their twenty-page court complaint document that their client was able to specify a "distinguishing characteristic" of Bill Clinton's penis; just the kind of detail to leap from the page of a dry, legal document.

The tangle of media, politics and the law lay at the heart of the Paula Jones case. Eager to tap the expertise of sympathetic constitutional experts as he sought to compel a sitting president to testify, attorney Davis contacted Kenneth Starr who had not yet become independent counsel. In late May 1994 Starr had laid out legal arguments against the current presumption that a president was immune from civil suits while in office, during an appearance on PBS's *MacNeil/Lehrer Newshour*. In conversation with Davis, he seemed willing to file what is known as an *amicus curiae* brief supporting the Jones suit. Davis also elicited advice from Paul Rosenzweig, a DC-based attorney who, later, while working for the Starr investigation, would be instrumental in bringing Linda Tripp to the independent counsel to disclose the Lewinsky affair. Other conservatively minded attorneys were eager to assist Corbin Jones's legal team, notably George Conway, now better known as a vociferous Trump critic, despite being married to Kellyanne Conway, Trump's celebrated media defender. Conway was able to link the Jones team to conservative publicist Ann Coulter and to internet gossipmonger Matt Drudge. In the spring of 1994, however, none of them had any connection to Robert Fiske's ongoing investigation.

What would be characterized by the Clintons as a "right-wing conspiracy" was a gradual build-up of mutual interests. It was not an orchestrated conspiracy as such, but the Clintons' well-financed and politically motivated opponents responded pragmatically to the succession of scandals from Whitewater, via Foster, to Trooper-gate, and then via Jones to Lewinsky, boosting each one in turn. When Jones's attorneys presented their case to the US Supreme Court, their arguments had been refined in collaboration with Robert Bork, Nixon's former Solicitor-General and Reagan's failed nominee to the Supreme Court, and with Theodore Olson, a key legal player in the defence of both Reagan and Bush in the Iran-Contra scandal. Ironically, in 1988 Olsen had argued unsuccessfully before the Court that the independent counsel law was unconstitutional. Neither man wished Clinton well, and neither would casually offer their considerable expertise for free.

Adding substance to the Clintons' conspiracy theory was the decision not to allow Fiske to continue. In the fall of 1992, conservative Chief Justice Rehnquist had quietly replaced the elderly Judge George MacKinnon with Judge David Sentelle on the panel that oversaw independent counsel appointments. MacKinnon was known to avoid strongly partisan appointing counsels whereas Sentelle was openly Republican. He was joined on the three-man panel by Joseph Sneed, whose outlook was even more conservative. This left John Butzner as the lone Democrat, and when the panel met to consider the position of independent counsel in July 1994, Sentelle favoured appointing Kenneth Starr rather than reappointing Robert Fiske. Virtually ensuring Starr's appointment was the high regard that Sneed had for him due to their shared time at Duke Law School, Richard Nixon's alma mater. As a Duke faculty member, Sneed had taught Starr in the early 1970s and admired his plain, Texan origins and strong, moral code. Using the excuse that Fiske had been appointed by Clinton's Attorney General rather than by the independent panel, Judge Sentelle announced that Starr would be the new independent counsel in accordance with the newly signed law. It was later revealed that shortly before the announcement, Sentelle had lunched in the Capitol with North Carolina's two Republican senators, McLauchlin Faircloth and Jesse Helms. Despite Sentelle's insistence that the trio had spent more time discussing their prostate problems than the independent counsel question, both senators were known to feel that Fiske had not probed the President's dubious actions hard enough. Starr was more likely to get to the bottom of things.

Fiske and Starr maintained professional courtesies in the handover of responsibilities but most of Fiske's team decided not to stay on, and Starr's recruits brought a more adversarial style. Hickman Ewing, who took charge of the Little Rock office, for instance, shared Starr's fundamentalist Christian mindset, and Jackie Bennett joined the Office of Independent Counsel (OIC) because he was convinced that Clinton was morally "corrupt." If sections of the American public seemed less than scandalized by Clinton's behaviour, Starr's top lawyers retained that capacity. As many of Fiske's most highly qualified hires decided to return to their pre-Whitewater careers, their roles were filled by young, ambitious, and relatively untested newcomers, some with anti-Clinton prejudices. Four years out from Yale Law School, the future Supreme Court Justice Brett

Kavanaugh joined as an associate counsel having previously worked with Starr when the latter was Bush's Solicitor-General. To try to protect his investigation from charges of bias, Starr hired Sam Dash as OIC ethics adviser. Dash had served with distinction as chief counsel for the Senate Watergate Committee and had helped to craft the first independent counsel law. Ultimately Dash would resign when Starr felt he had an obligation to testify to Congress in favour of impeachment, a move which Dash saw as overtly partisan.

Of the rolling mix of defendants in Starr's sights as 1994 ended, the first to face charges was Webster Hubbell who confessed to defrauding the Rose Law firm and its clients and to filing false tax returns. Bargaining cooperation for a reduced sentence, Hubbell has always insisted that he told the investigators all he knew. However, they were disappointed that he provided no case against either of the Clintons or any other player in the Arkansas financial follies. The OIC next tried to use David Hale, whose credibility was wafer-thin, given the scale and diversity of his own con-schemes. He had already admitted to fraudulently obtaining Small Business Administration loans, and state prosecutors were set to indict him for a burial insurance scam; the latter had also disclosed his affair with his secretary, largely because he had simultaneously swindled her grandparents out of $486,000. Worse still for the investigation, the person most likely to be able to corroborate Hale's suspect testimony was Jim McDougal. But should Starr rest his hope of conviction in a complex trial on a volatile individual with manic depression and other health conditions? Jim's ex-wife Susan was another OIC target, but she was now involved in a bizarre scandal all her own, being charged in California with embezzling $150,000 from Nancy, the eccentric wife of renowned conductor Zubin Mehta. Offered immunity for her cooperation in March 1995, Susan made it clear that she knew nothing that would incriminate either Bill or Hillary Clinton. Thus, the Starr team felt compelled to use Hale's evidence to prosecute the McDougals fully as well as Arkansas Governor Jim Guy Tucker on multiple counts of fraud, in the hope that the threat of prison might stir the defendants' memories of Clinton complicity.

On 29 April 1996, with the trial against Hale, Tucker and the McDougals under way, federal prosecutors arrived to take Bill Clinton's videotaped testimony. This was the fourth time he had testified about Whitewater and his priority this day was to cast doubt on Hale's claims that he had played a part in securing loans for the McDougals and Tucker. He denied that the meeting at Jim McDougal's office that Hale alleged he attended, ever happened. Meanwhile, the Whitewater scandal had resurfaced in the media in January 1996 because of the discovery of 116 pages of supposedly lost records, largely related to Rose Law Firm billing, that detailed Hillary Clinton's legal work for the McDougals and their Madison Guaranty S&L. Webster Hubbell had told the Senate Whitewater Committee that Vince Foster was the last person he had seen with these papers, but they had not been found in his office after his suicide. Now they had rematerialized in the White House residence, and they raised doubts about Hillary's sworn testimony that she had little or no involvement with the McDougals, specifically at the time when they were seeking funds via Hale's dubious schemes.

Convicted along with Hale, Jim and Susan McDougal had divergent responses to the OIC's renewed invitations to cooperate. Jim, whose mental health problems were worsening due to his multiple addictions, seemed ready to help the OIC formulate a narrative trail that might trap the Clintons. Desperate, he was ready to consider anything to avoid prison. Susan, by contrast, was resolutely uncooperative. Irked, the Starr team reported to the sentencing judge that the former Mrs McDougal had played an active role in Hale's fraudulent loan schemes, had refused to cooperate with their investigation, and had attempted to camouflage her criminal acts. Taking this into account, the judge sentenced her on 20 August 1996, to two years in federal prison, 300 hours of community service, and fines and restitution totalling $305,000. On 4 September, Susan appeared before the OIC's Little Rock grand jury, where her refusal to answer questions resulted in her being jailed for contempt. Unusually, the US marshal processing her imprisonment placed her in shackles and leg irons for the short walk to a prison van. It made for a compelling TV image.

Feeding the media was an integral part of the legal and political manoeuvres that kept the Clinton scandals alive. As Whitewater subsided, the Paula Jones suit came back to the boil. An anonymous female caller, tentatively identified as Kathleen Willey, contacted Jones's lawyer Joe Cammarata in the summer of 1996. He did not have time to check out her claim that Clinton had grabbed her and sexually molested her in a room adjoining the Oval Office, but he was sure that journalist Mike Isikoff at *Newsweek* would pursue it, if he told him. It was Isikoff who identified Willey, but more importantly learned that she had confided in a co-worker, Linda Tripp, already known to the OIC as the last person to see Vince Foster alive. Tripp shared her inside knowledge of this new accusation against the President with a young co-worker, who, like her, had previously worked in the White House before being transferred to work at the Pentagon. Thus, Monica Lewinsky learned that her beloved president was facing another scandal, breaking just as the Jones case was scheduled before the US Supreme Court; so, she sent him a warning. Tripp, on the other hand, was already testing whether her inside knowledge of Clinton's misbehaviour could win her a lucrative book deal.

Having earned a psychology degree from Lewis & Clark College in Oregon, Monica Lewinsky had moved to Washington at the invitation of her divorced mother, Marcia, who had previously worked for the *Hollywood Reporter*, but was now moving east. Marcia had opted for an apartment in the Watergate complex. In 1996, under the pen-name Marcia Lewis, she published a gossipy account of *The Private Lives of the Three Tenors*. While detailing the many loves of Luciano Pavarotti, José Carreras, and Placido Domingo, she dropped heavy hints that she knew Domingo particularly well. When her daughter's affair with the President became the talk of the nation, reporters were apt to imply that Monica had followed in her mother's star-struck footsteps. One of Marcia's many wealthy friends had helped Monica get a job in 1995 as a summer intern at the White House, with a view to boosting her pending grad school applications. Monica started work in Chief-of-Staff Leon Panetta's office handling correspondence. On 10 August 1995, she joined other interns at a surprise forty-ninth birthday party for Clinton. She would later tell the grand jury that she felt "an intense connection" as soon as he shook her hand. That evening she read her new bookstore purchase – Gennifer Flowers's autobiography, *Passion and Betrayal*. The federal governmental shutdown that Republican House Speaker Newt Gingrich staged in an attempt to pressurize Clinton to approve huge budget cuts unwittingly facilitated the start of Lewinsky's relationship with the President. Newly appointed to a paid position in the East Wing of the White House, Monica was one of a small group manning the phones. On the evening of November 15,

Clinton invited her into his study where he asked if he might kiss her, and she consented. Later that night, they met again, and their intimacy grew to include – as Monica testified: "Everything up until oral sex."

Two nights later, Lewinsky was able to meet Clinton again on the pretext of delivering pizza. In a rear study area, they were "physically intimate again." Their clandestine meetings grew in frequency over the next few months, and the President made late-night phone calls during which they would engage in sexual banter. On Monica's side, the relationship was more than simply sexual and had elements of genuine depth and affection. One might see her as infatuated. She confided to her parents that she had been able to see the President and go to the Oval Office during the lockdown, but she did not disclose the relationship's full character. When her family visited in June 1996, they were impressed when the Secret Service welcomed Monica by name, and amazed when they were able to have a group photo with Clinton in the Oval Office. After a year, however, the illicit relationship was faltering as Bill belatedly recognized his folly but struggled to disentangle himself. "Dump Day," as Monica labelled it, came in May 1997. She recalled the crest-fallen President told her that he wanted "to do the right thing in God's eyes and do the right thing for his family." However, unfortunately for Clinton, the young and vulnerable Lewinsky had coped with the rollercoaster of their relationship by confiding in Linda Tripp, who, in her own version of events, depicts herself as maternally wanting to save Monica and to call Clinton to account for his misuse of power.

Had the Lewinsky affair not reignited a media frenzy about Clinton's character, there were signs in 1997 that the OIC investigation might prove anti-climactic. Having painstakingly gone over the Foster suicide and found no evidence of foul play and Clinton plotting, and with the prosecutions of Whitewater-associated fraud on track to indict neither of the Clintons, even Kenneth Starr by February 1997 felt his investigation was losing steam. He therefore listened with interest to overtures from Pepperdine University School of Law in California, which was seeking a new dean. Dismayed by Starr's failure to nail the Clintons, conservative pundits responded to rumours that he might now jump ship with angry recriminations. Some have seen Starr's spring troubles in 1997 as a watershed when the under-fire investigation pivoted towards the issue of Clinton, sex, and women. The conviction of the McDougals in April seemed to mark an end to the Whitewater chapter, and if Clinton had been able to settle the Jones case before her attorneys' pursuit of a "pattern of behaviour" by him towards other women had led them to Lewinsky, this scandal-ridden presidency might not be forever associated with impeachment, and a semen-stained dress.

Jones's Virginia lawyers had managed to extract a settlement offer of some $700,000 and they tried hard to convince their client that this was far more than a jury would award her, or worse, that she might not win. But Jones's husband Steve did not favour an out-of-court settlement and conservative publicist Susan Carpenter-McMillan, also steered Paula away from the deal. Irked by this grandstanding by the plaintiff, federal judge Susan Webber Wright granted Davis and Cammarata their motion to withdraw as Jones's counsel while ruling that they remained entitled to payment for their services. She also stipulated that the case must be fast-tracked for trial since she suspected that the plaintiff might value her current celebrity status more than justice.

In late September 1997, the OIC filed its hefty report on Vince Foster's death, which simply affirmed what Robert Fiske had concluded in 1994: suicide by gunshot. By November, Starr had decided that the Whitewater scandal had run its course, too, and gave his staff the confidential task of assessing whether what they had on Bill Clinton was enough for them to report to Congress with a view to impeachment. Starr also asked Paul Rosenzweig to assess the case for indicting Hillary Clinton for her part in the scandal. Two checks were crucial to proving that the President lied when he said he had no part in McDougal's efforts to secure funds for the failing Whitewater project from David Hale. One for $27,600, payable to Bill Clinton, had been found bizarrely in the trunk of a car that was on the brink of being crushed in a junkyard. The other for $5,081.82 was signed by Susan McDougal and drew on Jim's account at Madison Guaranty. The sum was for the exact amount outstanding on a previous Clinton loan and had the notation "Payoff Clinton" on the reverse side.

Weakening the case, however, was the fact that neither Clinton's signature nor his fingerprints were on either check, and the OIC knew that Jim McDougal had gotten into the habit of moving money around in other people's names without their knowledge. Similarly, while it was plausible to query both Clinton's sworn statement that he knew nothing about Hale's fraudulent loan to Susan McDougal's company and his insistence that he had no recollection of asking Jim McDougal to give legal work to Hillary at the Rose Legal Firm, there was a big gap from "plausible" to "proven." Accordingly, Starr's own team agreed that they should not send this report to Congress; Starr shelved it in the faint hope that the jailed Susan McDougal might have a change of heart. He was not prepared to join the swelling call for impeachment from conservative pundits that fall. But the chorus was audible before the Lewinsky story broke.

On Christmas Eve 1997, Monica Lewinsky worked her last day at the Pentagon and pressed ahead with plans to move to New York where her mother was now based. The least her former love interest could do, she told the President was to help her find a job there. Clinton asked his friend and renowned power broker Vernon Jordan if he could help, and he agreed. Unbeknown to both men, the OIC's Jackie Bennett received a phone call on 12 January 1998, from a woman who said she had proof of an affair between Clinton and a White House intern. More importantly, she said that the intern had been coached to lie about the relationship in a deposition in the Paula Jones case. The call was not a surprise to the OIC lawyers. An old law school friend of Paul Rosenzweig, Jerome Marcus, had been helping the Jones legal team and he had heard talk of another woman involved with Clinton, who had lied on his behalf, and that Clinton had asked Vernon Jordan to get her a job in return. Better yet, there were tapes to prove it. Rosenzweig recalled that Vernon Jordan had already been a subject of interest to the OIC because they had wanted to check whether he had secured work for Webster Hubbell to pay off the tarnished attorney for not telling all he knew about the Clintons. In retrospect, it seems that Marcus's lead was part of a calculated, political steering operation and the IOC took the bait.

The Clinton-Lewinsky-Jordan storyline worked especially well on Jackie Bennett. Bennett already knew that Clinton was set to be deposed in the Jones case on 17 January so this offered a chance that he might lie under oath. But Bennett knew he had to be careful since press coverage of the OIC's recent attempts to interview the Arkansas troopers about Clinton's sexual escapades had badly damaged the investigation's public image. For Starr and the rest of the team, it was the alleged role of Vernon

Jordan as a "Mr. Fixit" that made them believe that they had to follow up all stories about the President's buying the silence of witnesses. Except that this discovery was carefully stage-managed. As soon as Rosenzweig phoned Marcus to say that if the person with the tapes wanted to approach the OIC, they would be welcome, news of the invitation sped to Linda Tripp's New York-based literary agent Lucianne Goldberg, who eagerly passed along Jackie Bennett's phone number. A specialist in kiss-and-tell books, the flamboyant Goldberg had spied for Nixon back in 1972 and now had friends at *Fox News*, Roger Ailes's still new, conservative cable channel. The Lewinsky scandal would prove a goldmine for cable news.

If the OIC had hoped to handle this matter discreetly, they were operating alongside others with the opposite intention. As Bennett worked late preparing for his deposition of the First Lady on outstanding Whitewater matters, Tripp's halting, husky voice came on the line. She was calling on behalf of a friend who needed to know that if she helped the OIC, it would grant her legal immunity because she had learned that it was illegal to tape phone-calls. Once Bennett reassured her that immunity could be given, Tripp dropped the pretence and revealed she was set to have lunch with Lewinsky the next day. She also reminded Bennett that she had already testified to the grand jury over both Vince Foster's death and the Travel Office scandal. Even though it was 10:15 at night, he told her that he and other staff would visit her immediately to prepare her for her meeting with Lewinsky. She gave directions to her home, forty-five minutes' drive away.

Listening to Tripp's knowledge of Monica's affair with Clinton, Bennett and the FBI agents who sped to Maryland that night all agreed that she was a credible witness. She came across as smart, if not particularly pleasant. They were disappointed to learn that the tapes were not in her possession but with her lawyer. She still worried that those tapes were illegal and said that her lawyer had suggested she carry an audio-bug to her lunch meeting and induce Lewinsky to repeat afresh the "greatest hits" from their taped phone conversations. Bennett said that she would certainly be wired by the FBI who would ensure a professional record was kept of any crucial conversations. The next day, 13 January 1998, Tripp went to the Ritz-Carlton Hotel in the Pentagon City Mall and was fitted with a concealed, state-of-the-art, recording device ahead of her rendezvous with Lewinsky. She coaxed her young friend to talk about Clinton and the Jones case and got Monica to say that if Tripp confirmed Monica's denial of an affair with the President, she would be indebted to her for life. Tripp would always insist that she broke Lewinsky's confidences because she felt the country had a right to know the kind of man who was their president, and she characterized Clinton as not just sexually adolescent, but arrogant and reckless. Lucianne Goldberg saw her client as a patriot, motivated by moral outrage. But she also saw her as dangerously naïve if she felt that the move would benefit Monica. "You realize the press will destroy her," she told Tripp, adding that simultaneously the Clinton people would be out to destroy them both. Tripp was undeterred, although her overtures to the Starr team grew partly from her fear of Clinton retribution.

Ideally, the OIC wanted proof that Clinton had used his friend Vernon Jordan's influence to secure employment for Lewinsky in return for her perjury. On 7 October 1997, Monica had written the President an angry letter asking for his help in finding a job and suggesting the UN since she had been organizing international conferences while at the Pentagon. Within weeks, Monica had an interview with the UN Ambassador Bill Richardson, who offered her an entry-level position in the UN's public relations section. But Monica's mother had checked out the UN complex in Manhattan and had been struck by the many Arabs working there; maybe this wasn't the right place for a nice Jewish girl? Monica relayed back her preference for a job in the private sector and met with Vernon Jordan in early November. On 5 December, Lewinsky's name was included in the witness list faxed to the President's lawyer by Paula Jones's new, Texas-based attorneys and on 11 December, Monica met Jordan a second time and was given contacts at three major New York corporate offices. She has always insisted that there was never any discussion of a *quid pro quo*, even though the contacts helped her to secure a $40,000 a year PR job with Revlon. This was less than she had earned at the Pentagon and that job offer disappeared when the media frenzy erupted in January 1998.

On 19 December 1997, Lewinsky was served a subpoena to testify in the Paula Jones case. Two nights earlier, well after midnight, Clinton had called and said that she might be able to sign an affidavit to avoid testifying if subpoenaed. A freaked-out Lewinsky called Jordan when the subpoena arrived, and they met the same day. He asked her directly if she had ever had sex with the President and Monica immediately replied, "No." He read the subpoena and said he would find her a good lawyer. Days later, as Jordan drove her to attorney Francis Carter's office, she confessed that she and Clinton had engaged in "phone sex." Jordan raised an eyebrow and Monica attempted to describe what this might entail, but Jordan indicated that he did not want to know. He was savvy enough to realize that the less he knew the better.

The subpoena required Lewinsky to present a list of items that connected her to Clinton, including greeting cards received, photos, gifts and thank you notes. At their first meeting Carter asked Monica to bring them to him in two days' time and listened while she explained that she didn't know why she had been subpoenaed and really didn't want to be involved in a scandalous case like the one Paula Jones was pursuing. Accordingly, he agreed to argue to the judge that requiring his client to testify would be a needless embarrassment when her only fault was that her work as a White House intern had brought her into proximity with the President. Carter also alerted Jones's attorneys that he was seeking an order to quash the subpoena and contacted the President's lawyer Bob Bennett to check if he knew of any reason why this young intern was on the list. Bennett replied he hadn't a clue why her name was there. On 7 January, Carter gave Lewinsky her copy and sent the affidavit to Judge Wright in Arkansas by FedEx.

Judge Susan Webber Wright was already weary of the Paula Jones suit, especially since the plaintiff had rejected a reasonable settlement that might have ended the matter ages ago. Jones's new attorneys came from a small Texan firm committed to conservative causes. On 12 January, Wright felt compelled to warn both sides that the continuing media coverage showed that her gag order was being ignored. She cautioned that if she identified who was leaking, especially from California (where the Joneses were living by that point), she would issue contempt orders. She scheduled the President's deposition for 17 January at his personal attorney's office, although to the outside world it must be "at an undisclosed location." She also sternly urged the parties to settle. She warned the Jones's side that in her view, it was unlikely that a jury would find for the plaintiff and that she would be reading Bennett's motion for a summary judgment of dismissal with care.

Among the female witnesses for the plaintiff, each listed anonymously as "Jane Doe" in the court papers, was Monica Lewinsky. The Texas lawyers had chosen her because her age, employment status, and Clinton's request for oral sex all paralleled Corbin Jones's experience. Defending the President, Bob Bennett urged Wright to deny the relevance of these witnesses since their main purpose, he argued, was solely "to embarrass the President." Certainly, most of them had no relevance to a case that claimed workplace discrimination. Wright ruled that only a limited and reasonable exploration of sexual contact would be permitted, and she excluded matters that predated the alleged Jones incident by more than five years or involved non-employees. She warned that she would keep a tight rein on cross examination. Lewinsky's testimony was nonetheless permitted.

When Bob Bennett asked at the White House about Monica, or "Jane Doe #6" as she was listed in court documents, he was told that there was no cause for concern. When he called Frank Carter, he was assured that Lewinsky's affidavit spoke of nothing more intimate than the delivery of pizza. This reinforced Bennett's confidence. He had already interrogated Corbin Jones about her own sexual past and felt no jury would credit her claims to purity or naivety. If needed, he also had expert medical testimony that anyone claiming that Bill Clinton's penis bent to one side, like some kind of leaning tower of Pisa, was clearly someone who had never actually seen his entirely normal penis.

Bennett's namesake, Jackie Bennett at the OIC, came to the White House on 14 January 1998, to take testimony from Hillary Clinton, and recalled thinking to himself that clearly neither the First Lady nor her lawyers had any idea of what was coming. The same evening the Starr team debated how to encompass the Lewinsky evidence that Linda Tripp had brought them. Bennett opposed the idea that Starr should ask the Justice Department to hand over this new allegation to a fresh investigative team. He wanted permission to move quickly so that Clinton would testify at his scheduled deposition in the Jones case without being tipped off. Adding to Bennett's unease, he had a call from journalist Mike Isikoff, who had moved from the *Post* to *Newsweek,* signalling that the press already knew about Lewinsky. Tripp's literary agent, Lucianne Goldberg was working to ensure that this scandal broke quickly. The only upside was that this strengthened Bennett's argument for letting the Starr team press ahead.

There might be a window of just thirty-six hours to flip Lewinsky. Since any delay might be seen as corruptly benefitting the President, Attorney-General Reno felt she had to let the Starr team proceed.

On the same day, 14 January, Monica Lewinsky handed Linda Tripp a typed, three-page document labelled "Talking Points." It advised Tripp to follow the same steps that Lewinsky had in the Paula Jones case: namely, file an affidavit to avoid having to testify. It largely consisted of guidelines of what to put in and leave out of her affidavit. According to Lewinsky, they were largely ideas that Tripp herself had raised in previous conversations. Tripp, on the other hand, insists that the document must have been passed to Lewinsky by one of Clinton's many lawyers. Interpreted that way, it was evidence of an attempt to induce a witness to perjury and thus obstruct justice. The OIC was inclined to see the "Talking Points" in that way, too.

From this point on, the OIC's actions grew more aggressively hostile to the Clintons. While it is fair to say that its prosecutors had no duty to warn the President lest he lie in his scheduled deposition, they equally had no call to induce Isikoff to delay his story in order to ensure that his reporting did not forewarn Clinton or Lewinsky. The knowledge that the scandal was about to break pressed the Justice Department to request the judicial panel to extend Starr's authority and that hasty decision tainted the investigation. It suggested that their main concern had become how to "get" Clinton. They proceeded on an assumption of guilt rather than of innocence, and in the hope that the Tripp tapes would document that Vernon Jordan had helped Lewinsky explicitly to ensure her false testimony; in fact, they didn't. Monica Lewinsky would experience this new aggressive strategy first-hand.

On 16 January 1998, a tearful Monica, apprehended as she met Tripp for lunch, was escorted by FBI agents to a room at the Ritz-Carlton Hotel. OIC attorney Mike Emmick immediately tried to question her, but she was too distressed to respond coherently. Agents tried to calm her. They were keen to induce her to cooperate with their investigation by agreeing to entrap others. More damaging to the OIC's subsequent reputation, however, they did not respond appropriately to Lewinsky's repeated, legitimate request to contact her lawyer, Frank Carter. Seemingly denied legal counsel, a distraught Monica said she needed her mother. Jackie Bennett took over the questioning from Emmick. She wasn't a child, he sneered. In his view this 23-year-old didn't need to call her mommy. Instead, she needed to face up to the fact that lying in a legal document was a serious thing.

But, as time dragged on without progress, Monica was allowed the call. To her mother's ears, she sounded hysterical as she reported that the FBI had grabbed her. Monica asked the OIC men to explain and a worried Marcia said she would come to Washington on the next train from New York. Having alarmed Lewinsky by saying that both she and her mother might be facing charges, Emmick tried to secure her cooperation by offering immunity if she was prepared to cooperate; by phoning Clinton's White House secretary, Betty Currie, for example, to secure taped evidence of her complicity. Bennett was not happy that Emmick had offered mother and daughter blanket immunity. Monica's mother, Marcia arrived at 10:16 pm. The attorneys then brusquely told her that her daughter was facing up to twenty-seven years in prison for witness tampering and filing a false affidavit. Securing evidence on others was their prerequisite for immunity.

Marcia was stunned by the severe repercussions of her daughter's ill-judged liaison. She informed the OIC staffers that she had phoned her ex-husband from the train, and he wanted to talk to them from Los Angeles. Meanwhile, Bernie Lewinsky, a physician, had contacted a lawyer friend Bill Ginsberg whose specialty was medical malpractice. If the Lewinsky family had wanted an attorney with discretion and skills specific to their daughter's predicament, Ginsberg was the wrong choice. His first mistake was not taking the offer of blanket immunity that Emmick made over the phone, instead he berated him for keeping Monica under questioning without counsel for several hours. Since it looked as if hopes of a deal were gone, both Monica and her mother were given subpoenas to supply all tangible items indicative of Lewinsky's relationship with Clinton and allowed to leave. That night, Monica remembers thinking whether everyone would be spared the unfolding nightmare if she found an efficient way to kill herself. The personal damage from the Clinton scandals was growing.

The next morning President Clinton's deposition was set for 10:30 am in his attorney Bob Bennett's office. If he was not tipped off, there was still a chance that his sworn testimony would contain perjury and thereby revive the hugely expensive and lengthy investigation which might otherwise prove inconclusive. Understandably, Clinton was in a dark mood that morning. He has always insisted that Paula Jones's allegations were completely false and sustained by the pursuit of celebrity (otherwise why reject a generous cash settlement?) and by vicious politics. This civil case nominally sued him as a private citizen, but it would not have lasted if he had not been president. Had he been an unknown Arkansas male, it would have been summarily dismissed, and the scandal would have faded. At the outset, Jones's attorney presented a definition of "sexual relations" so that Clinton would know the scope of what was under discussion. Reluctantly, Judge Wright accepted but edited his definition so that it referred to actions that knowingly engaged or caused "contact with the genitalia, anus, groin, breast, inner thigh, or buttocks of any person with an intent to arouse or gratify the sexual desire of that person."

The "intent" aspect of the definition would ultimately prove crucial to Clinton's response. His testimony would be recorded (ostensibly for the benefit of the jury) and his responses to questions on the topic were likely to fuel at least gossip and most likely, scandal, if they leaked. After Clinton had categorically denied the groping accusations made by Kathleen Willey, cross-examination moved on to Lewinsky. Clinton's counsel Bob Bennett interjected that both sides were aware that Ms Lewinsky had filed an affidavit that denied sexual relations. Nevertheless, Clinton was asked if he had spent time alone with Lewinsky and asked if he had given her gifts. Eventually, James Fisher as Jones's lead attorney asked: "have you ever had sexual relations with Monica Lewinsky, as that term is defined in Deposition Exhibit 1, as modified by the Court?" and to this Clinton responded that he "never had." Most would conclude that he lied. It was a lie largely peripheral to the Jones allegation itself and in April 1998, her case against Clinton would be dismissed. But it was the moment that would lead to impeachment.

Back at the White House, media enquiries flagged that a story was about to break about the Starr investigation and perjury in connection with someone called Monica Lewinsky. Having privately asked and been assured that there was no sexual relationship, attorney Bob Bennett used his time at the deposition to reinforce Clinton's corroboration of Lewinsky's affidavit: there was no sexual relationship and any suggestion that she had received or been denied employment or other benefits on the basis of accepting or rejecting a sexual relationship was false. Clinton's denial of Paula Corbin Jones's allegations was quickly summarized, and the White House team left the deposition feeling upbeat. The mood within the Lewinsky family was very different, especially once the story broke and made Monica a topic of global fascination. The scandal quickly engulfed her separated parents with commentators speculating over whether Monica's inappropriate relationship with the President stemmed from missteps in their parenting. Her mother Marcia faced the legal threat of indictment if it could be demonstrated that she had more knowledge of her daughter's actions than she acknowledged in sworn testimony to the OIC. She was bewildered at how rarely people accepted that a daughter might not confide unreservedly in her mother.

Having arrived in Washington, Lewinsky's attorney Bill Ginsburg continued to make life difficult for OIC prosecutors, many of whom felt that he was relishing his position as attorney to the currently most famous client in the world. He rarely refused an invitation to speak on television. Hardliners like Jackie Bennett were ready to tell Ginsberg that if Monica could not provide the OIC with the evidence it needed, she would be prosecuted to the full extent of the law. Ginsberg was equally ready to insist that his client would not be part of the entrapment of the President unless it involved a crime on a par with espionage or treason. At the same time, he warned Monica to ignore efforts by the White House to contact her via Betty Currie; his job was saving her, not Clinton. The result was that meetings between the Starr team and Ginsberg did not go well. By 21 January 1998, the Lewinsky story was in the *Washington Post, Los Angeles Times* and on *ABC News* and was set to dominate the news cycle in a way not seen since Watergate.

President Clinton had a prescheduled interview with Jim Lehrer for *PBS*'s *Newshour*. During this, he said emphatically: "There is no improper relationship." In later interviews he insisted he would cooperate with the Starr investigation, adding that he didn't ask anyone to lie. Such was the level of mistrust across the media that Clinton's use of the present tense to describe his relationship with Lewinsky was seized upon; at present it was true that there was no improper relationship, but had there been in the past? Pondering how best to respond, Clinton conferred with his disgraced former political consultant Dick Morris, whose own use of high-end, DC call-girls had prompted his dismissal from the 1996 campaign. Quickly and discreetly, Morris commissioned a poll which found that if it were just adultery, the public would forgive and forget, but 60 percent of respondents would back removal from office if Clinton had committed perjury or encouraged Monica to lie. Morris advised Clinton to prepare the ground for an admission of adultery, while insisting that he had not obstructed justice by suborning perjury. Vernon Jordan swiftly reduced his own vulnerability by stating publicly that Lewinsky had assured him that she had not had a sexual relationship with the President, and he had consistently advised her to tell the truth.

Still striving to prove that Clinton had not just lied under oath himself but had encouraged Lewinsky to do the same, the Starr team interrogated not just Lewinsky and her mother, but the Secret Service agents assigned to protect the President. Quickly, however, the White House counter-attacked, charging that the endless media stories about the scandal could only occur because of calculated press briefings by the OIC in a gross breach of restrictions protecting grand jury evidence. Clinton himself on 26 January made a televised speech in which he reiterated his denial. Wagging his finger, he declared "I did not have sexual relations with that woman… Ms Lewinsky," adding "I never told anybody to lie, not a single time, never." The next day in an interview on NBC's *Today* show, the First Lady rose to her husband's defence, complaining that the press was in a "feeding frenzy" over tabloid gossip and neglecting the bigger story of a "vast right-wing conspiracy" that had been conspiring against her husband ever since he announced his candidacy.

Hillary Clinton had made similar accusations before and her conviction had grown since in her view, the news media seemed fixated on "gotcha" journalism, rooted in the belief that politicians always lie. From November 1993 until early February 1994, the *Washington Post* had published sixty-two articles on Whitewater, a relentless level of coverage that reflected the legacy of Watergate at the newspaper that essentially broke the story. It also reflected personal judgment. Editor Len Downie believed that it was the *Post*'s duty to compel government officials to tell the truth, and he saw Bill Clinton as a skilled liar. He had not told the truth as a candidate about his efforts to avoid the draft nor his pot-smoking. He had also made an unwelcome pass at a *Post* reporter, so Downie's overall assessment was that Clinton displayed an arrogance of power that needed to be checked. Hillary Clinton in turn believed that Downie was simply out to get them, and her hostility and refusal to supply documents deepened the *Post*'s own suspicions. To an outsider, however, to see the liberal-leaning *Post* as part of a right-wing conspiracy verges on paranoia.

Fuelling the First Lady's frustration was the reality that there were right-wing interests with deep pockets eager to damage the Clintons whenever the opportunity arose. They had believed that the Republican surge in the 1994 mid-terms had set the stage for Clinton's defeat and his 1996 re-election had been a bitter blow. James Moody, one of a succession of attorneys advising Linda Tripp, was a member of the right-wing Federalist Society, whose members also included Kenneth Starr, as well as Jerome Marcus and George Conway who had discreetly assisted the Paula Jones suit. Moody was recommended to Tripp by right-wing publicist and *Fox News* pundit Ann Coulter. Tripp later testified that it was Moody who had turned over her tapes to Coulter to be copied. This enabled the material to leak and thus galvanized negative press coverage. When *Newsweek* decided to delay Mike Isikoff's story on 18 January, conservatives were still able to keep the story flying by leaking the imminent news of a new Clinton sex scandal to the online *Drudge Report*. In the ratings and circulation war that shaped media decision-making, this compelled news channels and mainstream newspapers to pursue the story. Trying to catch up with *Newsweek*, *Time* reporters called White House sources. At *NBC* and the *Washington Post*, reporters sought to verify the *Drudge Report* story via sources at the OIC. Rush Limbaugh, the right-wing shock-jock, did not bother to verify anything. He just told his millions of radio listeners that another sex scandal loomed. The Lewinsky affair would feature on his program for nearly a year.

By the time Bill Ginsberg met with OIC lawyers, the latter already knew that the story had broken and therefore Lewinsky's value to them had plummeted since she could not entrap others and thus bolster their case against Clinton. There was no longer a pressing case for granting immunity. The subsequent media dissection of Lewinsky and her family added another dimension to the price that the scandal extracted. The longstanding tension between the principle of individual personal privacy and the right to free expression was laid bare. If the Clintons could berate the media for failing to respect a "zone of privacy" where the First Family could escape public scrutiny, surely the Lewinsky family had even greater grounds for complaint? A private choice by their daughter had brought every detail of their lives into the media spotlight, and speculation, innuendo and opinion echoed across the planet.

The Lewinsky scandal also exposed the harsh character of both litigation and politics as fields in which this sex story unfolded. Legal prosecution is a process dedicated to amassing compelling evidence that the accused person has acted contrary to the law. As trained prosecutors, the OIC attorneys saw Lewinsky simply as a potential resource. Protecting herself and her family from imprisonment and other penalties, in their view, should have provided sufficient motivation for her to cooperate. If she had helped the OIC obtain taped evidence implicating Clinton's personal secretary Betty Currie, it would enable them to press her over any attempts made by Clinton to ensure that she and Monica lied to protect him. Even better, if Lewinsky could be used to elicit incriminating testimony from Vernon Jordan or Clinton himself, she would help the OIC prove that the President had called in favours to protect himself, and thus abused his power. Since Monica refused to do either, the OIC had to assess whether Lewinsky's account of her own experience was sufficient to support serious allegations against Bill Clinton. In practice, this meant that the Starr investigation systematically gathered the salacious details of the Clinton-Lewinsky affair in order to prove that his sworn statement in the Jones case was false. It then presented this evidence to a grand jury to see whether the evidence justified charges, and finally since the constitutional remedy for presidential misconduct is impeachment, the OIC sent its report, complete with its detailed account of sexual interactions, to Congress for the House of Representatives to determine whether articles of impeachment should be presented to the Senate.

Impeachment is a political process, framed by partisan divisions and by the unending struggle over public opinion. In early 1998, it remained the case that just one president, Andrew Johnson (back in 1868) had been impeached, and none had been removed from office via the process. The Nixon precedent was to use the combined pressure of public opinion and political calculation to force resignation. On 6 February 1998, Clinton insisted at a press conference that he would not resign. At that stage, although the OIC had been given permission to investigate, and the media were pursuing the sensational story, the demand for impeachment was largely confined to conservative zealots. But the investigation and the story would not go away. Both were replenished from the deep wells of gossip, which included not just Monica's taped conversations with Linda Tripp, but her sharing of intimate details with others. Eventually, the Starr Report listed eleven confidants.

Among the details disclosed was the existence of a dress worn by Monica during a sexual encounter with Clinton and stained with his semen. When OIC prosecutors interrogated Lewinsky's mother, Marcia, over a three-day period in February 1998, the recovery of this dress was seen as important to their offer of immunity. The tawdry stuff of gossip – blowjobs and illicit encounters – had become headline news, and political and legal ammunition. Starr's investigators used White House entry logs, phone records, and subpoenaed interviews with staff, including the Secret Service agents assigned to protect the President, to establish every occasion on which Lewinsky was alone with Clinton. Eventually, the Starr Report would state bluntly that Ms Lewinsky wore the dress on 28 February 1997 and that DNA testing had established that the semen stain originated with Bill Clinton. Few felt that this ejaculation threatened the Republic's integrity or survival in the way Nixon's, Trump's, or arguably even Reagan's, machinations did.

For the first six months of 1998, Clinton tried to maintain his denials and impede the OIC requests to interview senior staff. On 2 April, Judge Wright granted a motion to dismiss the Paula Jones suit, but this was immediately appealed. The case still hung over Clinton in the summer when he relented and agreed to testify partly because the claim of executive privilege was stengthening the comparison with Richard Nixon. On 2 June, the Lewinsky family wisely replaced Bill Ginsberg with two veteran Washington attorneys, Jacob Stein and Plato Cacheris, who reopened negotiations with the Starr team to secure their client's immunity. On 28 July, they confirmed an immunity deal and preparations began for Monica's testimony. The next day Clinton agreed to testify voluntarily before the grand jury. Since Lewinsky appeared first, the jurors had already heard her testimony before they listened to Clinton via video link on 17 August. That evening he went on television to address the nation and change his story from his January denial. He confessed: "Indeed, I did have a relationship with Miss Lewinsky that was not appropriate. In fact, it was wrong. It constituted a critical lapse in judgment and a personal failure on my part for which I am solely and completely responsible." In his carefully managed appearance before the grand jury, Clinton maintained that his denial of sexual relations in the Jones case was not untrue since it was guided by the precise terms of the definition of sexual relations used.

A trained lawyer, Clinton felt able to exonerate himself through a technicality. In his reading of the definition, the key issue was who was receiving sexual gratification. Oral sex performed on him did not constitute sexual relations because it was not done to gratify Monica Lewinsky. This legal hair-splitting ensured that when Kenneth Starr transmitted his report to Congress on 9 September, his team felt that they had to demonstrate that Lewinsky's testimony proved her sexual gratification and that hence the President had lied on oath. It also ensured that the 445-page report and its 36 boxes of supporting evidence contained enough salacious detail to make it a magnet for reporters and others in search of titillation. Many readers shook their heads over Bill's use of his cigar. Ironically, Starr himself felt he had to complete and send his report in haste to avoid accusations of interfering politically in the November mid-term elections. He entrusted Brett Kavanaugh with the task of crafting the case for impeachment. Starr also assumed that the report and its details would be considered confidentially by the House Judiciary Committee and that Congress would then decide how much material needed public disclosure. Instead, without reading its content, Congress authorized the report's complete public release with just forty-eight-hours delay. Protective parents and the easily shocked were faced with unprecedentedly lurid news accounts.

On 5 October 1998, the House Judiciary Committee chaired by veteran Republican Congressman Henry Hyde of Illinois recommended an impeachment inquiry. Three days later, the House voted to commence the inquiry with thirty-one Democrats supporting the motion. Nevertheless, despite the torrent of headlines, there was no conspicuous tide of hostility towards Clinton from the American public, most of whom considered him an effective president, while lamenting his lack of self-control and moral judgment. This was confirmed by the November elections which saw the Democrats gain five seats in the House and maintain their numbers in the Senate; it is more common for the president's party to lose ground in mid-term elections. Polling at the time showed that six out of ten voters felt that

Clinton should not be impeached, and they credited the President for the strong economy. On 13 November, the Paula Jones suit was finally settled for $850,000, although in March the following year, Judge Jones ruled that all but $200,000 of this sum should be assigned to legal costs.

Despite some calls for Congress to consider a vote of censure against Clinton as an alternative to impeachment, the Republican-led inquiry proceeded in early December. On 16 December, with the House poised to vote on articles of impeachment, Clinton accepted his National Security Council's recommendation of air strikes against Saddam Hussein's Iraq for failing to allow UN weapons' inspectors to complete their work. In a clear instance of life imitating art, the decision mirrored the plot of the 1997 satirical movie, *Wag The Dog*, in which a White House spin doctor recommends military actions to distract from a presidential sex scandal. On 19 December, the articles of impeachment passed the House. Its debate had been enlivened by the resignation of Republican Congressman Bob Livingston of Louisiana who had been set to become Speaker when the new Congress convened in the New Year. But a full-page ad in the *Washington Post* by the owner of *Hustler* magazine, Larry Flynt, offering bounty payments for "evidence of illicit sexual relations," had exposed a range of liaisons enjoyed by Livingston. Calling upon Clinton to resign the presidency because of the damage he had done to his office, Livingston dampened Democratic catcalls by saying he would set the President an example by asking his family's forgiveness and vacating his Congressional seat.

While the Lewinsky scandal held public attention because of its prurient elements, Bill Clinton was not impeached because he committed adultery, or as he put it, had had an "inappropriate relationship." He was accused of two "high crimes and misdemeanors," which are the constitutional basis for impeachment. Both flowed from his oath of office in which he pledged to ensure the faithful execution of the laws and they referred to his behaviour in relation to the Paula Jones trial. Firstly, he was accused of perjury, giving false testimony under oath, and secondly, that he had encouraged and induced Monica Lewinsky to give false testimony. Together, these amounted to a breach of his oath of office. It was also implied that he had used the power of his office to influence others to assist him in his scheme to present false evidence in federal court. Overall, his accusers argued that his conduct tarnished his office, eroded public trust, and undermined the rule of law.

Impeachment requires that two-thirds of the Senate vote in favour. When Andrew Johnson was impeached in 1868, he survived by just a single vote. In 1999, the odds for President Clinton were far better since the Republicans needed to muster a super-majority of sixty-seven votes, which set them the mountainous task of persuading twenty-two Democrats to vote with them. This challenge was deepened by the likelihood that some Republicans too would decide that they did not believe that the mistakes Clinton had made rose to the level of a high crime or misdemeanour that warranted removal from office. Republican Arlen Specter of Pennsylvania voted "not proven" on both charges and that was held to be equal to a "not guilty" vote. Moderates in both parties felt that Clinton had behaved badly on a personal level, but they also felt that while his actions might warrant censure, he did not deserve to be removed from office, especially since there was a growing sense that once its attention switched to Clinton's sexual misdeeds, the Starr investigation had ceased to be an independent probe and become more of a witch-hunt. As Representative Robert Menendez said during the House debate on 18 December: "Monica Lewinsky is not Watergate." This view was shared by the public who continued to give Clinton positive job approval ratings, reaching 73 percent immediately after the House voted to impeach. Public opinion never turned against Clinton in the way that it had against Nixon in the summer of 1974.

While the Senate impeachment trial proceeded in January 1999, Clinton was scheduled to deliver the State of the Union address. Studiously avoiding his present difficulties, he was able to give a positive report on the economy and outline how growth had produced more jobs and a budget surplus that could support key entitlement programs, such as Social Security and Medicare. On 12 February, the Senate voted on impeachment along party lines with both articles failing to meet the required two-thirds majority by a clear margin. The accusation of perjury against Clinton mustered fifty-five votes (twelve short), while the charge that he had obstructed justice by inducing false testimony drew fifty (seventeen short of the needed total).

In the eyes of conservative Republicans, "Slick Willie" had escaped again. For Democrats, the brazen partisanship of the new conservative coalition had been exposed because the punishment sought greatly exceeded the nature of Clinton's offense. In the eyes of the law, however, Clinton deserved to be punished. Two months after the Senate vote, Judge Susan Webber Wright found him guilty of contempt for his false testimony in the Paula Jones case. She ordered him to pay $91,202 in legal and associated costs and announced that she would refer his conduct to the disciplinary committee of the Arkansas Supreme Court which would consider disbarring him from legal practice. By October 1999, Kenneth Starr had concluded that the course of events had made his leadership of the OIC untenable; he had been branded as a Clinton-hater and so delivering an objective view on whether the President should be prosecuted was no longer feasible with him in charge. He was replaced by Robert W. Ray, who had the challenge of determining whether the time and dollars spent investigating the Clintons would yield an indictment as soon as the President left office. In mid-September 2000, ahead of the election, Ray felt it proper to announce that his review of the Whitewater probe, the Travel Bureau scandal and related matters did not justify further action. But he had not finished. In December he summoned Monica Lewinsky and met discreetly with President Clinton. He told Clinton to settle the disciplinary matter before the Arkansas Supreme Court's Professional Conduct Committee, which he did by accepting a $25,000 fine and a five-year license suspension. Ray also required Clinton to admit publicly that he gave knowingly evasive answers in his Paula Jones deposition, and as his hours in office ticked away in January 2001, Clinton made the required press statement via his lawyer. Others had suffered more: Jim McDougal had died in prison and his wife Susan was only released after receiving a pardon from Clinton in his final days in office.

Some still see Bill Clinton as one of the most successful presidents of the post-Watergate era, but it is also impossible to separate him from the scandals that consumed so much of his time in office. For his apologists, the endless stream of accusations stemmed from the ideologically fuelled hatred that inspired his political adversaries. For his critics, it reveals the devious and opportunistic nature of Clinton himself. And for cultural commentators, it illustrates how the new media landscape, especially the emergence of cable news and the internet, produced a market for "news" that readily incorporated gossip. There was no longer the same layers or filters between on the one hand, the speculation and commentary that had always circulated inside certain social networks, and on the other, the mass media supposedly entrusted to report the facts to a wider public. The appetite for scandal and for celebrity storylines was growing exponentially, even forming new media genres sometimes called "info-tainment" and "reality TV." Like Watergate, the Lewinsky scandal soured public opinion towards politicians and the media. Neither could command trust in the way that they had, and the tendency to retreat into partisan silos intensified. The world in which Never Trumpers and Trumpites coexist in separate Americas had begun to take shape. It was a world in which large sections of the public were simultaneously scandalized by the wickedness of their opponents and unmoved by or even dismissive of the scandalous revelations about their chosen champions. It was a world in which scandal seemed to lose meaning and substance as it became an almost daily or ubiquitous phenomenon and one all too readily dismissed as a political manoeuvre.

Chapter 4

Electoral Scandals: Bush v. Gore (2000) and Russia-gate (2016)

It is fair to say that politicians have a mixed reputation. Some, usually with hindsight, get the Mount Rushmore treatment and are extolled as heroes. Most, especially while in office, are viewed by some as akin to snake-oil salesmen; they are slippery customers. Elections, therefore, can be likened to H.L. Mencken's view of multiple marriages: they are the triumph of hope over experience. But America has generally been seen as the world's foremost modern democracy and its transition of power from one president to another in a peaceful way (until 2021) has been held up as a model for other nations around the world. It is therefore shocking, and indeed scandalous to discover that the US election process can be flawed in a whole series of ways, beginning with the reality that elections are very much shaped by politicians as they strive to gain an advantage for their party. The fact that elections can be manipulated, and that mistrust has grown were vital elements behind Donald Trump's insistence that the 2020 election was stolen.

Electing American presidents is neither quick nor simple. The national conventions formally choose the party's nominees in the summer before the November election, but increasingly, delegates to these conventions are already assigned to specific candidates based on caucuses and primary elections that begin in Iowa and New Hampshire in early February. Nor is that the real beginning. To stand a realistic chance, presidential hopefuls announce they are running during the previous year and then spend months boosting their candidacy in terms of fund-raising and promoting themselves to the public. Getting the message out is as urgent as breathing for political campaigns. In 2019 the Democratic National Committee set fund-raising and polling thresholds for candidates to qualify for a place in the televised debates that are seen as crucial. The first was held over two nights (26-27 June) to accommodate twenty candidates.

By February 2020 the list had been reduced to six candidates, although it included a latecomer, billionaire Mike Bloomberg, a media tycoon and former Mayor of New York, rich enough to fund his own campaign and qualified by increasing his polling numbers. Bloomberg's emergence underlined the reality that money talks and that you cannot win the presidency without it. His candidacy was brief and unsuccessful, as the contest suddenly swung into a two-horse race, but even the radical candidate Bernie Sanders, who lasted into April, demanding Medicare for All and embracing democratic socialism, was reliant on a vast on-line fund-raising operation. The marriage of money and political campaigning ensures that corruption is a perennial feature of American politics and if you follow the money, you often find a scandal.

Ironically, the expensive race for the presidential nomination via primaries and caucuses emerged as a reaction to the fact that past national conventions were corrupt. The historic image of a "smoke-filled room" where shadowy figures cut deals prompted reforms in the early 20th century that saw the introduction of primary elections and caucuses where parties select their candidates through a public process. This was supposed to reduce the power of political bosses and restore choice to the people. But what was supposed to ensure a more open and less corrupt process then created its own problems. First and foremost, it made the running for political office, especially the presidency, hugely expensive by making campaigns into lavish marketing operations. In order to compete for the nomination, candidates have to be either rich themselves, like Donald Trump, Mike Bloomberg or Ross Perot, or be able to attract donations, usually by a combination of mass fund-raising among ordinary citizens and by accepting donations from wealthy interests often via what are called Political Action Committees or PACs. Scandals related to the influence of money in American politics have therefore not diminished, and the so-called "campaign finance" issue remains an unending source of debate.

We have already seen that one of Richard Nixon's earliest scandals was campaign finance-related, prompting his televised "Checkers" speech, and many of the suspect activities surrounding the Watergate scandal, arose from the fund-raising operations and expenditures of CREEP (Campaign to Re-Elect the President). Even the morally upright Jimmy Carter, elected in 1976 as the antithesis of all that Nixon and Watergate represented, quickly found himself under scrutiny for alleged campaign finance violations largely centring on his close adviser and Georgia banker, Bert Lance. Press reports of suspicious bank loans from Calhoun First National to members of the Carter family business in Plains, Georgia compelled Lance to resign as director of the Office of Management and Budget. The loans were seen as having illegally funnelled money into Carter's presidential campaign. Lance was eventually acquitted of nine charges of bank fraud in 1980, but the media storm damaged Carter and tainted his claim to be a different kind of politician.

After Watergate, attempts to regulate campaign finance saw the establishment of the Federal Election Commission (FEC) and the setting of limits on contributions from individuals, political parties, and political action committees (PACs). The need to raise money to cover the high cost of campaigning has meant that the rules have largely inspired campaign managers to find ingenious ways of getting around the restrictions. Since most PACs represent business, labour, or ideological interests, their influence continues to be a source of scandal, at least in the eyes of hostile observers. The significant contributions given by petrochemical or pharmaceutical industries, or by the cluster of often evangelical Protestant groups sometimes referred to as the Moral Majority, or by the National Rifle Association, or by groups backing immigrant or transgender rights, can all be regarded as akin to bribes, pressing candidates to maintain a certain stance on significant policy issues. In 2010, the US Supreme Court ruled that corporate entities making communications and independent expenditures in the context of election contests are exercising the right to free speech as guaranteed under the First Amendment. This has led to the emergence of so-called Super-PACs, which do not contribute directly to parties or candidates in ways that are legally limited. Instead, they have the right to spend without restriction to advocate positions that either support or oppose specific candidates. It's also often unclear where all Super-PAC funds originate. In 2014, the Supreme Court also ruled that aggregate limits on the amount an individual may contribute during a two-year period to all federal candidates, political parties, and other political committees violated the First Amendment. Thus, the recent trend has been to strengthen the leverage of wealthier interest groups, and for some, that is scandalous.

But not everyone is scandalized. To understand the controversies surrounding recent presidential elections requires an understanding of how the actual election process works and why it can be misused. Political scandals have always co-existed alongside a popular acceptance that politics is a dirty business associated with dubious practices. A major function of political parties, for instance, has always been "getting out the vote." In practice, this has always involved not just ensuring that all supporters are able to cast their ballot effectively, but also placing obstacles in the way of rivals. This occurs in all phases of the electoral process including the technicalities of filing as a candidate in an election. The Constitution requires that presidential candidates should be at least 35 years old and that they must be natural-born citizens who have resided in the United States for the fifteen years prior to taking office. Notoriously, when Barack Obama (who was born in Hawaii and lived for a time in Indonesia) was running for the presidency in 2008, right-wing pundits, including Donald Trump, star of the high-rating TV show *The Apprentice*, alleged that Obama, whose father was Kenyan, had not really been born in America, and they pressed to see his birth certificate.

In June 2008 the Obama campaign published a certificate of live birth from the Hawaii State Health Department, but even this did not stop the rumours, which were spread widely by right-wing operatives, like Jerome Corsi, who would later feature in the Mueller investigation of possible Russian and Trump campaign collusion during the 2016 campaign. In 2020, Joe Biden's selection of Kamala Harris, who is the daughter of immigrant parents from India and Jamaica, prompted a weak repeat of the "birth certificate" claim. This was articulated by John Eastman, a law professor who would also feature in attempts to block the counting of Electoral College votes in 2020. Eastman suggested that if her parents were in the US on temporary visas, this in some way cast doubt on Kamala's birth right citizenship which is guaranteed by the Fourteenth Amendment. More salient to election outcomes is the fact that individual states historically control which candidates appear on the ballot; for instance, in 1948, Alabama chose not to have the Democratic nominee and sitting President Harry Truman on the ballot because local politicians opposed the national party's civil rights policies. Thus, in elections, the saying holds: *you have to be in it to win it.*

When it comes to winning elections, voter registration is also crucial. Generally, the more difficult it is to register, the less likely it is that socially and economically disadvantaged groups will vote. This has always been highly politicized because the electoral machinery is run by the local politicians in power. Especially where state or local government draws constituency boundaries, it creates a situation where politicians try to choose their voters before voters choose their politicians. Normally, you can only vote in the district where you reside, and its boundaries can be drawn so that different sides of the same street vote in different districts. And as we shall see, that can be scandalous. But equally crucially, you can only vote if you can prove that you are eligible; by successfully registering to vote ahead of polling day. For example, across the former Confederate states after the Civil War, the Republican Party largely relied on the votes of African Americans, but once the Democrats took control of state governments after 1877, they adopted measures to drive down African American voter registration.

Evading the Fifteenth Amendment prohibition on limiting the right to vote on the basis of race, creed, colour or previous condition of servitude, state governments used literacy tests, poll taxes, and proof of residency requirements to disfranchise African Americans and if needs be, others, for generations thereafter. In the very same period, major cities in the North such as Chicago or New York had Democratic political machines that tapped the often multi-ethnic, and mobile electorate to ensure that their candidates were victorious. With the machine in charge of administering the election, votes in the form of willing if dubiously qualified electors were readily found. Fraud was the norm. A famous Chicago ward captain declared: "We don't know how many votes we got, till we know how many votes we need." "Good government" or "progressive" reformers tried to clean up this situation by introducing measures that tightened registration and voting procedures so that the individual voter was correctly identified and "assistance" at voting places was limited.

Much the same debate is seen today. African American and Hispanic voting blocs are identified with the Democratic Party and high voter turnout by these groups typically benefits Democratic candidates. Early efforts to limit the impact of the 1965 Voting Rights Act by drawing boundaries that placed minority voters in constituencies where their vote would be diluted were outlawed by the courts and replaced in the 1980s by a practice of creating majority-minority districts. This has since been superseded by more elaborate, data-led redistricting along partisan lines that strives to make the outcomes of elections as predictable as possible. The Republican Party has control of most statehouses and governorships currently and has used this to magnify its electoral control, based on the 2011 and 2021 re-districting, and to pass measures designed to suppress voter turnout. Such partisan measures were evident in Florida which was at the centre of the 2000 election scandal. In 1998 the state passed a law requiring a voter registration purge to clean the system of ineligible electors. The move was prompted by voting irregularities in the 1997 Miami mayoral contest that saw the result legally overturned.

The purge would remove most obviously the deceased and individuals who were registered to vote in multiple locations. It also removed those declared mentally incompetent and most controversially, convicted felons whose rights had not been formally restored. The registration purge law also stated that it was the responsibility of any voter deemed ineligible to prove their eligibility. Accordingly, a list of 58,000 names was circulated to county supervisors, who were then required to send a letter to each named person alerting them and advising them of their right to challenge their ineligible status. The list was initially distributed in June 1999 but was re-sent in January 2000 after some 8,000 citizens were found to have been wrongly identified. Wrong names predictably produced wrong addresses and so non-delivery of these crucial notifications of ineligibility. Of those excluded in Dade County on the basis of felony convictions who then appealed because of inaccuracy, nearly 50 percent were successful. The rigor with which the purge occurred varied considerably. In Broward, Palm Beach and Volusia counties, for instance, it emerged that the list was simply ignored, while in Sarasota, the only felons purged were those who took the trouble to reply to the notification and admit their ineligibility. However, on election day 2000, some ordinary voters were wrongfully denied the right to vote due to the purge and this added to the anger over the tightly contested presidential race.

The record voter turnout by African Americans associated with Barack Obama's election victory in 2008 was followed by a tightening of registration procedures across sixteen states. This was generally accompanied by the charge that there had been widespread fraudulent voting. The changes typically ended late registration, limited organized registration drives to a finite period ahead of the scheduled election, eliminated early voting opportunities, and required that a photo ID be presented that matched exactly information held by either the state driver vehicle registration agency or the federal Social Security system. The American Civil Liberties Union argues that up to 15 percent of low-income Americans do not have the appropriate photo ID, and that included 25 percent of African Americans. Low-income groups, especially Hispanic migrants, are also more likely to have incomplete or inaccurate Social Security records. In the 2016 election, African American voter turnout, having exceeded 66 percent in the previous two elections involving Obama, fell back to 59.6 percent. While this was partly due to their doubts about Hillary Clinton, it was also affected by the new regulations, which have since been extended and strengthened in several states. As we shall see, the outcome can also be vitally affected by other stages in the process, particularly the nature of the ballot itself.

Earlier elections were not perfect either in terms of voter registration issues, but while these issues reached a crescendo after 2000, the immediate post-Watergate elections highlighted other tactics that gave rise to scandal. While Jimmy Carter's 1976 campaign did not escape the taint of a campaign finance scandal, his re-election bid ran into different challenges. Going into the final weeks, most commentators felt that President Carter had the edge over former film star, Ronald Reagan, when it came to mastery of policy detail. They assumed that the only scheduled, televised debate on 28 October 1980 would highlight this contrast to the President's advantage. However, having trailed Carter by eight points among registered voters (and by three points among likely voters) right before their debate, Reagan moved into a three-point lead among likely voters immediately afterward, and won the 4 November election by ten points. It subsequently emerged that a Reagan "mole" placed in the Carter camp was able to smuggle out a copy of the briefing book, used to prepare the President, and thus gave his challenger an unprecedented advantage. Reagan's performance, sometimes remembered for his genial but dismissive comment: "There you go, again!" was certainly not adversely affected by having this additional intelligence. It did, however, create a scandal and a Congressional investigation when it was uncovered in 1983.

There were several reasons for Carter's defeat, including a still depressed economy, but the ongoing Iranian hostage crisis in which staff at the US Embassy in Tehran were held captive (in retaliation for Carter's decision to allow the recently deposed Shah to come to the US for medical treatment), was widely seen as crucial. Frustrated by the slow pace of diplomacy, Carter had ordered a risky military rescue operation in April 1980. A severe desert sandstorm caused the helicopters to malfunction, killing eight servicemen and aborting the mission. News of this setback deepened public doubts about Carter's effectiveness, but his staff were able to renew negotiations with the Ayatollah Khomeini's regime. Clearly, if the hostages' release could be secured before the November election, it would be a major boost. The Reagan campaign began to worry about what was termed the "October surprise." Rumours that they worked actively to delay the hostages' release until after the election eventually prompted a Congressional investigation in 1992. It found no credible evidence for this allegation and criticized press reports that had focused on the role of Reagan staff member and future CIA director William Casey as a supposed envoy to the Iranians. Reagan himself always denied the charge. More recently, new documents have emerged describing actions by Joseph Reed, senior aide to Chase Manhattan Chairman, David Rockefeller. The Shah was an important Chase client and the bank had been involved in winning him a safe haven in America, but Rockefeller himself remained an ardent critic of Carter's foreign policy, because the latter's emphasis on human rights weakened longstanding allies, allowing figures like the Shah to be toppled. In a letter to his family after Reagan's victory, Reed declared he had given his all in thwarting any effort by the Carter officials to pull off the long-suspected "October surprise." Hours after Reagan took the oath of office in 1981, the hostages' plane for home took off.

It is a basic rule of presidential campaigning that you try to create a stark choice, portraying your candidate in the most positive way, while simultaneously highlighting the other side's weaknesses and the negative consequences of choosing them. Both tactics make scandal more likely since the louder the claims of virtue made for a candidate, the more discrediting is the revelation of impropriety, and the opposition is likely to use every means available, no matter how morally dubious, to smear the other side. This is at the heart of what is termed "negative campaigning" and George H.W. Bush's 1988 campaign manager, Lee Atwater, was one of its acknowledged masters. He was convinced that people vote based on their fears rather than their hopes, and he strove to make his opponent the embodiment of their fears.

One technique that Atwater developed as a political consultant was "push-polling." At its simplest, this involves calling a list of potential voters ostensibly to conduct an opinion poll and inviting them to say how they would respond to hypotheses about a candidate. On the surface, this may appear similar to the marketing technique, "message testing," whereby you test the popularity of different approaches and avoid negative public reactions. But in the case of a push poll, the main purpose is to start a scandalous rumour. For example, it might be damaging to a liberal candidate, if they are said to have received support from conservative ideological groups or predatory business interests. The damage largely depends on whether the message or the poll is picked up by the media. In many ways, the modern push-poll is a technologically enhanced variation on an old dirty trick, familiar to Nixon operatives. Since Democratic Senator Edmund Muskie was seen as a potentially formidable opponent in 1972, Nixon operatives during the primary season printed flyers attacking his stance on Israel and placed them on the windshields of cars parked in the vicinity of synagogues. The flyers were done in the same style used by the rival primary campaign of Democratic New York Mayor John Lindsay, thereby fostering mutual recrimination. A key aspect of negative campaigning is to exploit divisions among the opposition while using polarizing issues to maximize solidarity on your own side. Since so-called social issues like abortion or gun control are powerfully divisive, negative campaigning has made it harder for moderate candidates to succeed in American politics, especially when campaign managers like Atwater are able to tap into the deep anxieties of the electorate.

A South Carolina native, Atwater had grown up in a racially segregated society and recognized that the growth of the Republican Party in what previously had been a solidly Democratic state reflected the strong legacy of racism. By the 1980s, the success of the civil rights movement had made it politically unacceptable to use the overtly racist language previously used to foster white solidarity against African Americans. Instead, Atwater used what became known as "coded racism." In the Reagan era, this meant that conservative candidates could depict their opponents as liberals eager to spend taxpayers' money on "welfare queens", and likely to be weak on law and order and permissive on drugs and other crimes. When Reagan contrasted hard-working Americans to "welfare queens" driving Cadillacs or insisted that he was going to strengthen the war on drugs, his white working-class audience could be left to assume for themselves that both the "welfare queens" and the drug dealers were not white.

Atwater's campaign against Democratic nominee Michael Dukakis in 1988 remains a textbook case of negative campaigning. The Bush team portrayed Dukakis as an extreme liberal. Dukakis, whose time as Massachusetts' governor had seen a strong economic recovery, was attacking Bush for neglecting domestic issues at the expense of international relations. The Democrat was promising to turn the national economy around just as he had in his home state, so the Bush campaign needed to switch the focus. Its media adviser and future founder of *Fox News*, Roger Ailes, created an attack ad, a TV spot known as the "Revolving Door." After initial "establishing shots" to convey that this was a prison, the ad showed male prisoners coming in and out of a revolving door. The audience heard: "As governor, Michael Dukakis vetoed mandatory sentences for drug dealers. He vetoed the death penalty. His revolving-door prison policy gave weekend furloughs to first-degree murderers not eligible for parole. While out, many committed other crimes like kidnapping and rape." The narrator concludes: "And many are still at large. Now Michael Dukakis says he wants to do for America what he's done for Massachusetts. America can't afford that risk."

Reinforcing this ad, but created and distributed by a PAC rather than by the Bush campaign itself, was the more notorious "Willie Horton" ad. This again focused on the prisoner "furlough program," but used the specific example of Horton, a convicted murderer who went on the run after a weekend furlough. He broke into a couple's home, beat the man and raped the woman. More importantly, the ad not only positioned Bush as a hard-line supporter of the death penalty, which Dukakis opposed, but offered its audience two mugshots of Horton: a tall, bearded, black man. The narration dwelt upon Horton's viciousness, detailing the nineteen times he stabbed his 17-year-old murder victim; the ten weekend passes he had been granted, despite his life sentence, and adding as a final detail that he "repeatedly" raped the woman. Much more racially charged than the official Bush ad, the "Willie Horton" ad not only exploited a fear of violent crime, which had actually risen during the 1980s, but linked that fear to the racist myth of black male sexual predatoriness. While the Bush team distanced itself publicly from the ad in the ensuing uproar, Atwater told campaign insiders that he would win the election by making Horton seem like Dukakis's running mate in the minds of the electorate. Bush won comfortably in November.

In the aftermath of Watergate, a more worrying trend and possible by-product of negative campaigning was the low level of voter turnout. In 1960 just under 63 percent of eligible voters participated in the presidential election, but by 1980 it was essentially 10 percent lower. In 1996 when Bill Clinton was re-elected, just 49 percent of eligible voters showed up. Over half of them stayed home. Americans were giving up on politicians in increasing numbers. We have already pointed out that it is normal for the different parties to make it more difficult for groups that are likely to support the other side to register and get to the polls. At the same time, the actual management of election day and the voting count can have a profound impact on whose vote counts. This was dramatically revealed in the 2000 election. Essentially a dead heat between George W. Bush and Al Gore, the outcome hinged on who won in Florida and since its governor at the time just happened to be Bush's brother, Jeb, this had all the makings of a scandal.

Before we get into the detail of how faulty voting technology and partisan administration affected the outcome, it is only fair to acknowledge that these were not the only reasons Gore lost. The presence of a serious third-party candidate, Ralph Nader, the Green Party candidate, who campaigned hard to secure 5 percent of the vote in order to qualify for federal election funding, had a bearing on the outcome. Nader was not the only alternative. TV personality and former Nixon speech writer Pat Buchanan ran as the Reform Party candidate, but he was generally seen as appealing more to potential Bush voters; Bush was also seen as more likely to lose voters to libertarian candidate Harry Browne. To some extent therefore the Nader effect on Gore's vote was offset by the votes taken away from Bush by Buchanan and Browne. This makes the accusation that Nader gifted the election to Bush by splitting the vote in Florida less credible than it at first appears. But the Republican Leadership Council had been confident enough that Nader would hurt Gore that they ran some pro-Nader ads. This is a tried and trusted, split-the-vote tactic, and the margin of Bush's victory was wafer-thin.

With only Florida undeclared, the results stood at 267 Electoral College voters for Gore and 246 votes for Bush. Victory came once either candidate exceeded 270 votes. Gore was 3 votes short, and Florida was worth 25 votes. However, the outcome there was delayed by multiple legal challenges by both parties which culminated in the US Supreme Court decision of *Bush v. Gore.* Delivered 12 December, it ended the recounting of disputed ballots that had been ordered by the Florida Supreme Court in the aftermath of the state's 26 November announcement that Bush had carried Florida by just 537 votes. By ending the election review process, the December ruling affirmed that Florida's 25 Electors were pledged to Bush, giving him 271 votes and hence the presidency. At the heart of this outcome lurked not one scandal but several. The most inflammatory charge was that the state government had administered the election in a way that ensured that the Governor's brother became the next president. A related scandal stemmed from documented cases of minority citizens, mainly African American and Hispanic, being denied the right to vote. Complicating the entire saga was the fact that in crucial ways the voting technology employed was faulty, leading to some ballots being disqualified or assigned to the wrong candidate. So, the 2000 election begs the question: which is bigger – a scandal that reveals that an election has been won by illicit means, or a scandal that shows that the whole darn process is unreliable and broken?

The suspicion that the 2000 election outcome was rigged grew because the electoral administration was so obviously partisan. In Florida, the secretary of state is responsible for overall administration of the vote and in 2000, Republican Katherine Harris held that elected post. She also happened to be co-chair of the local Bush campaign. The conflict of interests was glaring, and as voting count problems escalated, her decisions seemed blatantly partisan. On two separate occasions she refused requests for a delay in reporting vote totals, despite concerns over the accuracy of the count. Since the reported total gave the state to Bush, her narrowing of the criteria that would permit manual recounting was suspiciously self-serving. All three of her key decisions were overturned on appeal to the

State Supreme Court. At the same time, her advice that absentee ballots, received with a postmark after Election Day, should nonetheless be accepted, provided the ballot itself carried a date that indicated that the vote was "cast" prior to the election, was seen as an attempt to increase the number of military ballots since armed service personnel were believed to be likely Bush voters. Certainly, there would have been less scope for scandal had she recused herself from her role in favour of a non-partisan adjudicator.

Adding to the controversy was the way partisanship pervaded the lower levels of electoral administration since county supervisors of elections were themselves elected along party lines in all Florida counties except Miami-Dade. These elected supervisors had considerable discretion under state law, and media scrutiny of their actions in the 2000 election exposed clearly biased policies. In Seminole County (north-east of Orlando), the election supervisor invited the Republican Party's north Florida campaign chair to her office to correct absentee ballots from prospective Republican voters by adding the missing ID numbers that would otherwise have led to the ballots being rejected. The same opportunity was not extended to the Democratic Party. In Martin County, north of Palm Beach, the supervisor went a step further and allowed Republican campaign workers to take away absentee ballots in order to add missing ID numbers and then resubmit them. Incomplete Democratic or independent ballots in that county were simply ignored and judged invalid.

Part of the county supervisor of elections' job was to design the ballot itself to accommodate the names of the candidates in a clear and legible manner. Subject to each state rules, individuals could file as candidates for the presidency and vice presidency; it was rarely a two- or three-horse race. In Florida, the 2000 election had ten pairs of names for the office of US president and vice-president; more than ever before, and so, just fitting all the names on a punch-card ballot proved difficult. State law stipulated only that candidates should be listed according to the party vote totals in the most recent state election which ensured that the Republican Bush-Cheney ticket would come first in any layout. The ballot design had to match the voting equipment and since this varied in each county, so did the ballots. Even in counties that used the same type of voting machine there was no requirement that they consult on ballot design and subsequent investigations found they didn't. Consequently, voting in some places was easier than in others. Some mistakes were mind-boggling. In Duval County, centred on Jacksonville, the electorate was instructed on the supervisor-approved ballot to "vote on every page," even though pages 1 and 2 listed presidential candidates and by voting twice, as instructed, they invalidated their ballot. Over 22,000 votes for president were lost as a result: easily exceeding Bush's eventual margin of victory.

Once the election occurred, a crucial role was played by county canvassing boards. Unless the position was on the ballot, the election supervisor was automatically on the board, alongside an ostensibly non-partisan local judge and a second partisan selection. So, most boards, which oversaw the vote counting and reported the totals from each county, were partisan operations. Under Florida law, canvassing boards decided the validity of any indeterminate punch-card ballots. Absent a court order, they decided whether any manual recounting would occur, and when it did, they set the rules for how unclear ballots should be interpreted and determined whether absentee ballots were valid or invalid. Both Democratic and Republican controlled boards took such decisions in a self-interested way.

Most Florida precincts used voting machines that were based on pre-scored punch cards. These had been developed for the early data processing equipment used by companies like IBM with the punch cards operating through binary codes. By pre-scoring the card around the area to be punched, it should have been easier for a clean hole to be created and thus enable the votes to be mechanically counted. What makes the 2000 election such a far-reaching scandal is that the machines that malfunctioned were neither new nor confined to Florida. Broward County, for instance, had been using its machines since 1974 and Miami-Dade since 1978. Nationwide, 28 percent of voters relied on this type of voting machine. We know that the 2000 count was flawed, but potentially in lots of precincts across America, voting tallies in elections may have been inaccurate for decades.

Coverage of the disputed ballots in Florida made the phrase *hanging chad* widely known. Chads are the pieces of card that are supposed to be punched out of the ballot card by applying a stylus to the flat card held in the voting machine. Sometimes, chads are not cleanly removed. This can be because the machine isn't working properly, but it may also be because the voter doesn't insert the ballot correctly in order to ensure a proper alignment or fails to use the stylus properly. Either way, the result is a ballot where the chad remains in place and the computer cannot determine the voter's choice. Chads fall into categories. A chad attached by one corner is referred to as a "hanging chad." If two corners remain intact, it is called a "swinging chad" and if only one corner is detached, it's known as a "tri-chad." The glossary extends to chads that have varying degrees of damage suggestive of the voter trying to mark their ballot choice. These include a chad that remains attached but has a clear indentation, called a "dimpled chad" and a chad that has been pierced but not detached called a "pregnant chad." Where a manual recount was authorized in 2000, the county canvassing board had to set rules about what categories of chad should be accepted as proving a voter's preference.

Attached to the ballot holder is a loose-leaf booklet, reflecting the fact that in US elections there can be many federal, state, and local contests as well as referendum measures to be decided on the same day. When opened, the pages of this booklet should present the names of the candidates so that they line up with a guiding arrow pointing to a specific point in one long column on the ballot. Voters can then find their preferred candidate and use the stylus to punch through the card in the correct place. Once they have voted in one contest, they turn to another page, and this aligns with the next column in a way that should ensure that the voter can find one choice in each of the ballot's vertical lines. Usually, the candidates' names appear in the booklet on the left-hand side allowing the voter to punch to the right of a directional arrow. However, the large number of presidential candidates prompted some counties to print names on the left and the right side of the ballot with the punch holes in the centre in what became notorious as the *butterfly ballot*.

This created problems because the directional arrows did not always align clearly with one candidate and so the voter's choice was either in doubt or incorrectly recorded. It also placed fringe candidates higher up the list of options than they would have been on a ballot with names on one side only. All voters are supposed to check their ballot to ensure that their choices have been recorded correctly. Where necessary, the voters are advised to remove any chads that have not been cleanly removed. The 2000 election in Florida confirmed that many voters don't follow these instructions. Voters deposit their punched ballots in precinct boxes, and these are then returned to central counting stations where computers tabulate the punched cards.

The computers are programmed to read a designated spot on the card as a vote for a specific candidate in a specific contest. Since not all counties used the same machines or cards, the computers had to have programs that recognized the cards to be tabulated.

A different voting system, branded as *marksense* ballots, was used in certain counties and employed optical scanners, some of which were stationed at the precinct level. The voter was given a large ballot with contests and names which they marked in pencil like choosing numbers in the lottery. The completed ballot was placed in the scanner. Where this reading occurred at the precinct with the voter present, it was possible to spot errors and inform voters that their ballot would be invalid so that they could request a fresh ballot and rectify their mistakes. In two counties, Escambia and Manatee, the election supervisors ordered that this check on spoilt ballots be overridden, reportedly to ensure the count was completed without delay. In another, Gadsden, the ballots were not scanned at the precinct but brought in boxes to a central scanning point where, since the voter was no longer present, mistakes could not be rectified. The only African American majority county in Florida, and therefore a county that should have added significantly to Gore's total, Gadsden just happened to produce the highest number of uncountable ballots in the 2000 presidential election. But this may have been the result of incompetence rather than trickery.

Almost as soon as voting began in Palm Beach County, voters there started to complain that the *butterfly ballot* was confusing and hard to use. With names being fed from both left and right side, option 4 – the Reform Party ticket of Pat Buchanan and Ezola Foster – was positioned adjacent and to the right of the Democratic ticket of Al Gore and Joe Lieberman, which was confusingly labelled as option 5 because the top two punch holes were void and had made the Bush-Cheney ticket option 3. In this area of Florida with both Jewish retirees from north-eastern cities, like New York, and local African American and Hispanic service workers, option 5 should have been heavily selected. Subsequent analyses suggest that a combination of voting for Buchanan in error or voting for more than one candidate lost Gore over 10,000 votes, and with it the presidency.

But the scandal did not end there. Since the result was by a margin of less than 0.5 percent, Florida law required a recount. Supervisors were instructed to do this, and some, but not all, did. This first machine recount reduced Bush's victory margin to just 327 votes; later counts pushed it back up. The explanation for changing totals within an ostensibly mechanized system lay largely in the cards. As the cards went through the machine, hanging chads were sometimes shaken loose and swinging chads could swing back into place. It could also produce ballots where the intention of the voter was impossible for the machine to determine since the punched hole did not correspond to a recognized position on the ballot. This was where manual recounts and human discretion were required. It was the responsibility of each canvassing board to determine the nature and extent of a manual recount and local officials used their discretion, which meant in some cases that they chose not to recount. The Bush campaign marshalled money and resources to resist the Gore camp's demand for manual recounts.

Significantly, the Gore suit selected four counties (Broward, Miami-Dade, Palm Beach, and Volusia) with already high totals for Gore which might go even higher on review. James Baker III, a senior Bush advisor, who had served in both the Reagan and Bush Senior administrations, insisted that the recounts being sought would produce so many inconsistencies across the canvassing boards that they would inevitably create unequal treatment under the law. The Florida Supreme Court, affirming lower court judgments, extended the deadline for manual recounts. The counts in Volusia and Broward were completed and included in the final count. The Palm Beach recount was rejected by the state authorities since it was not concluded by the deadline, partly because election workers were encouraged to take their Thanksgiving Day holiday. Finally, the recount in Miami-Dade was aborted by its canvassing board at a meeting, conducted in an intimidatory atmosphere created by loud and angry Republican demonstrators who surrounded the office where it was held. Given the angry demonstrators wore tailored grey suits, this became known as the Brooks Brothers Riot. Roger Stone, later implicated in the Wikileaks publication of stolen Clinton campaign emails in 2016, was involved in this successful blocking of the recount. Secretary of State Katherine Harris then called the election for Bush on 26 November and the Gore team filed suit to contest the outcome.

Eventually by a majority verdict the Florida Supreme Court upheld Gore's challenge but dramatically insisted that where ballots had been machine read as having no vote for president, they should be manually recounted across the entire state. The court also warned that the margin of error in machine counting of punched ballots was so large as to warrant a reconsideration of the entire system. These legal contests culminated on December 12 in the US Supreme Court majority decision which ruled that no further manual recounts should be allowed since they could not be done in a way that ensured equal protection of every citizen who voted in the election and thus could not meet the standard set by the Fourteenth Amendment. The dissenting justices argued that it would have been better to remand the case back to Florida so that its courts could set a common standard for the interpretation of disputed ballots. Conversely, the conservative Chief Justice William Rehnquist in his concurrence with the majority opinion insisted that the disputed ballots were primarily the result of voters not following the instructions that were clearly posted in the polling places both in terms of how to use the machines and how to check that the ballot reflected their choices. In historical perspective, Rehnquist's opinion raised a sensitive topic since similar reasoning had been used to justify the literacy and understanding tests, used in many states to deny the right to vote until they were outlawed by the Voting Rights Act of 1965. A complicated machine that can be easily used incorrectly may operate as the equivalent of a test designed to reduce the electorate.

It should be clear by now why the 2000 outcome was so controversial and scandalous. However, what deepened the outrage for some was the experience of being denied the right to vote. Florida law permitted a prospective voter who found that their name was not on the voters list at the precinct on election day to file an affidavit declaring that they were registered to vote in that precinct. Only the election supervisor could approve a ballot for such a person and normally that was by phone and on election day calls into the election supervisor's office often received a "busy" signal. As a result, prospective voters were kept waiting or denied the vote or in some cases allowed to vote by precinct workers, even though the letter of the law had not been followed. During the 1990s, groups concerned about low election participation rates had secured measures designed to facilitate registration, including linking it to renewal of license plates on cars or so-called motor voter registration. Analyses of the 2000 election discovered that the transfer of registrant details from the license agency to the relevant election supervisor was inconsistent which resulted in some people being denied the right to vote. Such voter ID requirements are likely to affect poorer and minority voters disproportionately.

Further aggravating the sense of grievance was the different approach taken to another category of voter: overseas absentee ballot voters. Under pressure, Florida officials counted ballots in this category that clearly did not meet legal requirements. These included ballots with postmarks after the election, ballots with no postmark, overseas ballots that were posted within the United States, ballots without the required signature, and even some ballots where the voter was voting twice. All should have been disqualified. Lawsuits brought by the Republican campaign team asked for any discarded absentee ballot to be reconsidered in fourteen counties and their suits named the canvassing officers, a move which implied that they would be personally liable for any failure to comply. The officials were also targeted in an orchestrated media blitz labelling them as "unpatriotically" denying the right to vote to brave American service personnel who were prepared to give their lives for their country. All twelve counties won by Bush reconvened and accepted absentee ballots that had been rejected previously. The sheer partisanship of this process was underlined by the fact that the Bush team argued against accepting previously rejected ballots in those counties comfortably won by Gore since this seemed more likely to find overseas absentee ballots that added to his total.

As outrage simmered over the Bush victory by court ruling, a consortium of media interests and political scientists set out to review the different categories of discounted ballots in Florida. Some ballots had been rejected because it appeared the voter had voted twice – so-called over-voting. Others were rejected because no vote could be clearly identified – so-called under-voting. If all the over-vote and under-vote ballots were taken into consideration, this research suggested that Gore would have won by a very narrow margin; certainly, no more than 171 votes. But Gore's appeal to the courts had asked only for under-votes to be reviewed and that was what the state courts accepted before the US Supreme Court overruled them. If only under-votes in the four counties cited in the Gore suit had been manually determined, Bush would still have won by 225 votes, and if all the under-votes across the state had been recounted as the state Supreme Court ordered, Bush would have won by 430 votes. Thus, even if the legal battle had turned out differently, it would not have changed the result and the sense of grievance would not have diminished. The close contest had exposed deficiencies in the election system that were scandalous. Some of the flaws were mechanical – punch cards or optically scanned cards that did not work well – but others were political, stemming from the reality that elections were effectively run by the politicians not the people. When Donald Trump later insisted that the 2020 election was stolen, he was evoking recent memories, but he was also ignoring the fact that states had replaced the old machines with more secure and reliable technology. Most experts believe the 2020 election was the most secure on record.

By 2004, when George W. Bush ran for re-election against John Kerry, there had been widespread adoption of computerized voting machines. The Bush campaign, led by chief strategist, Karl Rove, made a determined effort to mobilize conservative voters through divisive social issues like abortion and stressed Bush's efforts to make America safe after the 9/11 attacks. His re-election victory, like his first, was determined by a single state's Electoral College votes, but this time it was Ohio that ensured Bush four more years. In the weeks before the election, pundits warned that another close race was likely to leave voters with a renewed sense of scandalous injustice. Already Republicans charged that the widespread call by Democrats for states to accept provisional ballots permitting voters who were not on precinct rolls to vote and then assessing their eligibility was a corrupt ploy to inflate turnout through fraudulent voting. In Ohio, the Republican secretary of state attempted to regulate late registration by insisting that any application should be on a prescribed thickness of paper and with a specific font size, which Democrats charged was an attempt to block voters who printed out the online form on cheap home copier paper and reduced the font to fit a single sheet (in other words, poorer voters).

At the time, Democrats also worried about the switch to computerized voting machines which would potentially leave no tangible evidence for any recount in a close contest and might be vulnerable to hacking. In the event, election day in Ohio was notable mainly for long lines because the state did not supply enough voting machines. To try to process all those who wanted to vote the polls stayed open well beyond the official closing time and hence the vote call was delayed. In many places people had to wait up to six hours to vote, and one can easily imagine how some grew discouraged and just walked away. Democrats alleged that the long lines outside understaffed polling stations in predominantly Democratic urban districts were no accident. The Kerry team concluded that the margin of their defeat (certified at well over 118,000 votes on 6 December) was too large to make litigation worthwhile. A recount ordered locally only reduced Bush's lead by a few hundred votes. The losing party's dissatisfaction, however, resurfaced when the new Congress convened on 6 January 2005. What is normally a polite ceremony in which Congress certifies the election turned into an acrimonious two-hour debate in the two chambers. The House voted to affirm the result 267-31 and, in the Senate, only Democratic Senator Barbara Boxer voted nay. This final twist suggested that no Republican was scandalized by the outcome and only a minority of Democratic politicians, thus signalling a split inside the latter party between establishment and militants that would continue to the present. Nonetheless, this was a precedent for the multiple Republican challenges to the certification process in 2021.

During the Obama years (2009-2017), Republicans continued to charge that fraudulent voting was a genuine problem in America's democracy and used their control at the state level to introduce tighter rules especially in relation to voter I.D. At the same time, in areas where the state legislatures had a major role in the redistricting of political constituencies after the 2010 census, the GOP followed a policy of re-drawing lines so that individual seats became uncompetitive. The new boundaries ceded certain, usually urban districts to Democrats, often with large African American and minority populations, and left others equally assuredly Republican. The politicians chose their voters. Ironically, since the general election outcome was pretty certain after re-districting, the real contest switched to the party primaries, and this tended to produce greater ideological rigidity. Democratic incumbents had to placate progressive challengers, while Republicans faced a growing threat from more ultra-conservative candidates especially those willing to champion hot button social issues and a libertarian, anti-government position. Ironically, some of the established Republicans who had overseen the partisan re-districting, like House Speaker, John Boehner of Ohio, found themselves forced out as the GOP moved further to the right. Overall, partisanship was intensified, and consensus diminished.

At the same time as these changes made it more difficult for establishment figures like Republican John McCain or Democrat Hillary Clinton to win presidential elections, a dramatically changing media market was reinforcing partisanship within America. When Richard Nixon had run for the presidency, the media scene was still dominated by the three major networks and there had been a consensual view of what kind of candidate would make a good President; a consensus that favoured the middle ground. With the advent of cable and then the internet and social media, broadcasting was superseded increasingly by niche marketing. An abundance of channels enabled people to get the news they wanted, and as the ascent of the conservatively inclined *Fox News* demonstrated, this meant that conservative voters did not need to listen to what the more liberally inclined *MSNBC* or *CNN* had to say. Barack Obama's campaign had also found that you could mobilize a lot of voters on the Democratic side through Facebook and text-messaging to mobile phones and the general trend was to decide elections in the old-fashioned way of ensuring turnout of the committed, in the case of older voters, and the enthusiastic in the case of younger first-time voters. Once the parties knew which issues energized their supporters, they could ensure that messages were sent that reinforced the saliency of these issues in this election. There was a convergence of trends therefore that made American politics more polarized, and which favoured divisive candidates who did not represent the consensus. Enter Donald Trump.

So now we turn to the question of Russian interference in the 2016 election and the related scandal about whether the Trump campaign colluded with Russia in efforts to beat Hillary Clinton. Even before the November election, the director of US intelligence and the director of homeland security jointly stated that their agencies were confident that Russian operatives were responsible for two episodes of hacking into the Democratic National Committee, and in particular, the downloading of the chair of the Clinton campaign, John Podesta's email files. The hackers passed the emails onto *Wikileaks*, which published embarrassing extracts from them on-line in the run-up to election day. The intelligence agencies told senior Congressional figures both before and after the election that they had concluded that the hacking was not done solely to interfere with the American election, but specifically to defeat Clinton. Democrats were universally outraged, but the Republican reaction varied. Chair of the House Homeland Security Committee, Michael McCaul of Texas, stated bluntly that such interference should not be allowed to continue. Senator John McCain, who led the Senate Armed Services Committee, declared that he was not surprised since the Russians had also targeted his presidential campaign in 2008. However, the then chair of the House Intelligence Committee, Representative Devon Nunes of California took issue with the claim that the Russians were trying to help Donald Trump. He insisted that the real problem was the Obama administration's failure to put in place stronger safeguards, particularly given its provocative strategy of "resetting" US relations with the Kremlin in an aggressive manner. As Obama's Secretary of State, Hillary Clinton had been a vocal advocate of a tougher line.

Candidate Trump was more openly sceptical about the intelligence agencies' conclusions, telling journalists that the hackers could have been based in China or even New Jersey. He also intimated that he would hope to foster a better relationship with Russian leader Vladimir Putin. Those around Trump also fed media conspiracy theories that implied that the hacking was a dirty trick done by the Obama administration as it tried to frame the Trump campaign as a Russian operation. This suspicion carried over into the Trump White House which tended to regard staff in various federal departments who had served the previous administration as untrustworthy "never Trumpers." This included the acting Attorney-General Sally Yates who was fired within days of Trump's inauguration, but controversy really took hold once Trump fired FBI Director James Comey on 9 May 2017. Comey had previously seemed a Trump ally. On learning that Clinton had used a personal email account while Secretary of State, intelligence agencies, including the FBI, had launched a probe to determine whether there had been a dangerous security breach. However, by the summer of 2016, their conclusion was that although Clinton had behaved imprudently, she had not endangered national security. Then, on 27 October, with the 8 November election day nearing, Comey announced that the FBI had reopened its investigation because of a newly discovered batch of messages.

The timing of Comey's announcement seemed at odds with FBI protocols on ensuring its actions were non-partisan, especially in relation to elections.

Democratic Senator Diane Feinstein said the announcement "played right into the political campaign of Donald Trump." Trump, who had energized his rallies with the chant – "Lock her up! Lock her up!"–repeated his charge that Clinton's use of private emails was "worse than Watergate." On 6 November, Comey announced that the fresh material had not altered the FBI's conclusions and Clinton would face no further action, but the damage was done. Speaking to donors after the election, Clinton singled out Comey's intervention as crucial in her defeat. Nonetheless, Comey's subsequent failure to protect Trump amid the growing accusations of Russian interference prompted the new President to fire the FBI director; a move which, as staff tried to warn him, triggered the appointment of a special prosecutor, Robert Mueller. Ironically, one reason cited for Comey's dismissal by Deputy Attorney-General Rod Rosenstein was that his conduct in the Clinton email case had tarnished the Bureau's reputation for impartiality.

Thus began, what Trump frequently called a witch-hunt. On 9 June 2016, Trump's son Don Jr., his son-in-law Jared Kushner, and his soon-to-be campaign manager Paul Manafort, met with a motley group of Russians in Trump Tower, New York. They had taken the meeting expecting to be offered damaging information on Hillary Clinton and the Clinton Foundation. This bait had been dangled during early phone and email exchanges, and Don Jr. had expressed enthusiasm at the prospect of getting dirt on the Democratic candidate. This might seem simply standard negative campaigning practice, except the information was being offered by a foreign power, and US law expressly prohibits candidates from taking anything of benefit from foreign nations. In practice, Natalia Veselnitskaya, a well-connected Moscow lawyer and the similarly murky, wheeler-dealer lobbyist, Rinat Akhmetshin, did not deliver. Given the US sanctions in place against targeted interests in the Russian Federation, it was a risky manoeuvre for the Trump team to attempt, especially given the dubious credentials of those involved. Akhmetshin was a US-based associate of Azerbaijani oligarch Aras Agalarov, whose pop star son Emin's publicist, Rob Goldstone, had helped set up the meeting. This has led some to speculate that the Russians never intended to provide information. Instead, their goal was to entrap the Trump campaign in a compromising relationship. Shortly afterwards, Wikileaks announced that it had the hacked DNC emails, a development that can either be read as evidence that the Trump camp was aware of a larger Russian program of assistance, or equally as further proof that the Russian scheme operated independently of a Trump campaign that was believed to be floundering in the early summer of 2016.

For Russia, Trump could become an asset who did not need to be aware of his role in order to be useful; a person sometimes referred to as a "useful idiot" in espionage circles. In this scenario, the overarching Russian goal was to foment polarizing divisions and generate distrust in America with recrimination on all sides. Whether one views the Trump campaign as blameless or not, one can still agree that the state of US politics in 2017 suggested that the Russian objectives were richly realized. After the Russian invasion of Ukraine and annexation of Crimea in 2014, the Obama administration in collaboration with the European Union had orchestrated an international response that included a wide range of sanctions. Integral to that effort had been Secretary of State Clinton, and during her presidential campaign she urged strengthening this tough line against Russian expansionism. In contrast, Donald Trump hinted that he might ease the sanctions already imposed. He had also floated the idea of greater US-Russian cooperation in handling both the Syrian crisis and the threat from Islamic State forces. These significant, and from a Kremlin point of view, positive policy developments raised alarm within the US foreign policy establishment particularly because of the many rumours already circulating about Trump and Russia.

On 11 January 2017, a website known for its scandalous revelations, *Buzzfeed*, published a confidential report drawn up by a former British intelligence MI6 officer Christopher Steele. The report was based on unidentified confidential sources within both Putin's and Trump's inner circle. Its contents rapidly gained notoriety, not least because it alleged that Trump had not only used the services of prostitutes while in Russia but that he had been particularly gratified by watching them urinate ("golden shower" style) on a bed previously assigned to President Obama and First Lady, Michelle. The larger part of the report was about corrupt commercial transactions, but it was the piss that caught the eye. It subsequently emerged that Fusion, the company that hired Steele initially on behalf of a Republican donor alarmed by Trump's candidacy, was in the end paid through an intermediary by the Clinton campaign; hence the Steele dossier was opposition research. Via Steele and his confidential sources, the Clinton campaign had arguably obtained negative campaign material comparable to what Don, Jr. had hoped to secure via the Trump Tower meeting. It is still claimed that this was done without the knowledge of Clinton herself. However, as with so many scandals related to Trump, his followers were as interested in the motivation behind the exposé as in the story itself. The Steele dossier was dismissed as fake news because it was funded by Democrats and involved obtaining negative stories from Russian sources.

Trump's real estate and media business dealings had had many Russian connections ever since the 1990s; precisely the period when the collapse of the USSR and the privatization of its primary resource industries, especially oil and natural gas, produced individual fortunes on a scale comparable to the "Robber Barons" of America's Gilded Age. Given the involvement of organized crime in these developments, the Russian Federation and other former Soviet states were referred to at the time as the "Wild East." The Russian oligarchs had billions in roubles, but their wealth was less secure and less productive until it was transferred to the West through a variety of money-laundering operations. One of the chief routes was via real estate, especially in New York and other fashionable American locations where luxury property, like Trump Tower apartments, could be bought through corporate intermediaries so that the actual purchaser was not disclosed. Ironically, the usefulness of acquiring a Trump property abroad for Russia's oligarchs diminished their interest in investing in Trump's eagerly touted Moscow plans. Despite regular visits to the country, he never succeeded in building a Trump Tower in the Russian capital.

In 1996 Trump had acquired the rights to the Miss Universe beauty pageant, which, like other media projects, he used to promote his brand around the world. This included staging the contest in Moscow. In June 2013, during the staging of the Miss USA pageant which he also owned, Trump met with the Agalarov family to discuss business over dinner at his Las Vegas hotel, accompanied by his then personal attorney Michael Cohen. Aras Agalarov was on stage with Trump when the future President announced during the Miss USA telecast that he was thrilled that November's Miss Universe contest would be in Moscow at an Agalarov-owned venue. During his November stay at the Ritz Carlton in Moscow, Trump boasted in an *MSNBC* interview about his great relationship with

Putin, noting that the Russian leader had done "a very brilliant job…. An amazing job… [that put him] at the forefront of the world as a leader in a short period." When Putin personally awarded Russia's prestigious Order of Honor to Agalarov shortly before the televised pageant, it confirmed the positive relationship the latter enjoyed with the Russian leader, previously signalled by government contracts that included the stadia that would host the 2018 World Cup. Agalarov was therefore a plausible intermediary between Trump and Putin.

When Trump's 2013 visit was scrutinized by the FBI and other agencies in the light of fears that he may have been compromised by Russia, Trump responded by saying that he had flown in for the Miss Universe event and then immediately flown back. Essentially, he could not have been at a hotel with prostitutes because he had only visited his suite there briefly to change clothes. As was often the case, the President's memory was inaccurate. He claimed to be in Moscow for twenty-four hours whereas he was there for forty-eight hours. Trump also hit back in March 2017 by trying to re-direct attention to his own allegations that the Obama administration had put wiretaps on him in Trump Tower. This counter-narrative that the real scandal of 2016 was the Obama administration's multiple, clandestine attempts to assist the Clinton campaign persisted. Trump's Attorney-General William Barr announced in April 2019 that, despite the Justice Department's declaration in court documents that neither it nor the FBI had any evidence of surveillance operations at Trump Tower, he was convinced that spying had occurred, and he wanted confirmation that any surveillance had due cause.

However, while the issue of collusion between the Trump campaign and Russia remained a simmering story for the entire period of Robert Mueller's investigation from May 2017 to March 2019, Russia's role in the election was far more significant in other ways. The final Mueller report was divided into two with only the second volume examining whether President Trump had obstructed investigators to conceal his collusion with Russia. In the first volume, US intelligence agencies show that the disinformation operations that the USSR had developed during the Cold War had been dramatically re-invented by the new Russia for a new age of cyber-warfare. Mass internet use is predicated on the commercial value of personal data as individuals leave behind a trail on the sites they visit.

With modern computers, such data provides the basis for richly textured profiles of individual consumers' character and preferences. This wealth of data is enriched further by social media with public messaging via Twitter, Instagram, or Facebook giving further insights into what makes people tick.

This extraordinary aggregation of personal data has value because of algorithms that have been developed to model how each piece of the puzzle connects. For example, the playlist of favourites that someone has on their Alexa speaker or Spotify channel can be used not just to identify other music that might appeal, but all the other items that are most likely to be desired by someone who listens to this type of music. Algorithms of this type can also identify the "hot button" issues for specific voters. By 2016, the Russian cyber-warfare operations had the advantage that talented Russian programmers had returned from key Silicon Valley operations with the algorithms they had helped to develop to create consumer profiles. The same programs that enabled US redistricting map makers to slice the population into carefully tailored subgroups whose political preference could be assumed were now available to a foreign power intent on deepening anger and division in America.

In 2011 when Putin was seeking a triumphant re-election to the presidency, Secretary of State Clinton had authorized a US influencing campaign in support of his opponents. Five years later it was payback time. Re-elected in 2012, Putin instructed his military intelligence agencies to amplify their cyber-warfare preparations. They created what were known as "troll farms," automated spamming and fake news outlets that could ensure that targeted subjects received messages that were highly likely to influence their behaviour, typically by reinforcing rather than changing political preferences. An early test of this project came after the Russian annexation of the Crimea in 2014. Moscow targeted Congressional aides with malware messages. So-called "click-bait" news items induced staffers to access material that then downloaded "Trojan" malware, and this in turn gave the Russians access to private Congressional deliberations so that they could see which politicians were opposed to the sanctions that the Obama administration was seeking to impose.

This limited and not entirely successful experiment (since the sanctions passed) provided the basis for a far larger effort in 2016. In assessing its impact, it's worth remembering that Trump's victory margin was in the

Electoral College, not in the popular vote and so, in key states it came from mobilizing a relatively small number of voters. In other words, it was a classic political operation that induced your voters to get out and vote, while at the same time encouraging the other guy's electors to stay home. One particularly effective tactic was to ensure that all negative stories about Clinton got to voters who might already be reluctant to vote for her, and there were various, usually Democratic-inclined, households where doubts could be amplified. Male, African American and white, blue-collar voters often had limited enthusiasm for a female establishment candidate who scoffed at Trump's "deplorables." When pharmaceutical boss Martin Shkreli shared his opinion that Clinton showed signs of early-stage Parkinson's Disease in August 2016, he gave the Russian bots a story line that resonated with all those Americans already worried that a female President would be a weak commander-in-chief. A month later when Clinton fainted at a 9/11 commemoration event, these rumours were reactivated. Just before election day itself, far wilder stories gained currency; most notoriously, bizarre allegations that Clinton and her aides ran a paedophile ring from the basement of a DC pizza parlour. In a media landscape of viral storylines, fake news of the most preposterous kind has a ready audience of people who want to believe the worst about a candidate they already dislike. Ultimately, this would feed into the growth of the Q-Anon online cult.

The core of the Russian operations was the creation of fake personal accounts. In 2014, thousands of linked Facebook accounts were created. The next stage was to build the audience for messages from these accounts and to do so in ways that validated their false identity. Hence, at this stage the messages tended to be warm or funny, human-interest stories. Once actual American Facebook users got used to liking or sharing messages from a fictional "Andrea" or "Alex," the platform was ready for the 2016 election. By early 2016, dozens of employees at Moscow's Internet Research Agency worked on creating and maintaining social media accounts, not only on Facebook but across Twitter, Instagram and other outlets. On Twitter, the agency created accounts that mimicked or resembled actual political groups, posing as members of the Tea Party, Black Lives Matter, and anti-immigration groups. They also recruited US-based staff to give their groups added credibility. For instance, the group "Black Fist" hired a self-defence instructor in New York to offer classes so local African Americans could resist police brutality.

Collectively, the Facebook accounts linked to the Russian operation generated over 80,000 messages sent directly to at least 29 million people, but potentially reaching an estimated 126 million Americans. Facebook also accepted $100,000 for 3500 politically motivated ads from Russian-backed accounts. Linked activities, including rallies in major cities (organized online), reflected the growth of fake organizations with over 300,000 people joining "United Muslims of America" ostensibly to fight Islamophobia; a quarter of a million belonging to the "Don't Shoot Us" group protesting police brutality; and over 130,000 backing the anti-immigration "Secure Our Borders" Facebook group. During the primaries, some ostensibly liberal progressive groups backed Bernie Sanders against Clinton, and once she secured the nomination, these fake groups focused on her failure to do or promise enough to justify the active support of progressives.

According to Twitter, in the ten weeks leading up to the 2016 election, the nearly 4,000 fake Russian accounts posted just under 176,000 tweets. The strategy was to try to induce US media to circulate these messages, thus giving them laundered value. Seventy US outlets did so and attributed it to a real person. Celebrity Twitter users were also targeted, and presumably unwittingly, they assisted the spread of Russian messaging. Former Ambassador to Russia, Michael McFaul, GOP political operative Roger Stone, *Fox News*' Sean Hannity, and Trump campaign staff Kellyanne Conway, Michael Flynn Jr., and Donald Trump Jr., all share with President Trump himself the distinction of having re-tweeted Russian messages. Russia also controlled 170 Instagram accounts that posted 120,000 pieces of content during a two-year period, and it is in the context of this multi-media platform that the Mueller Report's estimate that the content may have reached 126 million Americans makes sense. A University of Southern California study found that 20 percent of political tweets between 16 September and 21 October came from internet bots of unknown origin, further confirming that the Russian social media operation was of staggering proportions.

"GRU" is the English version of the Russian acronym ГРУ, which means Main Intelligence Directorate; in other words, Russian military intelligence. The Mueller investigation was able to identify the specific GRU units who hacked into the Democratic National Committee and leaked materials both via its own sponsored sites and via Wikileaks and hence into the election campaign. As a result, twelve GRU officers faced federal charges for crimes arising from the hacking of DNC computers, principally that of conspiring to commit computer intrusions. There remains little prospect that the accused will ever be handed over by Russia, however. Stolen documents acquired by the GRU included internal strategy documents, fundraising data, opposition research, and emails from the work inboxes of DNC employees, much of which might be of interest to Clinton's opponent, Donald Trump.

After the DNC announced that it had discovered the hacking operation on 14 June 2016, the GRU established a further cover story via a cyber persona Guccifer 2.0 who posted a web-post attributing the hack to a lone Romanian hacker. The same site was then used to publish the stolen materials selectively and tactically. Releases were organized around thematic issues, such as specific states (e.g., Florida and Pennsylvania) that were perceived as competitive in the presidential election. Wikileaks founder, Julian Assange, was known to be hostile to Clinton's candidacy, having characterized Hillary as a "bright, well-connected, sadistic sociopath." Hence, the publication of bulk tranches of records in the run-up to the November election was partly Assange's retaliation against Clinton's pursuit of him on espionage charges for leaking classified material obtained by convicted spy, Chelsea Manning. It was also a reflection of Assange's populist ideology that saw Clinton as a pillar of an exploitative, corporate capitalist, world order. Consequently, some applauded Assange, but others, who saw the Wikileaks founder's willingness to collaborate with Russian state hackers and to assist the Trump campaign as unprincipled and self-interested, felt scandalized.

One of Donald Trump's more striking characteristics is that he regularly appears genuinely scandalized. Whenever the mainstream media, such as the *Washington Post* or *New York Times* or the news channels, *CNN* or *MSNBC*, criticized his actions or decisions as president, he was apt to complain of "fake news." This was certainly his response to the widespread sense of shock expressed across such media when he won the 2016 election. Their hostility also fed his reaction to early coverage of his administration such as his Inauguration Day. Trump was incensed that anyone would challenge his demonstrably inaccurate claims that the 2017 crowds were bigger than ever before, or that it had not rained on 20 January. This was even more emphatically his response to the ongoing discussion of Russian interference, which he characterized as an attempt to deny his election victory and his legitimate claim to power.

President Obama had imposed further sanctions on Russia on 29 December 2016, and expelled thirty-five suspected Russian spies as well as ordering the closure of two Russian-owned compounds in Maryland and New York. This underlined the intelligence agencies' conclusion that Russia had meddled and made the question of collusion between the Trump campaign and Russia an understandably hot story. On 26 January, White House Counsel Donald McGahn learned that US intercepts had revealed that Trump's pick as National Security Adviser, Michael Flynn, had not been truthful in response to questions about contacts with the Russians. On 9 February, the *Washington Post* reported that contrary to his denials, Flynn had discussed the sanctions against Russia with its Ambassador Sergey Kislyak prior to Trump's inauguration. Joined by Chief of Staff Reince Priebus and Vice-President Mike Pence, McGahn reviewed the highly classified intercepts of Flynn's phone conversations with Kislyak. Flynn had previously assured Pence that he was innocent, and Pence had then backed up his claim that there was nothing in the story. Now the three senior White House figures read three phone-call transcripts in which sanctions were clearly discussed; the last of which had the Ambassador thanking Flynn and saying that the Russians would follow his advice on the sanctions question. The phone intercepts explained why Putin had not retaliated with a tit-for-tat expulsion of American diplomats in December. Flynn had given him reason to believe that the Trump administration would relax the sanctions policy provided the Russians showed restraint and patience. President-elect Trump had even praised Putin as smart for not retaliating.

For those Americans ready to believe that Trump was Putin's puppet, Flynn's behaviour was a predictable prelude to the administration's accommodation of Russian interests. It certainly did not ease suspicions to learn that Flynn had been paid $45,000 for a speaking engagement in Moscow or to see him chatting amicably at dinner with Putin himself in a 2015 photograph. Despite the rumours swirling around his National

Security Adviser, Trump chose to take Flynn with him to Mar-a-Lago for a weekend of meetings with Japanese premier Shinzo Abe as alarm grew over North Korean missile tests. On the Monday, as the Flynn story persisted, Trump included him in a lunch meeting with Canadian premier Justin Trudeau. This sign of presidential approval kept the Flynn scandal buzzing into the next news cycle.

Trump has always prioritized loyalty and unlike other military men and members of the intelligence community, Lieutenant-General Flynn had shown no doubts about Trump. In fact, he had acted as a warm-up act at Trump's 2016 campaign rallies. Equally significantly, he had been among the first in Trump's inner circle to whisper that he should not trust US intelligence agencies since they were part of the anti-Trump Washington establishment – the swamp, as it was nicknamed. Flynn had also been shrewd enough to realize that Trump's daughter Ivanka and her orthodox Jewish husband Jared Kushner, would be influential in the White House. He had therefore seemed happy to accommodate Kushner's heady ambitions, which included taking on a key role in relation to the Middle East policies, both towards Israel and Saudi Arabia. Aware of this, Ivanka and Jared were eager to back Flynn's appointment. Their voices, and Trump's own sense that Flynn was loyal, overrode the advice not to appoint Flynn that Trump received. Former New Jersey Governor Chris Christie, a hardened political operator, had endorsed the warnings of outgoing President Barack Obama, who had fired Flynn from the Defense Intelligence Agency for dubious judgment and questionable motivations. It was against this backdrop that Trump viewed the news that James Comey's FBI had interviewed Flynn in the West Wing on 24 January. Like the press, the intelligence agencies, Trump felt, just couldn't accept the fact that he had won. They were secretly plotting to bring him down before he had even begun. In this growing state of paranoia, Trump watched the Russia investigation grow.

A higher priority than loyalty for Trump has always been self-preservation, and Reece Priebus warned him that if Flynn remained, he would damage the presidency. Still loyal, Flynn promised Trump that he would go quietly and submitted his resignation on 14 February. The next day Trump told Chris Christie over lunch that with Flynn's departure, "the whole Russia thing was over." Christie doubted this. "Bad people are like gum on the bottom of your shoe," he remarked. "Very hard to make them go away." The same afternoon, the President was in a Homeland Security meeting. When it ended, he asked FBI Director James Comey to stay behind so he could talk to him privately.

Feeling that Flynn was being unfairly treated, Trump explained that he had to let him go, even though he hadn't done anything wrong. "I hope you can see your way clear to letting this go; to letting Flynn go," Trump pressed, according to Comey's contemporaneous notes of the conversation. "He is a good guy," Trump said of Flynn. "I hope you can let this go." For Trump, this was an ordinary conversation. He was simply asking a member of his organization to take care of something. Trump also felt that Comey owed him. After all, he had allowed Comey to continue as FBI head and assumed that he would show loyalty in return. Comey took a different view and the investigation of Flynn proceeded, culminating nine months later in his guilty plea on one count of lying to the FBI, which Flynn entered rather than face crippling legal fees defending himself on multiple additional charges. Before leaving office, Trump rewarded Flynn for his loyalty with a pardon.

On 2 March new Attorney General Jeff Sessions, regarded as one of Trump's closest allies because of his outspoken support for policies like "the Wall" on the Mexican border and immigration restriction more generally, announced that he was recusing himself from the ongoing Russia investigation. He had realized that during his congressional confirmation hearings he had claimed that he had had no communication with the Russians whereas the truth was he had had two conversations with Ambassador Kislyak. Justice Department rules plainly stated that no official can participate in a criminal investigation if he has a personal or political relationship with an individual or organization substantively involved in that investigation. And that meant any Trump person with Russian contacts. Sessions recused himself, despite receiving a clear message from Trump that he should not do so. Watching Sessions' news conference from aboard Air Force One, Trump was furious.

If Sessions had felt unable to oversee the investigation, Trump railed, he should have said so. Trump had expected Sessions to ensure that any Justice Department investigation would quickly overturn press speculation about his campaign's collusion with the Russians. Privately, Trump was hearing that there were lots of Justice Department people, mainly women, who despised him and wanted to use their lawyer skills to bring him down. They were *never Trumpers*, still appalled that the nation's first African American President had not been followed by its first female President. It was this kind of thinking that prompted Trump's early-morning, 4 March tweet accusing Obama of tapping his phones in an action that he labelled as identical to "Nixon/Watergate." Seizing another parallel, he complained that Sessions had not protected him the way Bobby Kennedy, when he was Attorney-General, had protected his brother Jack. Back then, FBI chief J. Edgar Hoover had known how to help his bosses, he declared. Trump adviser Steve Bannon reminded the President that times had changed. Something big had happened since the days of Kennedy and Hoover, he said, and that something was Watergate. Trump's anger foreshadowed his future reactions to legal suits brought against him. They were all presented as partisan efforts by "deep state" Democrats.

Without Sessions' protection, Trump pressed Comey for reassurance that he himself was not a subject of interest in the FBI inquiry. Privately, Comey nodded, but he was unwilling to go public. As the story persisted, Trump's anger grew. By 9 May, he could no longer contain his frustration and fired Comey, an action that on 16 May prompted the ousted FBI director to disclose his notes of their February conversation to the press, implying that the President, Nixon-like, was seeking to obstruct justice. Predictably, Congressional Democrats compared Comey's firing to Nixon's firing of the Watergate special prosecutor Archibald Cox.

Trump himself had hardly been tactful. On 10 May, he was photographed meeting with Russian foreign minister Sergey Lavrov and Ambassador Kislyak in the Oval Office. He was quoted as telling the Russians that he had just fired the head of the FBI whom he characterized as "crazy, a nut job." He had added that the "great pressure" that he had faced "because of Russia" was now "taken off." On 12 May, Trump taunted Comey with his own Watergate reference in a tweet that read: "James Comey had better hope that there are no "tapes" of our conversations before he starts leaking to the press." After a weekend's reflection, Comey leaked his notes to a journalist contact and the *New York Times* ran the story on 16 May. That evening on *CNN*, political pundit and veteran White House adviser David Gergen opined that the Comey firing had moved the Russia controversy into "impeachment territory." Gergen had been in both the Nixon and

Clinton White Houses when impeachment loomed, so his words had weight. The scandal was growing bigger, not smaller, and that was partly due to Trump's own actions.

Having provided legal cover for Trump's firing of Comey, Deputy Attorney-General Rosenstein felt compelled on 19 May to appoint a special prosecutor to investigate the collusion question and Russian meddling. He chose Robert Mueller, a previously long-serving FBI director and a figure of impeccable integrity. Trump had recently met Mueller while considering Comey's replacement and felt that his not asking him to return to the FBI gave Mueller an axe to grind. Mueller had also had a row in the past with one of Trump's golf clubs over fees charged to him. When Trump realized that a special prosecutor had expansive powers to investigate potential wrong-doing, he grew even more agitated; the scrutiny was equivalent to that applied during Watergate, Iran-Contra, and the Lewinsky scandals. Mueller could potentially dig through Trump's whole life and finances unearthing illegality wherever a case could be made. The investigation could be a scandal factory for the rest of his time in office. He could be impeached, disgraced, and then prosecuted. Trump was heard to say: "This is terrible. This is the end of my presidency. I'm F**K*D."

A casual glance at Trump's business career and past conduct more generally shows that he was not new to scandal and that his consistent response was to have his lawyers deal with it. After Sessions failed him, Trump lamented that his former personal lawyer Roy Cohn, an infamous fixer dating back to the McCarthyite era, was no longer alive; he would have got the job done. Now, his regular attorney was Marc Kasowitz, whose practice focused on divorce and bankruptcy; with both of which Donald was all too familiar. Aware of his inexperience, Kasowitz contacted several high-profile Washington firms, but they turned down the job. Defending the President from the various allegations might ultimately prove bad for their business, plus Trump had a reputation as a difficult and slow-paying client. Consequently, the choice was confined to those who were prepared to serve, and topping the list was John Dowd. Although his most prominent cases were in decades past, the 76-year-old Dowd knew how the Justice Department operated and had a network of Washington contacts. Appointed 25 May, Dowd, in turn recommended Ty Cobb, a veteran of the independent counsel investigations of the Clinton years.

Based on his review of the evidence, Dowd concluded that Mueller was unlikely to prove collusion between Russia and the Trump campaign, but he was less confident that the investigation would not uncover other charges. The most immediately serious for the President would be obstruction of justice, as this could form the basis for impeachment. White House counsel Don McGahn was prepared to resist requests for disclosure of documents from Congressional investigators through a claim of executive privilege, but Dowd convinced him that if his team could persuade Mueller that they were cooperating, this strategy would work against Congressional demands in a way that did not invoke executive privilege and so become liable to legal challenge. Certainly, a clash over executive privilege would generate further hostile headlines. Cooperation, Dowd argued, would be more likely to make Mueller see the President as having nothing to hide, and would be more likely to ensure that the investigation reached an early conclusion. As Dowd phrased it, "we'd get a hell of a lot more with honey than we would with vinegar." The likelihood of speeding up the process particularly appealed to Trump; he just wanted the threat lifted.

When Trump's legal team met with Mueller's about a month into the investigation, they tried to establish how far the focus was on the President. Mueller, however, was sphinx-like in his silence. The Dowd team argued that Trump's firing of Comey could not be interpreted as obstruction considering the broad powers given to any President to fire appointees. They also raised concerns about Comey's credibility as a witness given the timing of his release of his supposedly contemporaneous records, and more delicately they hinted that as a former FBI director himself, Mueller might face a conflict of interests that would undermine his role as an independent special counsel in this context. Dowd stressed that a prolonged probe would hurt Trump's ability to govern and spelt out that White House cooperation was based on its desire to expedite the investigation. Mueller replied: "You know me, John. I don't let any grass grow under my feet." This was in June 2017, leaving one to speculate how tall the grass had grown by the time Mueller submitted his report in March 2019.

As the first summer of Trump's presidency unfolded and media speculation about the Mueller investigation continued, the President faced other forms of negative news coverage. Most dramatically over the weekend of 8-9 July 2017, the *New York Times* ran its account of the Trump Tower meeting between Don, Jr., Paul Manafort, Jared Kushner and Natalia Veselnitskaya. On 17 July, Trump tweeted, in a Nixon-like complaint, that most politicians would have taken the meeting that Don Jr. had attended to get info on an opponent. "That's politics!" he wrote. Dowd reassured him that there was nothing to fear. This was just the usual case of liberal media selling a story. He also continued to deliver documents to Mueller's team. Eventually, the investigation received 1.4 million pages of records from the Trump campaign and a further 20,000 pages from the White House. Some thirty-seven witnesses gave interviews to the Mueller team voluntarily. As Dowd frequently insinuated to Mueller, such cooperation was hardly consistent with Nixon-style obstruction of justice. Other developments now complicated the special prosecutor's task. A quiet Justice Department investigation of the FBI's handling of the Clinton email investigation had uncovered an extramarital affair between senior counterintelligence supervisor Peter Strzok and FBI lawyer Lisa Page. Their intimate text exchanges revealed not just their relationship but an intense dislike for Trump and their clear preference that he should never become president. Strzok was immediately removed from Mueller's team, but the findings seemed to confirm that Trump could not expect fair treatment from the Bureau; indeed, maybe, his fears of a "deep state" operation, out to get him, were not so paranoid after all.

On 1 August, the special prosecutor's office received the draft of Trump's letter that fired Comey. Trump's lawyers claimed that the letter exonerated him by showing that he had no corrupt intent of ending the Russia probe, but instead regarded Comey's refusal to confirm publicly that the President was not under investigation as unreasonable and prejudicial. The continuing cooperation with Mueller offered a further advantage in law via the so-called Espy precedent, named after Mike Espy, who had faced investigation during the Clinton administration. Under its terms, a subpoena demanding testimony from the President was only permissible if it could be shown that the information sought could not be obtained in any other way. By offering detailed records and responsive witnesses, the White House was making it harder for Mueller to demand an interview with the President. Trump's legal team had watched him closely and like everyone, noted his tendency to embellish, fabricate, or just plain lie. Trump approached facts as something akin to raw food that would be so much easier to swallow with the herbs of hyperbole and other improving spices. While the lawyers did not think he had colluded with the Russians, they were also convinced that he could not get through a formal, sworn interview with investigators without perjuring himself.

At the same time, Trump could not disguise his impatience. Unlike previous presidents who read their briefing books, he spent much of each day watching cable news and reading press reports. The largely negative coverage flowing from the Mueller probe put him in a foul mood. "Can you believe how obsessed they are with this?" he would fume. This toxic atmosphere added to the general air of turmoil and dysfunction that fed a remarkable turnover of senior staff. Chief of Staff Reince Priebus departed 31 July 2017; becoming one of several staff to notch up a record for the shortest tenure in office. Priebus's successor, John Kelly helped to secure the removal of presidential aide and former campaign manager Steve Bannon, who had been the administration's leading Alt-Right, populist spokesman in mid-August by which time tensions inside Trump's National Security team had also produced multiple resignations. Press Secretary Sean Spicer, who was regularly scolded for failing to present Trump's position forcefully enough, left on 21 July. Anthony Scaramucci lasted just five days as director of communications. Health Secretary Tom Price resigned in September after press reports criticizing his use of private charters and military aircraft for personal travel at the government's expense. Such turnover diminished efficiency and was scandalous in itself.

Adding to the air of instability was a clear policy of clearing out holdover staff in certain departments. Attorney-General Sessions had demanded the resignation of forty-six US Attorneys on 10 March and accepted all but three letters of resignation. Secretary of State Tillerson was said to be decimating the career ranks of the State Department. Other staff had left in protest at the mayhem they witnessed. Director of Government Ethics Walter Shaub resigned on July 19 complaining that the administration was not vigilant about ethics. Wary of the confirmation process and aware that it strengthened a cabinet member's ability to dissent, Trump grew accustomed to working with acting secretaries. For those who valued sound government, whether in defense, diplomacy or domestic policies, the scandal-ridden administration was hard to work for, or with. Unfilled positions became a scandal in itself.

As Trump approached his second year in office in 2018, he wanted Mueller gone, too. On 19 January he learned of a Justice Department's probe into the FBI's use of FISA warrants. The 1978 Foreign Intelligence Surveillance Act (FISA) had established these procedures in the wake of post-Watergate revelations of the intelligence agencies' systemic misuse of their powers. The Act required agencies to apply to a special federal court to obtain any warrant and to provide evidence as to why a subject should be placed under surveillance. As the Act's name suggests, the warrants are expected to apply to foreign agents or US citizens who are acting as agents for a foreign power. Congressional Republicans, notably Devon Nunes from the House Intelligence Committee believed that the FBI had misled a federal judge in order to obtain a warrant against former Trump campaign adviser Carter Page. In their application to the court, the Bureau took evidence for their suspicion that Page was working for Russia from the Steele dossier, which, since it was designed as opposition research for the Clinton campaign, was, in Nunes's opinion, a tainted source. Accordingly, Trump believed that the probe had exposed a conspiracy by the intelligence and national security establishment to subvert his election victory. But the Justice Department did not support Nunes's interpretation and insisted that further investigation was needed. With no sign of the Mueller investigation ending, Trump decided he needed better legal representation.

By March 2018, Mueller's team had trapped more people in Trump's circle. Like former National Security Advisor Michael Flynn, George Papadopoulos, a campaign advisor on foreign policy, had pled guilty to lying to the FBI in a plea bargain that subsequently unravelled since he failed to provide the assistance he promised, notably with regard to the apprehension of a mysterious Maltese academic, Joseph Mifsud, who left the US a fortnight after Papadopoulos's first interview and whom the FBI believed to be a Russian agent. Trump's former campaign manager, Paul Manafort and his business associate Rick Gates, were also facing multiple charges, although since these did not relate primarily to Trump campaign matters, Trump felt able to brush them off as media attempts to build guilt by association. Far more worrying was the news that Mueller had delegated to the Southern District of New York US attorney's office the task of exploring Trump's murky finances, ostensibly to see if problems there might have given others leverage.

The Trump organization itself would be subpoenaed for records detailing its past financial transactions, particularly those involving foreign clients and known members of organized crime, whether it was a Trump Tower apartment or an Atlantic City casino operation that might serve to launder money. This long-lasting investigation would begin to produce charges against the company's top financial officers in 2021. Investigators would also take an interest in family members, especially Ivanka and Jared; after all, Jared's father Charlie Kushner, a New York real estate developer like Trump, had already served time in federal prison. As Jared gloomily explained to his father-in-law, this might mean not just impeachment, but financial ruin. On 22 March, Trump fired John Dowd. In mid-April, news leaked that Mueller was investigating a $150,000 donation to the Trump Foundation by Ukrainian billionaire Viktor Pinchuk, solicited by Trump's personal attorney Michael Cohen. Since the Foundation was being scrutinized as an illegal vehicle for campaign contributions, this was a potential breach of federal election laws. The Foundation was already facing ongoing questions from New York state prosecutors and Congressional investigators, which eventually resulted in its court-supervised dissolution in December 2018, the imposition of a $2million settlement against Trump for the misuse of charitable funds, and the requirement that his children Ivanka, Don, Jr., and Eric attend mandatory training sessions on the obligations associated with philanthropic board service. This was yet another example of the compendium-like range of Trump scandals that has continued to grow since he left office.

On the Mueller side, things were not getting simpler. After prodigious cyber research, his team were now confident that they could prove in court that Russian state-sponsored hackers had interfered systematically with the 2016 election. This was especially challenging because it had to be done without jeopardizing intelligence assets in Russia itself. They had also identified other "persons of interest" in Trump's campaign, notably Michael Cohen, whose office and home they raided on 9 April. As with Paul Manafort, the President's defense was that investigators were primarily interested in Cohen's own dubious business interests, but Cohen had certainly handled some of Trump's personal affairs, not least pay-offs to women with whom he had relationships, including Stephanie Gregory Clifford, a porn star working under the name Stormy Daniels. Such revelations were eagerly consumed by scandal-hungry cable news outlets. The net was also closing around Roger Stone who had begun his career learning dirty tricks during the Nixon administration. The eccentric Stone, known for his peculiar dress sense and propensity for boasting about his misdeeds, was always likely to provide a click-bait storyline. But his political dirty tricks were real enough. In 2000, he had taken a role in organizing the anti-recount demonstrations in Florida; during the 2016 campaign the FBI alleged that he was the one who reached out to Wikileaks's Julian Assange to ensure the release of Russian-hacked DNC documents; and in 2020-21, he had links with the Far Right, Proud Boys, a paramilitary group which played a role in the 6 January attack on the Capitol.

Trump's new legal team included one very familiar, public face. Former New York City Mayor, Rudy Giuliani, had once been a presidential hopeful in the wake of his leadership after the 9/11 attacks, but he was now largely just a Trump surrogate eager to talk, with varying degrees of sobriety and coherence, on cable news. He would continue in this erratic role right through the 2020 defeat and was a leading figure in the repeatedly defeated, legal attempts to challenge the election results. Less celebrated, but more useful, Trump's new attorneys, Jane and Martin Raskin, had worked as Justice Department prosecutors before subsequently specializing in good-quality defense work in Florida where they, like Stone, had supported Bush's opposition to the 2000 election recount demands. They also knew Bob Mueller from their time together prosecuting organized crime in Boston. On 24 April when the two sides met, Mueller greeted the Raskins warmly. Personal feelings, however, could not mask the tension that quickly emerged when Mueller explained that in order to assess the significance of certain actions taken by Trump, it would be necessary to consider the President's intent and that this could only be done by asking him in person via a deposition. When Mueller initially resisted their offer of Trump's responding to written questions via counsel, the lawyers countered by asking whether Mueller had adequately considered existing Department of Justice guidance on the constitutionality of prosecuting a sitting president.

This had always been a trump card, so to speak. The Justice Department's Office of Legal Counsel (OLC) had twice offered its written opinion on this question: once in 1973 during Watergate and again in 2000 in the wake of President Clinton's impeachment. On each occasion, it had concluded that a sitting president could not be prosecuted since the remedy provided in the Constitution was impeachment via Congress. Where the president was found to have committed crimes, any prosecution would have to await his removal from office. However, this deferment clearly did not prevent the investigation of those crimes in order to support the rule of law. The mid-term elections of 2018 thus took on an added significance. Currently, Republicans retained control of both houses, thanks partly to the strategic re-districting that had occurred after the 2010 census. However, it was normal for the ruling party to lose some seats in the mid-terms, and current polling numbers were predicting that the Democrats would regain control of the House of Representatives; significantly, that body is entrusted with the task of drafting articles of impeachment. The safety backstop for Trump remained the likely Republican majority in the Senate, which would hear any impeachment trial since there was little prospect of anti-Trump forces marshalling the required two-thirds majority to remove him from office. Learning perhaps from James Comey's misguided actions in the run-up to the 2016 elections, Mueller was more than ready to delay his report beyond November's election day.

As 2019 began, therefore, the Mueller investigation had essentially ended, but presenting its findings in relation to Trump's conduct was far from simple. In terms of the activities of Russian agents, Mueller largely agreed with Trump's counsel that there was not enough evidence to support the charge that his campaign team actively conspired with the Russians to secure their election victory. Conspiracy was the legal term, and it was more precise than collusion. It required evidence of active cooperation. The Russians certainly interfered and in a way that was hostile to Clinton, but that was not the same as showing that they operated at the behest of the Trump campaign or with their active participation. Inside the Mueller investigation there was genuine disagreement about the significance of other instances where Trump as president could be said to have obstructed justice. The team accepted that the OLC opinion meant they could not charge the President, but they were divided over whether they should include recommendations regarding impeachment. There was even disagreement among Trump's Democratic opponents. In January, Nancy Pelosi became Speaker after Democratic gains in the House. Her initial strategy seemed to be to give Trump enough rope to hang himself. She was pushing back against party militants who wanted impeachment immediately because she knew the votes were not there in the Senate; she even doubted whether the will was there in the country, although the federal shutdown that Trump had instigated when Congress failed to approve funding for his border wall with Mexico was pushing the president's already poor approval rating downward.

Equally important for Trump's future proved the changes at the Justice Department. Once William Barr had replaced Jeff Sessions as Attorney-General, Trump seemed to find the "team player" on whose loyalty he could count. Barr had signalled his credentials with an unsolicited memo on 8 June 2018, addressed to Sessions' Deputy, Rod Rosenstein, who oversaw the Russia probe, and Steven Engel who ran the Office of Legal Counsel, a job Barr had once held himself. The memo denounced the Mueller inquiry as "grossly irresponsible." He warned that by indulging what he called "the fancies of overly-zealous prosecutors," Mueller was threatening the nation's health and cohesiveness because "any claim of wrongdoing" by a democratically elected president had to be "based on evidence of a *real* crime – not a debatable one."

On 7 December 2018 Trump announced that he was nominating Barr for the Attorney-General post which, since Sessions' departure a month earlier, had been provisionally and unimpressively occupied by Trump loyalist Matthew Whittaker. In confirmation hearings on 15 January 2019, Barr promised openness. In the interest of transparency, he would ensure that the public and Congress were informed of Mueller's findings as fully as the law would allow. On 14 February, Barr was confirmed and by late February he learned that the Mueller report was imminent, but there were some loose ends arising from the 25 January FBI raid on Roger Stone's Florida home.

In the meantime, the unending media fascination with the probe was renewed via Michael Cohen's dramatic testimony before Congress in February. In a bid to limit his own prison time, Cohen was forthright in his condemnation of the President as a racist, a conman, and a cheat. Cohen had been very much involved in containing the Stormy Daniels' sex scandal, but his own misdeeds were predictably used by Republicans on the House Oversight Committee to attack his credibility as a witness. Of immediate relevance to Mueller, Cohen reported that Roger Stone had made Trump aware that he had spoken to Julian Assange ahead of the Wikileaks' release of the hacked DNC emails. The substance of Cohen's testimony went largely unchallenged by Trump's allies on the committee and while the media dwelt on the "mobster" style of language used by Cohen to describe Trump's mode of operation, the wider public remained firmly split into their separate worlds of Trump supporters and haters.

Barr's promise during his confirmation hearing that the Mueller report would not remain a confidential Justice Department document had sharpened disagreements within the Mueller team about how to summarize what the investigation had discovered about Trump. The OLC opinion prohibiting the prosecution of a sitting president was accepted by Mueller and his lifelong commitment to the political impartiality of the FBI inclined him to avoid any strong condemnation of the president. Eventually, this produced the blandest of observations: "If we had confidence after a thorough investigation of the facts that the President clearly did not commit obstruction of justice, we would so state." Thus, the accusations against Trump were rendered implicit. The report did not declare that he did not commit obstruction, rather it implied that he did but left it to others to judge the gravity of the offence. Barr learned that this was going to be the key finding when he met with the Mueller team on 5 March. During that meeting he asked specifically if the Mueller report's presentation of evidence but refusal to recommend prosecution, would allow the Attorney-General to make an independent decision based on the evidence, and he was told that it did. The independent report could ultimately give rise to a judgement by Barr and given Trump's enduring anger at Barr's predecessor Jeff Sessions for his failure to use his position to protect the President, Barr can have had little doubt what was expected.

Mueller also explained that his report would contain "6(e)" material; in other words, evidence and testimony gathered for the grand jury under subpoenas that stipulated that it must remain confidential. Consequently, sections of any published report would have to be redacted, and Barr asked for the Mueller team's assistance in identifying such material so that he could publish a report that complied with the rules but was still legible and issued promptly. On the afternoon of Friday, 22 March, the 448-page report arrived at the Justice Department. To the consternation of Barr and his associates, the Mueller team's help with identifying the "6(e)" material was via the footnotes. It had left the laborious task of redacting such evidence while maintaining legibility and comprehensibility to others. Preparing the text for publication would take time. Barr also knew that news of the report's delivery would leak and so it was imperative that his department publicly acknowledge its submission. There would be a scandal if this was not done, but there would also be a scandal if the contents of the report were not made known soon thereafter. He drafted a letter to Congress indicating that he was reviewing the submitted report and hoped to be able to disclose the principal conclusions "as soon as this weekend." He also reiterated his commitment to transparency. By early evening, the news media had their story and the clock had started loudly ticking.

Barr had also notified the White House, of course, but did not disclose the report's conclusions beyond confirming that no further indictments were being sought. This might just signal the Mueller team's acceptance of the OLC opinion barring prosecution of a sitting president; it left impeachment a possibility. Trump's personal lawyers scrambled back to Washington to prepare for any outcome since they had not been involved in the meeting at which Mueller had summarized his thinking for Barr and his Justice Department colleagues. Meanwhile Barr, Rosenstein and his acting deputy Ed O'Callaghan were reviewing the report to see if they felt that any of the ten documented episodes of potential obstruction were sufficiently proven to secure a conviction and survive an appeal. They each shook their heads. Disturbing though the behaviour was, in their view, it did not reach a level where they would recommend prosecution. But how could they communicate this to the public?

Barr decided to write a second letter to Congress detailing the special counsel's principal conclusions. The four-page letter of 24 March was inevitably selective. Acknowledging the extensive evidence of Russian interference, it quoted the last part of a sentence from the report to the effect that Mueller's "investigation did not establish that members of the Trump campaign conspired or coordinated with the Russian government in its election interference activities." The letter recorded that the special counsel had "ultimately determined not to make a traditional prosecutorial judgment" on the difficult legal issues surrounding the question of obstruction and ended this paragraph of the letter with a further quotation illustrating Mueller's determination to be a-political through equivocation:

"while this report does not conclude the President committed a crime, it also does not exonerate him."

However, Barr then went on to declare that the special counsel had effectively ceded the final judgment call to the Attorney General and that he and Rosenstein agreed that the evidence was insufficient to prosecute. He added that this conclusion was made independent of any consideration of the OLC opinion that a sitting president cannot be prosecuted, and he then further exonerated the President by saying that since the report was clear that it could find no evidence of the Trump campaign's active cooperation in Russian electoral interference efforts, the assumption of deliberate intent inherent in any obstruction of justice charge was hard to sustain. In short, if Trump had not been working with the Russians, why would he bother to block an investigation that was likely to prove that non-involvement? Barr ended his letter by promising to release as much of the report as possible, while protecting ongoing prosecutions and abiding by grand jury confidentiality rules.

Barr's letter was received with delight by the President at Mar-a-Lago and jubilantly by Trump's legal team in Washington. In one of his characteristic shouting conferences with reporters as he prepared to board Air Force One to fly back to Washington, Trump described it as "a complete and total exoneration." The Mueller team was far less happy. On 27 March Mueller wrote to complain that Barr's summary letter "did not fully capture the context, nature and substance of this Office's work and its conclusions." This was creating public confusion and risked diminishing public confidence in the outcome of his investigation. The next day, Mueller and Barr talked things through over the phone and Mueller seemed somewhat appeased by Barr's eagerness to get the full report out as soon as was feasible, which was likely to be mid-April. On 29 March, Barr tried to mend fences further by writing a third letter to Congressional leaders clarifying that his previous letter was never intended to be a substitute for the Mueller Report and that he was working to release the full report as soon as possible.

When the full report became available to them, the Trump legal team's euphoria soured. In their view, it must have been obvious to Mueller much earlier that there was no compelling evidence of a crime; certainly, nothing proving a conspiracy with the Russians to steal the election. Once that was clear, Trump's lawyers believed the obstruction issue became redundant; Trump was innocent. His only crime was that he had become a politician who could be slandered and placed under investigation for two years. That was a scandal. As Jane Raskin recalled saying to herself: "This should never happen again." At a press conference ahead of the report's release on 18 April, William Barr fulfilled Donald Trump's hope that his Attorney-General should sound like his personal lawyer, a loyal advocate and protector. The Mueller Report had stated that "collusion" was not a term used to describe actions under federal criminal law, but Barr now used the term that Trump regularly used to declare that the report had found "no collusion." He described the difficult situation the new President had faced in 2017 when confronted by relentless media speculation, illegal leaks, and a political opposition eager to use legal investigations as weapons to hamper his government. Mueller was far less outspoken in his defense, simply advising reporters to read his report. The scandal lost what little momentum it still had.

At his mass rallies in the summer of 2019, which continued to draw the faithful like televangelist services, Trump would elicit cheers as he made mocking references to the "Russian hoax." He would describe the special counsel's team as "18 very angry Democrats," ignoring the fact that Mueller himself was widely known to be an old-school Republican. He began to frame his re-election as a referendum on what he defined as a monstrous attempt by the electoral losers to overturn the choice of the people by refusing genuinely to concede, and instead ripping the country apart for two whole years with a phony investigation. This was the real scandal, he alleged, and his loyal followers roared approval. The fact that Mueller had documented the success of a Russian campaign to foment division in the country and determine the outcome of the presidential election was apparently of less importance. As we shall see, in 2020 when the election was called in Joe Biden's favour, he would insist that the people's choice was being denied even more brazenly and call upon his followers to "stop the steal."

We have looked at electoral scandals with very different outcomes. In 2000, the real election scandal was not whether Bush's brother Jeb stole the contest in Florida but about the systemic failure of the basic mechanics of electioneering. Too many votes went astray, and the scary thing was that this had been happening for years. The 2016 scandals suggest that the

Watergate model is misleading. By the summer of 1974 Richard Nixon felt compelled to resign since the likelihood of a successful impeachment for crimes related to Watergate had become tangible. In contrast, by the time the Mueller Report was complete, the prospect of a successful impeachment of Donald Trump over "Russia-gate" was fading rather than getting stronger. Why did the two scandals end so differently? Trump, like Nixon, faced considerable hostile media scrutiny and took office at a time when the nation was sharply divided over many issues. The mistrust of politicians, referred to in the 1960s as the credibility gap, was still there, but in a key sense it had mutated into something bigger and more dangerous to democracy: the development of what some have termed "cultural silos" or self-sustaining bubbles within which people only paid attention to the news that confirmed their opinions. Facts were forever disputed. As Rudy Giuliani insisted to a reporter in 2018: "Truth isn't truth."

Both Trump and Nixon had strongly established public personae before they entered the White House. Nixon had acquired the nickname "Tricky Dicky" and was both despised by progressives for his use of red-smear tactics and by some hard-line conservatives as too ready to shift his position whenever it was politically advantageous. When it came time to assess their own loyalties in 1974, Republicans could be said to have treated Nixon very much as he would have treated them: they ditched him. Trump, on the other hand, had emerged as a tabloid celebrity outside of electoral politics, reflecting public fascination with the "lives of the rich and famous." He cultivated his status as a billionaire businessman and established his media brand through his role as the Boss who hired and fired on the program *The Apprentice*. He also appeared increasingly on right-wing talk radio and on *Fox News*, breaching political correctness, engaging in what he would later dismiss as locker-room banter about sexual matters, and outlining stark positions on immigration and trade that appealed to the nostalgic politics of the Tea Party. By the time he declared his candidacy, he was seen as one of several uncompromising voices challenging the Republican Party establishment, which had been weakened by the unpopular legacy of the Bush years. In key states, there was a bloc of older white voters who liked Trump because he was not an egghead, because he was not a conventional politician, because he felt about immigrants the way they did, and because he offered simple solutions that they could understand. The last were epitomized in catchy slogans: Build the Wall, Drain the Swamp, and Make America Great Again. When Republican politicians had to choose whether to back Trump, all of them faced the stark fact that they could be punished in the next primary contests by these hard-line voters if they did not line up with the President. Hence, the GOP rallied around Trump as the scandal unfolded in a way that contrasted with what happened to Nixon.

In 2016, when Trump publicly appealed to Russian hackers to find Clinton's missing emails if they could, he might be seen as pursuing opposition research in the same way that Nixon had hoped that his break-in team at the Watergate might find materials that would help his re-election. Once the burglars were arrested, however, Nixon's associates became implicated in a cover-up that ultimately amounted to a blatant obstruction of justice as they paid defendants to ensure their silence. Investigators also found many more misdeeds that amounted to a pattern of illegal governance. Even though the Mueller team discovered that Russian state operatives were active in their efforts to hack into Democratic Party computers on the same night that Trump made his public appeal, it never found any trail of payments or instructions that would have shown Trump to be a co-conspirator. Some in Trump's circle, like Michael Flynn or Roger Stone had ill-advised contacts, but the meeting with Russian figures that Don, Jr., Paul Manafort, and Jared Kushner had at Trump Tower was not the "smoking gun" evidence that the Nixon tapes provided through their record of Nixon and Haldeman deliberations about involving the CIA to block investigators.

As an election scandal, 2016 saw the attention of the American public pulled away from the main story. The Mueller investigation had built on the intelligence agencies' earlier findings of Russian interference, but the media story was always Trump and collusion and then obstruction. In this sense, the Watergate model had misled. The big story was never "what did the President know and when did he know it?" If Trump had not colluded, the obstruction issue was indeed secondary to what should have been seen as the real threat. That threat was Russia's cyberwarfare, which had effectively targeted the weak spots in America's democracy. The Russian state had tried to deepen divisions inside the US by feeding stories to targeted groups and it had worked. It had tried to stop Clinton, a candidate Russia perceived as hostile to its interests. It had used cyberwarfare to expose weaknesses in her campaign and to the surprise of many, she lost. Trump's firing of James Comey, his anger at Attorney-General Sessions, and his railing against the witch-hunt may have appeared Nixon/Watergate-like but they were simply reflections of Trump's narcissism. He is rarely satisfied unless he is the centre of attention and is unable to accept criticism. When the Nixon tapes revealed the President's private conversation, there were Americans who were genuinely shocked, but the endless dissection of tweets and tantrums reported from the Trump White House surprised hardly anybody. He became the liberal media's pet troll.

If anyone questioned Trump's character, he tended to imply that the people knew who he was when they voted for him. But the closing phase of the Trump presidency drove home the multiple dangers of having a president like Trump. He could damage US foreign policy by suborning it to his own narrow self-interest. He could fail to protect his fellow Americans at home during a global pandemic, especially if health restrictions inhibited economic activities and thereby undermined his re-election. Finally, he could spread the big lie of the "stolen election" and maintain it in the face of mounting evidence and failed legal challenges until finally all that was left was disrupting the peaceful transfer of power. To these scandals we now turn.

Chapter 5

Making Scandal Great Again: The Trump Impeachments

For at least the first two years of his presidency, Donald Trump was watched by some in the media to see if he would become "presidential." One part of that process was implicitly acquiring a habit that might make him act or speak with greater caution. But once the Mueller Report failed to deliver grounds for impeachment, it became clear that the threat of scandal was no deterrent to Trump. No sooner was the Report delivered than Trump began pursuing a fresh plan to secure foreign efforts to boost his re-election chances. If the Democrats could have a witch-hunt over his campaign interactions with Russia, then it was only fair that an equally broad investigation should probe the dubious activities of Democrats in relation to Ukraine. In practice, this meant not only Vice-President Joe Biden's actions in the region, but those of his son, Hunter, who had been well paid for consultancy work with a Ukrainian energy company, Burisma. However, Trump's efforts to spark such an investigation prompted fresh controversy. In the words of the Democrat-led, House Intelligence Committee Report, Trump "subverted US foreign policy toward Ukraine and undermined our national security in favour of two politically motivated investigations that would help his presidential re-election campaign." During a 25 July 2019 phone call to the Ukrainian President Vladimir Zelensky, Trump clearly suggested that US aid, vital to Ukraine's efforts to resist Russian aggression, was dependent on "a favour;" namely, the announcement that Ukraine was investigating both a discredited theory that Ukrainian hackers interfered in the 2016 election and rumours that Hunter Biden, the son of eventual nominee Joe Biden, had engaged in corrupt activities while working for Burisma.

Zelensky had won a landslide victory three months earlier partly because he promised to root out corruption, which had been endemic under his predecessor, Petro Poroshenko. Trump's former campaign manager Paul Manafort had secured lucrative political consultancies in Ukraine during that earlier time, so Trump knew that dubious practices were widespread. The State Department had drafted talking points for the call that included encouraging Zelensky to press ahead with his anti-corruption drive. To increase his own leverage over Zelensky however, Trump had put a halt on the flow of aid and was still to confirm a promised in-person meeting with Zelensky that would signal US support internationally. Via the US Ambassador to the EU, Gordon Sondland, Zelensky already knew that well-publicized efforts to investigate the supposed scandals was what Trump wanted. These were not the priorities recommended by either the State Department or National Security Council; both had been shocked by Trump's decision to freeze aid at a time when official US policy was steadfast support for Ukraine in the wake of Russia's seizure of Crimea. Tensions between the White House and the foreign policy establishment resulted in the firing of the US ambassador to Ukraine, Marie Yovanovich, because she refused to collaborate with Trump adviser Rudy Giuliani who was leading efforts to uncover any scandal that could be damaging to Joe Biden.

As usual, the President's phone-call to Zelensky was monitored by several NSC and State Department officials. During the roughly thirty minutes of conversation, these listeners became increasingly alarmed. NSC staffer and army Lieutenant-Colonel Alexander Vindman immediately reported his concerns to his boss, Timothy Morrison, who passed the issue to the NSC's lawyers. Vindman, a decorated military veteran, had helped to prepare the President's talking points and he mistakenly believed that everyone else would share his sense of scandal at Trump's efforts to extract personal political advantage from national diplomacy. Vindman's twin brother, Eugene, was also attached to the NSC as an ethics officer, a role created in the wake of the Iran-Contra scandal. Alexander told his brother: "If what I just heard becomes public, the President will be impeached." Ultimately, what Sondland, Yovanovich, and the Vindman brothers would have in common was that their testimony about Trump's approach to Ukraine (delivered to Congress in the public interest) was rewarded by their removal from government service, once the impeachment failed.

Sondland and the Vindman brothers were fired and the already recalled Yovanovich was pushed out of the diplomatic service.

When Joe Biden formally entered the race for the 2020 Democratic nomination in April 2019, Trump's personal attorney Rudy Giuliani stepped up efforts to get a Ukrainian investigation of both the bogus claims about Ukrainian interference in 2016 and Hunter Biden's Burisma activities. With little to show, Giuliani's efforts drew some negative media attention, and in a pique, Trump downgraded the US delegation to Zelensky's inauguration. When it still returned with a positive impression of the new government's commitment to tackling corruption, Trump was disappointed. Everyone, he insisted, had to back Giuliani's efforts. Experienced diplomat Bill Taylor was so unhappy with this that he only agreed to return to his previous ambassadorial posting in Kiev as Yovanovich's successor after receiving assurances from Secretary of State Mike Pompeo that he would report to him rather than to Giuliani. On 28 June, the Department of Defense announced that in accordance with the Congressional appropriation, it was preparing to release $250 million in military aid to Ukraine. But days later in July, the Trump White House put a freeze on all funds to Ukraine, including an additional $141 million from the State Department.

By the time of Trump's 25 July call to Zelensky, both US and Ukrainian officials had expressed concern about the delay. Legal counsel at the Office of Management and Budget even queried the legality of withholding funds so clearly allocated by Congress. For his part, Ambassador Sondland reiterated to his Ukrainian contacts that for Trump the aid was part of a transaction – a *quid pro quo* in short; once Zelensky publicly announced investigations of Ukrainian interference in 2016 and of Hunter Biden's work at Burisma, the aid would arrive, and the White House meeting would happen. As subsequent events underlined, bolstering Ukraine against Russian aggression was clearly an agreed goal of US foreign policy with grave global implications; at least among the experts who knew the region and perceived Putin's Russia as an escalating threat. Trump's own attitude was far less clear cut. He had spoken positively about the Russian leader and at times seemed to envy his authoritarian governmental style. During meetings between US and Ukrainian officials earlier in July, divisions inside the administration were manifest. Sondland and Trump's Acting Chief of Staff, Mick Mulvaney, repeated that Trump would only agree a meeting after the desired investigations were publicly announced. This prompted Ambassador Taylor to leave the meeting in protest.

National Security Advisor John Bolton subsequently learned that the meeting had continued without Taylor. NSC Senior Director for Russia and Europe, Fiona Hill, reported that she and Alexander Vindman had insisted that any Trump-Zelensky meeting should be arranged through the normal State Department channels rather than via Rudy Giuliani. In her later testimony to Congress, Hill said that Bolton had responded that she should let the NSC's legal advisor know that Bolton had wanted no "part of whatever drug deal Sondland and Mulvaney are cooking up on this." The House Intelligence Committee seized upon this lurid phrase in its report, and it certainly signalled Bolton's sense of its illegality. The Committee also learned that in phone conversations after 25 July, Trump was only interested in when Zelensky was going to announce the investigations and never raised other important matters such as the continuing war between Ukraine and pro-Russian forces in the east of the country. The White House freeze on aid continued through August and Ukrainian officials fretted that this was starting to impact on their military operations. Ambassador Taylor also wrote to Secretary of State Pompeo expressing concern. He could not and would not defend a policy that effectively rolled back US commitments to Ukraine. He was equally emphatic to Sondland, saying: "it's crazy to withhold security assistance for help with a political campaign."

Just as President Zelensky was preparing to announce the investigations that Trump wanted in early September, news broke of the House Intelligence Committee's investigation into the 25 July phone call. Almost immediately, the Committee learned that in an unprecedented move, the Acting Director of National Intelligence had withheld notification of Alexander Vindman's whistle-blower complaint from the relevant Congressional committees. Scrambling to defend its actions in the face of the growing public and Congressional scrutiny, on 11 September, Trump lifted the hold on aid to Ukraine. But by that time, the Defense Department was unable to spend approximately 14 percent of the funds appropriated before the tax year ended. Congress had to pass a new law to extend the funding in order to ensure the full amount could be used by Ukraine to defend itself. The delay necessarily reduced the stockpile of US supplied war materiel that Ukraine had at the time of the Russian invasion in February 2022.

On 17 October at a press briefing, Acting Chief of Staff Mulvaney confirmed that the aid had been withheld to expedite investigation of both the spurious claim that Ukraine interfered in the 2016 election (a claim also used by Putin to deflect attention from Russia's actual interference) and the allegations about Hunter Biden. Mulvaney was unapologetic. "We do that all the time with foreign policy," he declared, adding: "I have news for everybody: get over it. There is going to be political influence in foreign policy." Ambassador Taylor, drawing on his decades in the diplomatic service, contradicted this, testifying that he had never previously encountered such a blatant subordination of the national interest to personal advantage. He explained in his testimony: "we condition assistance on issues that will improve our foreign policy, serve our foreign policy, ensure that taxpayers' money is well-spent," and not on specific investigations designed to benefit the political interests of the current President. In this context, Trump's behaviour was scandalous, but as the impeachment verdict showed, not scandalous enough.

Trump's reflex reaction to any challenge or criticism was to counterattack verbally and stall procedurally. He had little knowledge or understanding of the US governmental system and its separation of powers. For Trump, as for those involved in Iran-Contra under Reagan, nothing that Congress requested that was contrary to his own preferences was in his view legitimate. This was revealed conspicuously in his response to both the Ukraine investigation and his subsequent impeachment. As the House Committee made clear: he "ordered federal agencies and officials to disregard all voluntary requests for documents and defy all duly authorized subpoenas for records. He also directed all federal officials in the Executive Branch not to testify-even when compelled." The Committee explicitly likened Trump to Nixon who had refused to hand over incriminating evidence during Watergate, but it added that Trump had gone further by denying the fundamental authority of Congress to pursue an impeachment inquiry, a position contrary to the Constitution. This line of defence, used by Trump, was later amplified by the decision of the Republican-controlled House in 2023 to censor the previous chair of the House Intelligence Committee, Representative Adam Schiff, who led the first impeachment efforts against Trump.

The crucial context enabling Trump to act in this way was the partisan polarization of America. As House Speaker in 2019, Democrat Nancy Pelosi recognized that the decision to impeach Trump over his Ukraine actions was complicated tactically. She, like many Democrats, had hoped that the Mueller investigation would provide a strong basis for impeachment, and when it did not, she was faced with pressure from within her own party to hold the president accountable. At the same time, she knew that given the Republican majority in the Senate, there was little prospect of a successful impeachment, and that an unsuccessful attempt would in key respects entrench Trump's hold on the GOP by mobilizing his supporters in a way that would then impact on the Republican primaries (where moderate Republicans faced Trump challengers) and might enhance the President's already considerable fund-raising operations. It could make a bad situation worse. However, Trump's attempt to use foreign policy in a volatile area of the world to secure a purely domestic electoral advantage was so egregious that she felt she had to proceed or risk alienating those Democratic voters who were still seething from Hillary Clinton's 2016 defeat.

Aware that Trump had characterized their efforts as a witch-hunt, the Intelligence Committee's final report stressed that its right to investigate and secure documents and testimony was firmly established. It also reminded people that presidents previously impeached – Andrew Johnson in 1868 and Bill Clinton in 1998 (a third, Richard Nixon, was threatened with impeachment, but resigned) had complied with requests from Congress based on this legal authority. Nixon's initial refusal to hand over the tape-recordings of his deliberations to Congressional investigators had ultimately formed part of the draft articles of impeachment against him. Trump's obstruction was far more extensive. Confirming his suspect understanding of the Constitution, Trump had declared: "We're fighting all the subpoenas," and "I have an Article II, where I have the right to do whatever I want as president."

Article II of the US Constitution which deals with the presidency can in no way be summarized as giving the president the power to do whatever he wants. It featured recurringly in Trump's scandalous term in office, largely because he failed to read or understand it. It includes rules for the Electoral College and the counting of its votes, for instance, and a clause prohibiting the president from receiving benefits (so-called emoluments) from others beyond his salary while in office. The first would feature in Trump's attempts to block the count after his 2020 defeat and the second was an ongoing issue due to his blatant use of the presidency to benefit his company, not least by encouraging foreign governments and others to patronize the Trump hotel in Washington. It was later revealed that Secret Service personnel and others were charged exorbitant rates for room and board when they travelled with the president to his various properties.

Despite the argument that Trump was acting unconstitutionally when he refused to cooperate with Congress during the Ukraine investigation, most administration officials obeyed Trump's order and did not comply with subpoenas for their testimony. John Bolton, National Security Advisor, refused the House Intelligence Committee's request for voluntary testimony, and threatened a countersuit if he was subpoenaed. Dreading a lengthy court battle, Democrats backed down. Subsequently, Bolton himself indicated that if the Republican-controlled Senate required him to testify at the impeachment, he would, but Senate Majority leader, Mitch McConnell, judged that the trial would be less damaging if it proceeded without witnesses. Already out of the administration since September 2019 and like so many others, eager to demonstrate that he had not been a Trump yes-man, Bolton said that he might have testified if pressed by the Democrats, although he still maintained that the Ukraine episode was driven by the Democrats' hyper-partisanship.

During the Watergate scandal, what finally eroded Republican loyalty and popular support for Nixon was the accumulation of evidence of the concerted cover-up rather than the break-in itself, plus the cumulative disclosure of a culture of lawlessness at the heart of government. Seeking to develop the same momentum, the Intelligence Committee detailed not just Trump's unprecedented refusal to supply documents or permit officials to testify but his systematic efforts to intimidate anyone who did speak out or comply. This included warning of dire consequences prior to their appearance and followed by invective and mockery towards them once they gave evidence. Trump's use of social media, notably Twitter, meant that his animosity towards these individuals was transmitted to literally millions in a way that reasonably raised concern for their personal safety. When he railed against the anonymous whistle-blower who first raised a complaint about Trump's conduct formally, he acted directly contrary to federal law which explicitly guaranteed protection and anonymity in order to encourage public officials to file their concerns.

Nevertheless, by the time the House voted articles of impeachment in December 2019, it was clear that the Senate Republicans were overwhelmingly determined to acquit. Since impeachment requires a two-thirds majority, this meant that the trial would end in acquittal. The Senate trial did not begin until 16 January 2020, and procedural decisions indicated that the Republican majority was determined to limit proceedings and swiftly exonerate their President. Every attempt by the Democratic minority leader, Chuck Schumer, to secure authority to subpoena testimony from cabinet officials, State Department and White House documents, and communications generally regarding Ukraine was blocked by the Republicans (53-47). Party loyalty was undiminished by revelations that Trump had been cultivating Ukrainian sympathizers via various dubious intermediaries such as businessman Lev Parnas, who had worked with Giuliani. Since the trial occurred during the primary season when the two parties selected their candidates for the fall elections, backing Trump publicly was the safest move a Republican politician could make.

The timing of the trial also meant that Trump, like Bill Clinton in 1999, delivered his State of the Union address on 4 February, while facing impeachment, although by that stage, he was already confident that Mitch McConnell had GOP senators marshalled to acquit. The wider public was of course, divided, but even some Republicans felt that Trump's conduct warranted censure, and many were puzzled by the refusal to allow witnesses or secure documents that might provide a basis for assessing the President's guilt. The trial concluded on 5 February. Senators voted 52 to 48 to find Trump not guilty on the charge of abuse of power; (all 45 Democrats, Independent senators Bernie Sanders and Angus King, and Republican senator Mitt Romney voted guilty). Romney's vote marked the first time in American history a senator voted to convict a president of his own party. On the second charge, the Senate voted 53 to 47, in a party-line vote, to find Trump not guilty on the charge of obstruction of Congress.

The party-line vote was unexceptional in the sense that all three impeachments in US history have seen the same tendency. Romney's vote reflected the changing nature of the GOP. The Republican nominee in 2012 was one of many who had expressed misgivings about Trump in 2016.

He lamented then to *CNN*'s Wolf Blitzer that a Trump presidency could "change the character of the generations of Americans that are following" and might result in "trickle-down racism," "trickle-down misogyny," and "trickle-down bigotry." The 2008 nominee had been John McCain, who was equally scornful of Trump; a stance that Trump fully reciprocated. Trump's absence and the presence of all other living presidents at McCain's funeral in September 2018 reflected the intensity of that feud. Senate Majority leader Mitch McConnell, according to Romney, was equally unequivocal about Trump's inadequacies as a president but only in private. Like most long-serving senators, McConnell felt that Trump's idiosyncrasies would be funny, if he were not president. "Everyone gets the joke," was the way Romney summed up the situation.

But Trump was president and the Mueller probe and then the Ukraine impeachment trial had made him even more convinced that he was unfairly victimized, and he wanted a chance to be avenged. Trump's own rancour was mirrored by the animosity of his opponents. His 2016 victory had dismayed many. After all, numerically, a majority voted for Hillary. More concentrated in the major cities and often better educated, such voters continued to see his election as scandalous, and the almost daily headlines across liberal media deploring Trump's words or actions reflected and reinforced the fact that large sections of the country were unreconciled to his presidency. Conversely, in the eyes of his devoted followers – those who flocked to his rallies – such people could be dismissed as "Never Trumpers." This was the real scandal, they insisted: this "Deep State" conspiracy that refused to accept "crooked" Hillary's defeat and who worked actively to prevent Trump's doing all that he promised, like building the Wall. Impeachment, in their eyes, was just the latest episode in this scandal. Even after Trump left the White House, they read every attempt to hold him accountable through the same lens: he was being persecuted.

To the few who tried to be objective, Trump was sometimes unwittingly scandalous because he just seemed unable to conduct himself with the decorum expected of an American president; unable to be sophisticated, or tactful on the public stage, and apt to tweet or say something that deepened divisions. His inaugural address illustrated this trait. Typically, a new president accepts that elections are divisive and uses his speech to urge his fellow countrymen to reunite and offers to work cooperatively. Trump, on the other hand, dwelt on what his supporters saw as the evils that had grown larger during the previous eight years. With his predecessor Barack Obama seated close by, Trump described his election as a restoration of power to the people after a period of rule by an uncaring establishment that had protected itself while allowing ordinary working people to suffer in what he termed an "American carnage." Seated with other former Presidents, George W. Bush was heard to murmur that this was "some weird shit."

On top of the Mueller investigation and Trump's daily tactlessness, and even before the first impeachment, the Trump administration had gained an unenviable reputation for instability evident in the rapid turnover of personnel. Officials who are generally seen as the President's key advisors, such as his Chief of Staff, National Security Advisor, or Communications Director are sometimes referred to as his "A Team." Trump's A Team had a 92 percent turnover in a single term compared to Obama's 71 percent across two terms. Having temporary appointees who had not been confirmed in their positions became normal for Trump. Forty percent of the top positions in the Defense Department that require Senate confirmation were without a confirmed appointee at the time of his 2020 election defeat. In other departments, Trump's own policies exacerbated the vacancy rate. He came to office strongly committed to cutting federal jobs. A businessman, he had little sympathy for the work done by the Department of Labor which had sued his company in the past; it experienced a nearly 12 percent cut in its workforce. The Ukraine scandal that triggered Trump's first impeachment deepened his strained relations with career diplomats and foreign policy analysts in the State Department and it witnessed the same job loss rate as Labor.

The same pattern was evident in agencies that employed highly trained scientists. Both the Environmental Protection Agency (EPA) and the federal Center for Disease Control (CDC) struggled to recruit. Trump's Executive Order 13771 required that for any new federal regulation introduced, two should be rescinded. This was felt particularly in the EPA since many of its controls had never been enshrined in law. Addressing the climate crisis, the Obama administration had launched a Clean Energy Plan (CEP) in 2015 to reduce CO2 emissions. Trump has never accepted the scientific consensus on global warming and in October 2017 suspended the CEP. Eventually the Affordable Clean Energy (ACE) program was offered as its replacement, but the EPA's own impact analysis reported that ACE would increase CO_2 emissions by sixty million tons by 2030 and in alarm twenty-two states sued to force a reversal. For ecologists, the damage done by Trump deregulation may yet prove the greatest scandal of all. Coupled with other steps to reduce the EPA's regulatory role and enable businesses to pollute, these policies made it hard for conscientious scientists to work for his administration. They were simply too scandalized.

With ominous significance for the future, the *Washington Post* reported in May 2017 that there were nearly 700 vacancies at the CDC due to an ongoing hiring freeze, many for senior positions in the Office of Public Health Preparedness and Response; in other words, positions pivotal in overseeing federal support during a public health crisis. At the time, the agency was also without a permanent director after Tom Frieden (an Obama appointee) stepped down following Trump's inauguration. The departing Frieden, who had managed the response to the Ebola virus outbreak in Africa as well as two coronavirus-type incidents in Asia, told reporters that his biggest fear was a flu-style pandemic. A strong advocate of the annual flu vaccination program, he stressed that the CDC would need to have systems in place that could be rapidly scaled up in response to disease outbreaks and should not rely on having the ability to organize afresh. His words were to prove prophetic when the COVID-19 pandemic emerged.

One of the most sobering aspects of the 2020 election is the fact that, were it not for the pandemic, Trump would probably have secured re-election. Given his questionable, and sometimes incompetent actions during the pandemic, it is arguably the only scandal for which he has been punished. Each of the previous scandals in this book had an element of incompetence. If Richard Nixon had been able to manage the hidden taping system competently, it would not have been there to prove his guilt over Watergate. If the Reagan administration had conducted foreign policy with greater attention to the State Department experts who warned of the dangers of clandestine deals to trade arms for hostages, the Iran-Contra deal would not have been able to proceed. If the Clintons had not got themselves involved in financial wheeler-dealings with Arkansas associates of limited business competence, the Special Prosecutor would not have been pursuing them in the manner that exposed Bill's lies on oath about his relationship with Monica Lewinsky. If the US election machinery was not so riddled with flaws, the narrow Bush victory in 2000 would not have occurred – at least not in a way that generated so much mistrust in the election process. In this way, the 2020 lie of a stolen election had its roots in the broken election system of 2000.

Even in Trump's case, the fact that his 2016 team saw nothing wrong or risky in seeking dirt on Hillary from Russian sources raises questions about their competence as political operatives. The pattern continued even in victory when Michael Flynn was unable to recognize that his phone conversations with the Russian ambassador during the transition needed to be limited and conducted with some sense of the risks he ran if they were exposed. Even more glaring, Trump himself barely paused to re-group from the Mueller investigation before attempting to use US aid as a bargaining chip to compel Ukraine to investigate Hunter Biden's commercial activities. The impeachment of Trump may have failed, but it still deepened the impression that he, like Nixon, would do anything to win. Consequently, as the COVID-19 pandemic began to erode the economy that was central to his re-election hopes, he sought to wish it away to the neglect of his leadership responsibilities and with a callous disregard for the cost in American lives. In contrast to Joe Biden's overt compliance with health guidance, Trump's behaviour seemed scandalous.

But with the pandemic as with so much else, Trump was inconsistent. On 2 February 2020, he imposed a ban on travellers from mainland China that he subsequently cited as the strong action he took to protect Americans. On 20 March, he extended travel restrictions to Europe as the surge in COVID-19 cases became evident there. At the same time, however, Trump spent the early spring reassuring Americans that the new viral strain was no more serious than the usual winter flu and they should continue business as usual. He even suggested that with warmer weather it would simply fade away. He said all this, even though, in private conversations with veteran journalist Bob Woodward (of *All The President's Men* fame), he showed that he knew differently. In a 7 February phone call, he called it "deadly stuff," that it was "more deadly than even your strenuous flu" and admitted that airborne transmission made it hard to contain. When Woodward challenged him about his downplaying of the threat in further taped conversations on 19 March, Trump acknowledged that he had, and said he still liked "playing it down" because he didn't want to create a panic.

His choice of the word *panic* reflected his belief that ordinary people are easily led by their emotions but more especially his concern that the health crisis would hit the economy, which he saw as crucial to his re-election bid.

With the World Health Organization (WHO) officially declaring COVID-19 a pandemic and state governors issuing emergency declarations to try to contain transmission, Trump's conflicted approach (which usually gave priority to economic recovery over safety) drew gasps of horror from healthcare professionals. In other ways, he zigzagged. On the one hand, he signed the CARES Act on 30 March that released $4.5billion in vital federal aid to cities and states as they struggled with the deepening crisis, and on the other, he tried to use the crisis to reward powerful lobby groups and push his more controversial policies. He strongly backed suspension of royalty payments from the oil industry to state and federal authorities as a COVID response, a move that (long before Putin's war on Ukraine filled its coffers) promised to give the industry a windfall worth billions of dollars. At the same time, COVID-19 was used as a rationale for denying admission to migrants seeking entry to the USA and was highly effective in driving down admission numbers. The Wall, promised to Trump's nativistic followers, was eventually built of bureaucratic hurdles rather than metal fencing, and the Biden administration was slow to dismantle it.

Ever since becoming president, Trump had shocked traditional observers by his habit of making rash and ill-informed comments across a range of topics and by taking advice from random pundits or family members rather than trusting the considered judgment of senior officials. The first impeachment can be seen as flowing from Trump's inability to speak the carefully weighed language of diplomacy. When this same fault emerged during the pandemic, it proved even more controversial and damaging to his re-election hopes. On 10 April, despite receiving guidance from the Center for Disease Control (CDC) that face masks slowed transmission, Trump joined other Republican leaders in reassuring Americans that there was no need for them. At the same time, he lent his credibility to an unproven antimalarial drug, hydroxychloroquine, as a treatment for COVID-19.

On 12 April, America's leading epidemiologist, Anthony Fauci, suggested in an interview that applying more stringent measures earlier might have slowed the virus's spread. Trump took to Twitter to rebuke Fauci and implied that he would soon be dismissed. However, this did not occur because Trump was warned that keeping experts like Fauci on board was crucial to retaining public confidence. Two days later, it was revealed that as part of his general scaling back of federal operations, Trump had allowed the so-called PREDICT program to lapse in October 2019. Established in 2009, it had worked in thirty countries including China to monitor new viruses globally and build up global capacity to respond following the SARS, Ebola, and MERS outbreaks. Meanwhile, Trump paused US funding for the WHO citing its failure to gather and distribute data on the initial COVID-19 outbreak in China. His decision showed two characteristic features of his policymaking: he liked to pin the blame for America's difficulties on outsiders and he saw no inherent benefits in multilateral international organizations. Organizations were good only if they benefited Trump's America specifically. He had little time for a worldview that stressed the long-term benefits of altruism.

The same sense that Trump was guided by the question – *what's in it for me?* emerged over the distribution of key equipment from federal stockpiles to individual states. By 15 April, Democratic leaders at the state level were complaining that it was unclear how they could get federal resources. The President's son-in-law, Jared Kushner, seemed to have a personal role and Trump himself implied that resources went quicker to those governors most likely, as he put it, "to treat us well," which suggested favouritism rather than an objective assessment of need. Trump still consistently undercut the advice of medical experts who stressed that viral transmission was more likely when people gathered in indoor spaces. Hoping to retain the strong approval he enjoyed with evangelical Protestants, he had urged churches to stay open for Easter services and generally resisted calls for a systematic reduction in activities that required face-to-face contact. Despite the death rate in the US reaching a new high in mid-April, Trump was already floating the idea of a rapid reopening of the economy although he left the key decisions to state governors, thereby making them directly responsible for any negative consequences. At the same time, he tweeted his support for protesters opposing COVID-related restrictions in Michigan. The tweet read: "Liberate Michigan." Such protests ultimately escalated into a plot to kidnap Democratic Governor Gretchen Whitmer that was foiled by the FBI. Most conspicuously, Trump became the face of the "no mask" movement.

As the death and infection rate in the US climbed, the President continued to insist that the new virus was largely "harmless." He even complained that the testing program was giving a bad impression since the more you tested the more infection you found. He disputed the merits of mask-wearing and failed to respond to the clamour from healthcare professionals over chronic shortages of personal protective equipment (PPE). To energize his faltering re-election campaign, he resumed mass rallies including controversial events like the one in Tulsa, Oklahoma. This had to be rescheduled when it was belatedly realized that it fell on Juneteenth (19 June), the day African Americans celebrated their emancipation from slavery and was to happen in a city addressing the centennial of a brutal anti-black race riot in 1920; and all this in the inflamed context of continuing nationwide protests over the George Floyd killing by police in Minneapolis. Prospective attendees at the Tulsa rally could sign up online. Thousands did, despite warnings that it risked being a super-spreader event. This led the Trump campaign to boast recklessly of a bumper crowd that would exceed the venue's capacity. But many of these online subscribers proved to be hostile hoaxers who had no intention of attending, thus leaving the Trump team embarrassed by media images of a half empty stadium.

By the end of June, only one in six Americans polled approved of the President's handling of the pandemic. He just did not seem to care. Among his critics, Trump had long been perceived as so deeply self-centred as to be clinically narcissistic. During the pandemic, it sometimes appeared that the only person for whom Trump felt pity was himself. Visitors and callers to the White House grew accustomed to his "woe is me" preamble to every conversation. The pandemic, he would lament, was undoing the "greatest economy" that he alone had built; the "fake news" refused to give him credit for anything; as demands for financial disclosure about his taxes intensified, he complained the courts were not protecting his privacy; and now some dumb police officers had killed a black man in their custody sparking widespread protests for racial justice. Everything was happening just to cause him difficulties. At a time when the nation needed an empathetic figure, it had instead a president who was sorry for himself. This represented a golden opportunity for Trump's opponent Joe Biden, who as early as January 2020 had written an op-ed in *USA Today* insisting that Trump's repeated failures of judgment and rejection of science made him the worse possible leader for America during a global health crisis.

The stark difference between the two was symbolized by the ongoing mask controversy. In early April 2020, the National Security Council's Asia Director Matt Pottinger had placed a copy of studies demonstrating the effectiveness of masks in briefing folders for all members of the COVID-19 task force. Using the same studies, the CDC concluded that masks were a vital element in curbing the virus's spread. Yet even after a task force meeting had affirmed this conclusion, Pottinger was pointedly reminded that no masks would be worn at the next meeting. Trump made himself a symbol for all those complaining that public health restrictions were an attack on liberty. He not only mocked a reporter who wore a mask at a press conference, he even toured a mask-making factory in Arizona without a mask. At a visceral level, Trump regarded mask-wearing as a sign of weakness and took it as a sign of disloyalty in others. Mask-wearers were "Never Trumpers." Even after he contracted COVID-19 and required emergency treatment, Trump's choreographed return to the White House culminated in the defiant removal of his mask for the cameras and a call for his fellow Americans not to be afraid. Meanwhile, his Democratic opponent abided by public health guidelines. Staying home, wearing a mask, and maintaining social distance in public settings, Joe Biden defined the alternative to Donald Trump and underscored the idea that the election should be seen as a referendum on whether Trump was able to keep Americans safe.

Trump's habitual, factual inaccuracies and his divisive attacks on anyone whom he felt had crossed him had already generated active concern at social media companies like Facebook and Twitter by July 2020. This became especially true when he offered misleading or inaccurate guidance on COVID-19. In late April, he caused consternation by implying that bleach or other strong disinfectants might be effective remedies via injection, prompting medical professionals to warn that any ingestion of such cleaning agents was harmful. Even members of Trump's inner circle began to urge him to step back from the daily televised briefings. By July with US infection rates far exceeding those in other advanced countries, his apparent indifference to the nation's plight had campaign pollsters worrying that he was alienating suburban women voters (a perceived swing group). In August, as the Republican Convention neared, and even though the US death rate from COVID-19 remained close to its previous May peak, Trump continued to urge the return of children to classrooms and the reopening of businesses and public events.

On 2 October, it seemed that Trump would pay for his reluctance to comply with anti-infection protocols. Both the President and First Lady tested positive for COVID-19 and in what was said to be a precautionary step, Trump was admitted to Walter Reed National Military Medical Center. In reality, his blood oxygen level was falling dangerously, and he needed supplementary oxygen. At Walter Reed, he was treated with a powerful steroid dexamethasone whose status as a treatment was still experimental and which had significant side effects including "psychic derangements," sometimes tipping towards psychosis. He also received other experimental treatments including monoclonal antibodies and a new antiviral drug, Remdesivir. Such treatments were not available to ordinary Americans. Nevertheless, on his return from hospital, Trump tweeted: "Feeling really good! Don't be afraid of Covid. Don't let it dominate your life. We have developed, under the Trump Administration, some really great drugs & knowledge. I feel better than I did 20 years ago!" To critics, this seemed bombastic, turning the focus firmly onto himself and showing no regard for the grief of relatives of the more than 200,000 Americans who had lost their own fight with COVID-19.

By the autumn of 2020, another disturbing development was becoming more evident, and one that would culminate in arguably the gravest scandal: Trump's refusal to accept the election result and to encourage his supporters to contest the peaceful transition. As states responded to the pandemic by facilitating more voting by mail rather than in person, misinformation about the integrity of this process mushroomed. Zignal Labs, a media insights company that monitored topic prevalence across social media and mainstream news outlets reported that nearly a quarter of false claims – 3.1 million mentions – related to voting by mail. This was nearly five times the level of vaccine misinformation. Its closest rival (1.2 million mentions) was misinformation about the Clintons, including the claim that they were part of a secret paedophile ring. The Clinton allegation was particularly prevalent among followers of Q-Anon, a mysterious online conspiracy network that explained world events via the actions of a concealed satanic cabal. During September, the false claims about mail-in ballots began to crystalize into six main categories: the false idea that it was inherently an unreliable way to vote (410,918 mentions); misleading stories about criminal conduct involving mail-in ballots (345,040 mentions); the claim that in states with strict voter ID laws, mail-in ballots had been dumped (31,021 mentions); asserting that "foreign powers" were counterfeiting millions of votes (11,857 mentions); ballot "harvesting," a loaded political term used by President Trump for any form of ballot collection, a process that is legal in twenty-six states where someone other than a family member can drop off your absentee ballot for you (10,562 mentions); and finally, warnings of a "rigged election" (10,140 mentions).

The growth of a conspiracy theory that voting by mail would be used to steal the election also coincided with the appointment of a controversial figure as US Postmaster-General, Louis DeJoy. DeJoy was an important Republican Party donor who had previously been on the board of XPO Logistics, a private shipping firm that acts as a subcontractor for the United States Postal Service (USPS). He made it clear that cost-cutting was central to his vision for the USPS. He banned overtime and over 600 high-speed sorting machines were scheduled for removal, along with mail collection boxes in many cities; all measures that seemed likely to jeopardize the smooth operation of postal voting. Democratic protests and scrutiny from the independent Inspector-General for the USPS paused this process, and in October litigation eventually secured a commitment to reverse all measures that might negatively impact the election. Ironically, the persistent Trump claim that the election was being stolen concealed the reality that in several ways his team tried to steal it for themselves by derailing mail-in voting and intensifying voter restrictions. The prevalence of COVID-19 made the number of Americans considering postal ballots rise, and at the same time, Trump insisted that mail-in ballots were inherently fraudulent. In this way, two strands merged.

After leaving hospital in October, Trump hit the conservative news channels to prove that he was recovered and at the same time to spread false claims about mail-in voting. In an hour-long interview with Maria Bartiromo on *Fox Business* he was asked about a recently released video featuring FBI Director Christopher Wray that sought to reassure voters that postal ballots were safe and secure. Trump was having none of it.

Speaking of Wray, Trump declared: "he doesn't see the voting ballots as a problem. There's [sic] thousands of ballots right now! You pick up any paper in the country practically, and they're cheating all over the place on the ballot. So how is that not a problem? That's a much bigger problem than China or Russia. If you look at it, it's a much bigger problem." This directly contradicted not just Wray, but the federal Department of Homeland Security which had warned that there was clear evidence that Russia was seeking to interfere in the 2020 election.

As the election approached, Trump insisted that the United States had "turned the corner" as far as the pandemic was concerned. But the actual death and infection levels in the country ensured that COVID-19 remained the key election issue for voters. The persistence of the pandemic in the US could be partly blamed on the reluctance of the Trump administration to back CDC calls for greater restrictions; seen most glaringly on the issue of masks. In September, the CDC had drafted a sweeping federal order requiring all passengers and employees to wear masks on all forms of public and commercial transportation in the United States, but according to two federal health officials, it was blocked by the White House. A "culture war" had developed around masks. Trump supporters felt that Biden's diligent mask-wearing was unmanly. This sentiment had potentially deadly consequences since it boosted infection rates among blue-collar men in loyal Trump areas.

An October Gallup poll found American women were more likely than men to take precautions against COVID-19, including the wearing of masks outside the home. Other polls found that for his handling of the pandemic, men gave higher marks to Trump than women did. "To admit you're threatened is to appear weak, so you have to have this bravado," observed Peter Glick, a professor of social sciences at Lawrence University. If you wear a mask, Glick concluded, "the underlying message is: I'm afraid of catching this disease." Trump's behaviour and comments after his hospitalization, despite a widening COVID-19 outbreak within his circle, had revealed a White House that flouted the recommendations of its own health experts. Many American men who looked up to Trump accordingly chose to forgo the protective measures that health officials said were crucial. In one of his first rallies after his hospitalization, Trump told a Florida crowd on 12 October that he felt "so powerful." He joked that he was ready to "kiss everyone in that audience." Despite locally high COVID-19 levels, he declared: "I'll kiss the guys and the beautiful women. Just give you a big fat kiss." Many rallygoers did not wear masks, including some of those chosen to stand behind the President's podium and within the camera shot.

Increasingly, Trump mocked the media's focus on the pandemic and dwelt instead on other issues. Campaigning in North Carolina in late October, he railed against the media obsession with the disease. "That's all I hear about now. That's all I hear, turn on television," he said at a campaign event in Lumberton. "COVID, COVID, COVID, COVID, COVID, COVID," a refrain he recited across the state. He used his own experience of the disease, his weekend of hospitalization and his subsequent recovery as grounds to argue against the severity of the pandemic, even though by that stage it had cost more than 224,000 lives in the United States out of more than 8 million cases. "By the way, I had it, here I am," he would tell the audience with a smile. Even in Republican circles, some faulted his strategy, urging him to dwell on the need for a strong economic recovery and to claim that the way the economy had grown prior to the pandemic was proof that he could make it happen again. Instead, he chose increasingly to warn his supporters that postal voting could "steal" the election for Biden. He even did so as he cast his early postal ballot in Florida. "It's the only way we can lose," he said, citing the size of crowds at his rallies compared to Biden's scaled-down, COVID-19-secure events as proof of their relative support.

Thus, two different scandals – the first relating to Trump's response to the pandemic (where most might concede that he showed a chronic insensitivity) and the second relating to his insistence that any election that he did not win was "stolen" came together in the closing weeks of the campaign. In the final days, voters who were predisposed to vote for Trump could read in right-wing news outlets a variety of stories about how mail-in voting would permit massive fraud. With the country facing a potent third wave of COVID-19 infections, the number of Americans opting to vote by mail was growing and more than twenty-five states had expanded access to postal voting. The *New York Times* reported on 26 October that so far that month the website *Breitbart* had published thirty stories tagged "voter fraud." Often the stories reported the finding of illegally discarded mail-in ballots, cast in favour of Trump in battleground states like Pennsylvania and Wisconsin, but then failed to report or give prominence to further information that refuted these claims. Trump similarly tweeted links to the articles but rarely to the corrections. His supporters were thus fed a steady diet of misinformation.

Alongside the pandemic with its economic ravages and the significant boost to mail-in voting, Trump's 2020 campaign had to deal with the escalating racial protests that flowed from the murder of George Floyd by Minneapolis police officers on 25 May. In the White House, Trump's inner circle witnessed a rare display of empathy from Trump, and he privately expressed disgust at the police misconduct. On 27 May, he met with Attorney-General William Barr and press secretary Kayleigh McEnany to devise his response. He tweeted that Floyd's death was "very sad and tragic" and proposed that the FBI and Justice Department investigate the police for civil rights violations. In the context of the nationwide protests, this was a modest response. On 29 May, he spoke by phone to the Floyd family to express his sorrow and added that the family was "entitled to justice." However, his gesture did not go to plan since the family reported that Trump barely gave them a chance to speak and kept the exchange brief. Although most protests were peaceful, police in forty-eight cities had made over fourteen thousand arrests by May 29 and there had been clashes close to the White House in Lafayette Square. Trump's reaction was to boast of the security arrangements. Behind the perimeter fencing, he warned, there were "the most vicious dogs and most ominous weapons I have ever seen."

Most Republican campaign officials recognized that higher turnout by African Americans was usually to the advantage of Democrats, but at the same time violent racial disorder could also mobilise white voters to turnout for Republicans. Thus, Trump had to tread carefully. His comments, however, alleging that the protests were orchestrated by professional agitators and laying the blame for the D.C. clashes directly on Democratic mayor Muriel Browser, did little to calm the situation or address African American concerns. The next Sunday night, 31 May, a fire broke out in the basement of St. John's Episcopal Church in Lafayette Square, a venue which had hosted every president since James Madison at least once. By then, Trump was already furious because someone had leaked the fact that during the May 29 clashes, the Secret Service had placed the president in the White House security bunker as a precaution. Afraid of appearing weak, Trump denied going in but then implied that he had simply inspected the bunker as a matter of routine. At the same time, Trump aide Stephen Miller was pressing him to show strength by deploying the US military in Washington and other protest flash points. Joint Chiefs of Staff Chairman Mark Milley forcefully countered this suggestion by outlining how the Pentagon was monitoring the urban unrest and that the latest data showed that local law enforcement and National Guard units were more than sufficient to contain the disturbances. Milley was opposed to the domestic use of his troops. They were neither trained nor equipped to police civilian disorder and just as importantly, their deployment would damage what he saw as the vital principle of their political neutrality. He sensed that Trump's priority was to rally support for himself through a display of overwhelming strength rather than to calm the nation and protect its constitutional traditions.

Still smarting from media suggestions that he had cowered during the earlier protests, Trump accepted the idea that once additional security measures were in place, he should walk to Lafayette Square and visit St. John's. Aides suggested that he read a passage of Scripture or meet with faith leaders, but Trump was only willing to carry a Bible and hold it aloft as the cameras rolled. Attorney-General Barr, General Milley, and Defense Secretary Mark Esper were asked to return to the West Wing to hear an update from the president. Unwittingly, they were being summoned as extras in Trump's planned display of strength. Outside, protesters were removed using tear gas, flash grenades, and baton charges, even though there had been no serious disturbances that day. This occurred while Trump told a TV audience that he was both the "President of law and order" and "the ally of all peaceful protesters." After finishing his address, Trump had aides ask Barr, Esper and Milley to walk behind him as he headed to the church. Realizing that he was becoming a prop in a political photo op, Milley exited, but the image of him in his military camouflage gear had already been captured by reporters. From that point on, a scandalized Milley insists, his priority was to protect the Republic from a president who did not respect its principles. For his part, Esper told a press conference that he opposed Trump's threatened use of the Insurrection Act in order to deploy US troops to suppress the ongoing protests; he knew that Trump would be furious at this and expected to be fired. Later he told journalists that trying to prevent this egregious use of troops domestically became his goal for the remainder of Trump's term. Thus, both the head of the Joint Chiefs of Staff and the Defense Secretary believed there was a distinct possibility that Trump would use his powers as commander-in-chief to remain in power. They feared a coup.

As the election neared, and despite the raging pandemic, Trump continued to draw energy from his mass rallies, held in stark contrast to Joe Biden's insistence on social distancing and mask-wearing. At the same time, however, Trump's polling numbers worried his campaign team. In the seventeen states that his managers judged to be competitive and essential for his re-election, he was losing ground. Independents and some Republicans were joining Democrats in the view that Joe Biden would be better at managing the pandemic. Trump had lost his key asset – the healthy economy – and was losing ground with a key demographic – white suburban women. Rallies remained at the heart of Trump's campaign style, even though he was associated with the use of social media, like Twitter, to get his message out and generate further news coverage. In the last forty-eight hours of the campaign, he held thirty-three rallies – evidence of his prodigious stamina – mainly in the key swing states of Pennsylvania, Michigan, Wisconsin, and North Carolina. This would prove insufficient since only North Carolina stayed with Trump; the other three swung to Biden with a combined Electoral College vote of 46, and effectively, a clear margin of victory. Despite frantic appeals from Republican Senator David Purdue that Georgia was up for grabs, Trump only visited it once. All the time, he publicly ignored health warnings about COVID-19 and told his crowds that they could only lose if the election was stolen.

Trump's advisers had tried to prepare him. They had warned that the initial voting numbers would be misleading since they would be based only on in-person voting. This would favour Trump since he had directed his supporters away from mail ballots, but in several key states the result could then be reversed once postal ballots were counted. However, knowing that Trump did not take kindly to bad news, the team had also sprinkled some encouragement. For instance, they assured him that he would probably win if he got over 66 million votes; in other words, more than Hillary Clinton's 2016 tally. This was understandable but it fed into his deep unwillingness to concede if the vote went against him. On election night, Trump felt confident and when *Fox News* projected that he would win Florida, his belief surged since winning that state had been a watershed moment four years earlier. This time, the bubble burst quickly. Minutes later, the same Trump-leaning *Fox News* called Arizona for Biden, an unexpected outcome since it had not gone Democratic in a presidential election since 1996. By the early hours of the morning, Trump was incandescent. He had received more than 77 million votes, yet his analysts and the media were talking of a Joe Biden victory.

The ultimate scandal of the Trump presidency – his wilful refusal to allow the peaceful transfer of power – began to unfold. Even in 2016 Trump had been non-committal about accepting the result if it went against him. Now, he was prepared to listen to people like Rudy Giuliani, who advised him: "Just say we've won." While others tried to nudge Trump towards acceptance, Giuliani was one of several key figures, according to Congressional investigators, who encouraged efforts to overturn the election. On election night, some ascribed Rudy's words to inebriation, but in the coming weeks, his stance remained the same: denial and defiance. He became the most conspicuous figure in Trump's legal team attempting to overturn the result. His media appearances, including one where what appeared to be hair dye dripped down his face as he spoke and another where he led a press conference outside Four Seasons Landscaping in an obscure Philadelphia neighbourhood rather than at the downtown Four Seasons hotel, drew ridicule, but Trump loved his loyalty and his eagerness to continue the fight.

Giuliani's team lost dozens of legal challenges in multiple states with federal judges, even those appointed by Trump. The judges uniformly found no compelling evidence for Giuliani's allegations of systematic miscounting of ballots. A measure of the weakness of Trump's case was the extreme reluctance of law firms to represent him. Campaign legal counsel Matthew Morrison confirmed that virtually every firm that he had previously approached for support in the event of an election challenge refused to act once they heard the nature of Giuliani's claims and the evidence he had gathered. Other White House staff began to worry over their own legal position and tried to distance themselves from Giuliani. This begs the question: was the scandal simply the way Giuliani and others supported Trump's attempts to stay in power or did it extend to the failure of others to block those efforts?

If the latter, then many more people were culpable. Giuliani himself has had his license to practice law revoked by the New York Bar Association, a decision upheld in court where the judge declared that Giuliani had "communicated demonstrably false and misleading statements to courts, lawmakers and the public at large." The appellate court ruling added that the seriousness of Giuliani's misconduct could hardly be overstated. In public, Giuliani had repeatedly claimed that election machines had been tampered with to steal the election, but in sworn testimony he declared they had not done so. This discrepancy makes him a key part of the multi-million-dollar lawsuit brought by the Dominion company, the maker of the election machines. Worse still, some of Giuliani's wild accusations generated a real risk of harm to innocent individuals. Two African American election workers in Atlanta's Fulton County ballot counting centre were repeatedly named by Giuliani as active agents in the "steal." They received hundreds of threats by phone and were advised by the FBI to leave their homes after Trump supporters tracked down their home addresses.

State officials similarly ran the risk of personal attack when they refused to cooperate. Arizona House Speaker Russell Bowers, for instance, told Giuliani that the latter's plan to have an alternate list of pro-Trump electors created for the Electoral College vote was illegal. Subsequently, Trump supporters targeted Bowers' home; one even hired a truck that circled the neighbourhood with a placard alleging that the deeply religious Republican Bowers was a paedophile. Before 6 January 2021, Giuliani also knew that Trump planned to go personally with his followers to the Capitol to attend the formal count of certified Electoral College votes. The clear inference was that there would be intimidation of a kind that echoed the demonstrations outside the Miami-Dade County canvassing board in 2000. Judging by communications obtained by investigators, Giuliani seemed jubilant rather than mortified by this prospect. In the event, Trump's Secret Service detail refused to take him to the Capitol that day insisting that their protocols did not allow them to act in a way that placed the President at a heightened risk of attack. Trump raged at them at the time, but in hindsight, these agents unwittingly prevented Trump from providing incontrovertible evidence that he was fully behind the storming of the Capitol.

Between 4 November 2020 and 6 January 2021, the Trump campaign and its allies filed sixty-two separate cases challenging Joe Biden's victory. Thirty were dismissed by judges after preliminary hearings failed to demonstrate their merits. The remaining thirty-two suits secured one victory in Pennsylvania, but it related to such a small number of ballots that it could not affect Biden's victory in that state. Every other claim proved bogus. But even though courts rejected the claims as speculative, without proof or legal merit, President Trump, Rudy Giuliani, and others, nonetheless, continued to assert their validity in public, preying upon the loyalty and credibility of their supporters, and asking for their donations. Despite internal memoranda confirming that the voting machines had functioned properly, Giuliani on 12 November insisted on *Fox News* that Dominion voting machines had flipped votes at the behest of Venezuelan dictator Hugo Chavez. This claim that the software inside the machines was rigged to miscount Trump ballots had also been made days earlier by Trump lawyer Sidney Powell. By early December, judges in states as diverse as Arizona and Michigan had summarily rejected the suits and Dominion had begun libel actions. Still, Trump and associates continued to push the lie of the "steal." A full hand-count of ballots in the one Michigan county (Antrim) that Trump allies repeatedly cited as an example of the "steal" found a single misassigned ballot, despite Trump claims that the error rate was 68 percent.

Unwilling to focus on presidential matters as his term neared its end, Trump remained fixated on the election, and important policy matters were further adversely affected by fears among Cabinet members that in desperation, the President might trigger an international crisis with China or Iran or use the continuing protests in American cities as an excuse for domestic military intervention. Senior Pentagon officials and armed forces chiefs spoke among themselves about the need to "land the plane safely." Soon, Trump's intransigence began affecting the normal preparations for a transition to a new president. Chief of Staff Mark Meadows refused to allow the Biden team access to a White House computing system that is used to enable essential budgetary planning. When Ron Klain, Biden's future Chief of Staff queried in mid-November when the President-Elect would start to receive his daily intelligence briefings, he was dumbfounded by Meadows' response that no president really wanted daily briefings; clearly, Trump hadn't. The public received a stark reminder of the President's priority on 3 January 2021, when Georgia's Secretary of State, Brad Raffensperger, released a recorded phone call from the previous day in which Trump openly stated that all he wanted was for Raffensperger to find "11,780 votes, which is one more than [the 11,779-vote margin of defeat] we have, because we won the state." This would prompt a subsequent Georgia state grand jury investigation into the actions of Trump and others. Trump and eighteen others have been indicted on multiple charges arising from their efforts to overturn the election result in Georgia.

The Electoral College used to select the US President has its own procedures. Effectively, voters in each state select a slate of Electors. The College itself never meets as a single body, but instead, on the Monday after the second Wednesday in December, Congress requires the Electors to gather at their respective state capitals to record their vote and certify the results. On 14 December 2020, this went ahead. Each elector had to sign six times and a certificate of ascertainment was attached to confirm that they had done so correctly. Then copies were sent: one to the President of the US Senate (normally the Vice-President); one to the chief judge of the US District Court in which the vote occurs; two to the Archivist of the United States; and two to the state's election certification office (normally the State Secretary of State). Despite the many safeguards thus in place to prevent interference, Trump's advisors attempted to secure "alternate slates of electors."

This was mainly the brainchild of law professor, John Eastman. He had represented Trump as part of a Texas lawsuit that sought legal annulment of electoral processes and hence results in four other US states. The US Supreme Court quickly dismissed that case by affirming the lower court's view that Texas had no legal basis for interfering in the electoral processes of another state. Despite this rebuff, Eastman then concocted another plan to prevent the acceptance of the Electoral College certificates. However, everything hinged on Vice-President Mike Pence agreeing to act in a way that Eastman himself privately acknowledged would be illegal. As the House's 6 January Committee discovered when it secured Eastman's private memoranda, he recognized that the Twelfth Amendment gave the Vice-

President simply a ceremonial role. He opens the envelopes containing the certificates; it does not give him a role in their counting. As president of the Senate, he presides over the count but has no discretion as to its conduct under Section 15 of the Electoral Count Act of 1887. Eastman implicitly signalled confirmation of such illegality when he chose to plead the Fifth Amendment (protecting an individual from self-incrimination) in his deposition to the 6 January Committee. Senior legal advisers around Trump repeatedly told him that what Eastman proposed was illegal. Like Giuliani in New York, Eastman would eventually face disbarment from practicing law in his home state of California.

Nevertheless, in the run-up to the January confirmation of the election by Congress, Trump supporters attempted to create alternate slates of electors in the contested swing states. These alternate slates were supposed to provide a pretext for Vice-President Pence to stall the certification process, particularly when combined with challenges to the legitimacy of the vote from Trump supporters in Congress. This impasse, it was argued, could allow Pence to return the matter to Republican-controlled state legislatures. Accordingly, Trump and his associates repeatedly pressed Pence to cooperate. They also sought to summon an intimidating mob. On 18 December, four days after the genuine slates of electors had been certified at state capitols, Trump tweeted "Big protest in D.C. on January 6th. Be there, will be wild!" Trump supporters had already secured a permit for a rally at the Ellipse on the Mall, and Trump now tried to expand its purpose.

Tracking the actions of leading figures in the subsequent assault on the US Capitol, the House Intelligence Committee uncovered a network of Trump sympathizers in far-Right groups like the Proud Boys and Oath Keepers. Across this network, Trump's call to gather was read as a call-to-arms. They were being summoned, they felt, to halt the certification of Biden's election by force, if necessary. Immediately prior to 6 January, intelligence reports made both the Justice and the Defense Departments aware that there was on-line chatter about an attack on the Capitol Building itself. By early January, despite receiving the same reports, White House staff indicated that Trump's plans for his rally included calling on the crowd to march down to the Capitol. On the day, it also quickly became apparent that many of those gathering had brought weapons. As part of its normal security precautions, the Secret Service had set up metal detectors to scan attendees before they were admitted to the Ellipse area, close to the stage where Trump was set to speak. A large cohort of his supporters chose instead to gather away from these detectors to evade the screening process.

According to Cassidy Hutchinson, a principal aide to Trump's Chief of Staff, Mark Meadows, the scene infuriated Trump because by thinning the crowds at the front of the stage, it might give the impression of a poorly attended event to TV viewers. She testified:

> I was in the vicinity of a conversation where I overheard the President say something to the effect of, "I don't F'ing care that they have weapons. They're not here to hurt me. Take the F'ing mags [magnetometers or metal detectors] away. Let my people in. They can march to the Capitol from here. Let the people in".

While Trump's immediate concern was ensuring the optimum visual effect from his rally, his comments also confirmed that he knew that his followers were armed before he invited them to march on the Capitol.

For anyone inclined to view Trump's actions on 6 January as tantamount to fomenting insurrection, the rhetoric used by him and his associates at the rally seems designed to inflame the crowd. Giuliani told them: "Let's have trial by combat." John Eastman repeated the disproven claims that the voting machines had been rigged and outlined how Vice-President Pence could stop the count and send the process back to the state legislatures. Trump himself made clear that he had talked to Pence about precisely that scenario and declared: "So I hope Mike has the courage to do what he has to do. And I hope he doesn't listen to the RINOs [Republicans In Name Only] and the stupid people that he's listening to." In this way, Trump directed the crowds' anger directly at Pence and when they stormed the Capitol, they responded with threats to hang the Vice-President once they caught him. Just to underline the strategy of intimidation, at 14:27, despite clear reports of the unfolding attack, Trump tweeted:

> Mike Pence didn't have the courage to do what should have been done to protect our Country and our Constitution, giving States a chance to certify a corrected set of facts, not the fraudulent or inaccurate ones which they were asked to previously certify. USA demands the truth!

Deputy Press Secretary at the White House, Sarah Matthews likened Trump's tweet to pouring gasoline on a fire. One of his closest aides, Hope Hicks read this tweet with disbelief. She texted a colleague: "Attacking the VP? Wtf is wrong with him." Aware of the damage that her father was doing to himself and the country, Ivanka Trump cajoled him into sending a further tweet at 14:38 which read: "Please support our Capitol Police and Law Enforcement. They are truly on the side of our Country. Stay peaceful!" Trump understood that support for law enforcement rather that militant protesters was the position that he had always staked out, and under pressure from aides and family, he sent another tweet at 15:13 (which still, of course, omitted any call for his followers to disperse). It read: "I am asking for everyone at the US Capitol to remain peaceful. No violence! Remember, WE are the Party of Law & Order – respect the Law and our great men and women in Blue. Thank you!"

Live television coverage ensured that most Americans and many people around the world witnessed the storming of the Capitol, the desperate attempts of the outnumbered police to block the mob, and shared footage from the rioters' mobile phones captured the scenes of Trump supporters entering the halls of Congress. At this point, the most conspicuous scandal in relation to Trump was his inaction. For 187 minutes, as the House Select Committee investigating the 6 January attack phrased it, he did nothing to protect and defend the core political institutions of the nation. Despite pleas from his own family, his inner circle, and political leaders of both parties, Trump refused to make any kind of call for his followers to desist and disperse. His speech had concluded at 13:10 local time, and he learned the gravity of the situation as early as 13:25, but it was not until 16:17 that he issued an appeal to his followers to go home. Instead, he was widely reported to be watching events on television, speaking by phone to sympathetic Senators and Congressmen about blocking the Electoral College count, but making no effort whatsoever to mobilize the security forces at his disposal as Commander-in-Chief.

Among the many Republicans appealing to the President to call off his supporters was House Minority Leader Kevin McCarthy who made repeated attempts to call Trump and connected with him at least once. According to Congressman Jaime Herrera Beutler who spoke to McCarthy shortly after the conversation, Trump did not agree to do anything. When pressed to call off the attack, he initially claimed that his supporters were not involved, and that the incursion was a leftist attack. McCarthy corrected him and told how his own staff were running for their lives as the mob raided offices in the building. Trump replied: "Well Kevin, I guess they're just more upset about the election, you know, theft than you are."

When Trump eventually agreed to deliver a video message asking his supporters to disperse, it was characteristically ambivalent. He said:

> I know your pain. I know you're hurt. We had an election that was stolen from us. It was a landslide election, and everyone knows it, especially the other side, but you have to go home now. We have to have peace.

He added: "We love you. You're very special." Even after the televised images of the storming of the building, even after scenes of graphic violence, Trump's first impulse was to empathize with the perpetrators, and spread the "Big Lie" of the stolen election, rather than to condemn the violence. Lest anyone mistake his message, at 18:01 he sent what proved to be his last tweet of that traumatic day, and once again the tone was one of justification rather than condemnation. It read:

> These are the things and events that happen when a sacred election landslide victory is so unceremoniously & viciously stripped away from great patriots who have been badly & unfairly treated for so long. Go home with love & in peace. Remember this day forever!

Apart from these communications, official records show he made no attempt to respond to the unfolding attack. He had no contact with the Pentagon, the Department of Homeland Security, the Department of Justice, the F.B.I., the Capitol Police Department, or the D.C. Mayor's office.

Given the enormity of what happened, and the damage it inflicted on the image of the US as a stable democracy, there was widespread condemnation that ultimately resulted in Donald Trump becoming the first president to be impeached twice. Conventionally, a key element in any scandal is that it has negative consequences; that's one reason why politicians are supposed to avoid scandal. However, of the many aspects of scandal that Trump upended, none has been more profound than the principle of accountability. Despite all that had transpired, that evening when Congress eventually reconvened, 147 House and Senate Republicans voted against the certification of Biden's election victory. Privately, some conceded that the brazen violence of the attack made them vote against certification. After all, if they voted for it, they would become likely targets. More generally, for those who wanted to remain viable in GOP politics, it was clear that this symbolic vote was another appeasement for the Trump-infused base that now dominated the party. To underline the point, consider the fate of those who did come out emphatically against Trump and the Big Lie: Congresswoman Liz Cheney and Senator Mitt Romney. The former had been tipped as a potential Speaker if the GOP regained the House, while the latter, the GOP's 2012 presidential nominee, had been branded a R-I-N-O after his vote during the first impeachment, and was sought by the mob during the Capitol invasion.

Cheney and Romney were quickly rendered relics with Cheney losing her re-election bid in 2022 to a Trump-backed challenger. The *realpolitik* faction in the Republican Party was far better represented by Senator Mitch McConnell who, after hinting that Trump had to take responsibility for what had happened, nonetheless refused to authorize a prompt impeachment trial in the Senate after the House passed articles of impeachment on 13 January. The delay was sufficient to ensure that the trial occurred after Biden's inauguration on 20 January, and this, in turn, gave Senate Republicans an excuse to vote against impeachment on the grounds that its punishment (removal from office) had been rendered redundant by Trump's departure. With ten House Republicans voting with the Democratic Majority, the House had passed articles of impeachment, and it seemed briefly that the principle of accountability might prevail. However, on 26 January the Senate only narrowly defeated a motion not to proceed in view of Trump's departure from office. With only five Republicans willing to proceed, it was clear that there would not be a two-thirds majority (sixty-seven Senators) to convict. The issue was raised again on 9 February since Trump's legal defense team argued that the Senate was not authorized to try a former president. On that occasion, the motion to proceed gained the support of six Republicans.

After a four-day trial, Trump was acquitted because the fifty-seven votes against him fell ten short of the super-majority needed to convict. At that stage, of course, he could not be removed from office via impeachment, but he would have been prevented from running for office again. Among those who had condemned Trump's behaviour over the storming of the Capitol, yet voted not to convict was Senator Mitch McConnell. He was still smarting from the fact that the run-off election in Georgia had raised the Democrats to fifty votes in the Senate and hence with the new Vice-President Kamala Harris able to vote in cases of a tie, had ended McConnell's time as Senate Majority Leader. Certainly, there were signs that McConnell had not forgiven Trump. He reminded the media that other institutions could still hold Trump to account, declaring: "We have a criminal-justice system in this country. We have civil litigation. And former presidents are not immune from being accountable by either one."

McConnell was certainly not wrong about litigation since cases against the former President have accumulated since he left office with new suits joining those already begun. In December 2022, a New York state court found the Trump Organization criminally liable for a tax-dodge scheme that entailed seventeen separate fraud charges. Its Chief Financial Officer and lead payroll executive will go to jail, and Trump will once again find it harder to finance his company's operations via US banks. The verdict also adds momentum to a separate prosecution related to Trump's practice of valuing his properties low when reporting for tax purposes but much higher when seeking loans. If upheld, that second case would compel the company to pay at least $250 million in fines plus the money Trump allegedly pocketed from the misled banks. It would also ban Trump and his three eldest children – Donald, Jr., Ivanka, and Eric, who have all served as Trump Organization executives – from running a company in New York state. Worst of all, the suit threatens to pull the Trump Organization's New York papers of incorporation. Without them, Trump could not do business in the state and might have to file for bankruptcy. The judge concluded in September 2023 that the Trump Organization and co-defendants acted fraudulently, but no doubt any negative verdict will be appealed.

There are also criminal investigations arising from Trump's efforts to overturn the 2020 election result. A special grand jury in Georgia has recommended indictments arising from Trump's efforts to overturn his defeat there. Several of those indicted, notably Trump's attorney Sidney Powell, have pleaded guilty to lesser charges in deals that will see them testify against the others. Meanwhile, the Justice Department is assessing the evidence and recommendations handed over by the House's January 6th Committee which linked the former president to the attack on the Capitol in multiple ways. However, the decision to prosecute Trump has placed Biden's Attorney General Merrick Garland in a difficult political position, which he has tried to escape by appointing a Special Prosecutor Jack Smith. The latter has subpoenaed Mike Pence, Ivanka Trump and her husband Jared Kushner among others, but it remains to be seen whether cases will be concluded before the 2024 election, especially if Trump is once again the Republican nominee. Disappointing results in the 2022 mid-term elections, notably for Trump-backed Senate candidates, have reduced Trump's influence within the party as demonstrated by the emergence of rivals like Ron DeSantis of Florida and Nikki Hailey of South Carolina as candidates in the presidential nomination race. Thus, Trump's chances of escaping accountability for scandalous conduct cannot be separated from his political standing. During 2023, the apparent willingness of former Trump allies like Chris Christie and William Barr to state openly that Trump should not be the Republican nominee in 2024 has signalled some erosion of support. But this has been offset by polling that shows that none of the other Republicans in the race command anything like Trump's level of support with Republican voters. Ongoing court cases will coincide with the primary contests.

In the summer of 2021, it seemed possible that Trump would be held to account for his cavalier approach to presidential matters in the most mundane way. He contravened federal laws that require Presidents to place the records of their administration in the National Archives. An FBI raid found classified documents at his home of Mar-a-Lago. This was on the back of litigation by professional historians who had heard multiple stories of Trump destroying documents during and after meetings, even flushing them down the toilet, and followed the reluctant and belated return of fifteen boxes from Mar-a-Lago after months of wrangling. However, the subsequent discovery of classified materials from both Joe Biden and Mike Pence's time as vice-president on their property deadened the sense that Trump was especially guilty, even though Biden and Pence have shown a markedly more cooperative approach than Trump ever did. This investigation too was handed over to Special Prosecutor Jack Smith to consider and in June 2023, Trump was charged with thirty-seven offences that detailed that he illegally retained and failed to return highly classified documents. Significantly, there was an emphasis on his refusal to comply with requests to return such material and on evidence that he knew that he had material that he was not legally entitled to have, even boasting about it in private conversations. Several commentators have noted that he could have avoided prosecution had he complied with the requests. The case has become a classic binary issue. Trump opponents are outraged that he has such a sense of entitlement that he cannot see that taking documents is wrong. Trump supporters are equally incensed that he is facing criminal charges whereas others did not.

The sheer number of cases Trump faces is striking and confirms the fact that he is routinely involved in hostile litigation and his main tactic is to stall, deny, protest, and either exhaust the resources of his opponent or ultimately settle in a way that does not hold him fully accountable. Eleven Democratic House members and two US Capitol police officers have filed suits charging that he incited the violence of the mob that attacked the Capitol, endangering their lives and leaving them with physical and psychological injuries. Trump's initial effort to insist that his status as president at this time grants him immunity from civil suits was dismissed by a federal judge in a blistering opinion and has been appealed by Trump's lawyers. It is likely to go all the way to the US Supreme Court given the importance of the principle involved. But it joins an already full docket of cases for any lawyer willing to work for Trump, who is well-known for not paying his legal fees (as Rudy Giuliani, among others, has discovered.)

A new statute in New York, extending the time period in which victims of sexual assault can seek civil damages, reactivated lawsuits by journalist E. Jean Carroll, who alleged that Trump raped her in the mid-1990s. In characteristic style, Trump responded to her allegations initially by denying he ever met her and then by saying she was "not his type." Carroll's suit which sought damages for defamation as well as rape went to court in April 2023. On 9 May, in a unanimous verdict, the jury found that Trump had sexually abused Carroll and that he had defamed her in subsequent comments. Although they judged the accusation of rape unproven, they awarded Carroll damages of $5 million. Trump declared on television the next day that Carroll was a "whack job" who he didn't know and that he could not get a fair trial in New York. His lawyers have unsuccessfully tried to have the damages reduced on appeal and Carroll has amended her suit in the light of the subsequent defamation with a further trial date set for January 2024. Damages of $10 million are now demanded, and it is likely that Trump will seek further legal delay. His countersuit, alleging that Carroll defamed him by continuing to say that he did rape her when the jury did not find him guilty of this, was dismissed. But he will stall and appeal.

At the same time, the saga of Trump's relationship with porn star Stormy Daniels, the details of which were suppressed via payments to tabloids by his then "fixer" Michael Cohen, are the subject of a suit brought by Manhattan District Attorney Alvin Bragg. Against the backdrop of the Mueller inquiry, Cohen himself has testified under oath that he made the payments at Trump's direction, and he pleaded guilty to federal campaign finance violations in 2018. Bragg is claiming that in addition to breaching state laws relating to business accounting practices, Trump broke federal laws relating to election campaign expenditures by concealing the payments. A trial date is provisionally set for 25 March 2024, which falls in the midst of the presidential primary election season. Currently, negative court rulings and indictments seem to be consolidating Trump's support and amplifying his ability to raise money so this may bizarrely work to his advantage in securing the nomination. However, pundits also suspect that it may also make his defeat in the general election more likely by siphoning away some swing voters. Efforts by the Republican controlled House to generate momentum for the prosecution of President Biden's son, Hunter, while seen as blatantly partisan, have also yielded some results in terms of charges for tax evasion and perhaps more importantly, headlines and talking points for Trump defenders. A Special Prosecutor has been appointed and hard right Republicans in the House are demanding that President Biden face impeachment, despite the fact that they have not found clear evidence of his acting on behalf of his son's foreign clients.

It is worth pausing to note that prior to becoming president, Trump had already been obliged to settle cases involving discrimination in the rental of housing contrary to the 1968 Civil Rights Act, that he had been sued for improper employment practices by unions involved in his Manhattan construction projects, that he had been obliged to wind up his real-estate degree factory – Trump University (also known as the Trump Wealth Institute and Trump Entrepreneur Initiative LLC) – after class action suits (merging multiple cases) extracted a $25 million settlement in 2016, and that his children and himself were required to close the Trump Foundation in 2019. In the Foundation case, aware that Trump routinely settled on the basis that to do so was not an admission of guilt, the judge required him to acknowledge his personal misuse of Trump Foundation funds and to agree to both restrictions on future charitable service and ongoing reporting to the Office of the Attorney General, in the event he created a new charity. The settlement also included mandatory training requirements for Donald Trump Jr., Ivanka Trump, and Eric Trump, which the three children have now completed.

Unsurprisingly, Trump's pre-presidential business practices continue to draw litigation. He is accused of promoting a fraudulent multi-level marketing scheme via his TV show *The Celebrity Apprentice*. It is alleged that while Trump pocketed nearly $8.8 million from the scheme, investors were never likely to see a return on their money and in practice, lost thousands. Trump dismisses the case as just another politically motivated attack, and it is unlikely to reach the courtroom before 2024. Also pending is a suit for copyright infringement by the composer/performer Eddy Grant related to the use of portions of his hit single "Electric Avenue" as incidental music on an animated attack ad against Joe Biden posted on Twitter by Trump and his associates and viewed 13 million times. Trump counters that the ad was political satire and therefore protected by the First Amendment, and in any case that he just tweeted it and has no idea where it came from! Trump has made a similar "free speech" argument in response to charges that his 6 January speech incited the attack on the Capitol. Thus, on an almost daily basis, Trump seems to add to the scandals. He seems to embody the famous punch-line response to the question: "How do you know when a politician is lying?" Answer: "His lips are moving." By that logic, the scandals may only cease on his death. Certainly, at this juncture in the summer of 2023, the only thing certain is that the scandals involving Donald Trump will still grab headlines next year.

Conclusion

Scandals Are Not the Same

The scandals spread across these chapters have been very different but with a consistent trajectory. In 1974 when it became clear to Richard Nixon that he should not risk an impeachment trial, given the number of Republicans who might vote against him, their defection rested on the recognition that most Americans were appalled by the scandalous conduct of their president. On 4 March 1987, Ronald Reagan addressed the nation about the Iran-Contra affair, responding to the Tower Commission Report which had portrayed it as a product of independent actions that occurred partly because of Reagan's loose managerial style. It was an example of classic Reagan rhetoric, as illustrated by its folksy concluding paragraph:

> Now, what should happen when you make a mistake is this: You take your knocks, you learn your lessons, and then you move on. That's the healthiest way to deal with a problem. This in no way diminishes the importance of the other continuing investigations, but the business of our country and our people must proceed. I've gotten this message from Republicans and Democrats in Congress, from allies around the world, and – if were reading the signals right – even from the Soviets. And of course, I've heard the message from you, the American people. You know, by the time you reach my age, you've made plenty of mistakes. And if you've lived your life properly – so, you learn. You put things in perspective. You pull your energies together. You change. You go forward.

Thus, Reagan simultaneously accepted and sought to evade responsibility for the illegalities that took place under his presidency, and despite a profound dip in his popularity, the "Great Communicator" was able to "move on." That was largely due to the widespread public desire to avoid what was seen as the trauma of Watergate.

In January 1999, President Clinton faced his impeachment trial in the Senate. By a vote along party lines, the House had passed two articles of impeachment: the first, accused the President of perjury in his grand jury testimony, while the second alleged obstruction of justice because he had induced others to commit perjury to protect him; both actions that contravened the spirit and substance of his oath of office. In contrast to Nixon and Reagan, Clinton continued to enjoy high approval ratings from the American public, who drew a clear distinction between his private immorality for which he might rightly be censured, and his official actions that were seen as in keeping with his office. The outrage that the Republicans tried to nurture against Clinton, and which is a key part of any scandal, was perceived as thinly veiled, partisan warfare. On 12 February 1999, Clinton was acquitted (55-45 on the first charge; 50-50 on the second); neither article came close to the two-thirds majority (67) needed for conviction. The salacious component within the Clinton scandals ensured that for most of the previous year the Lewinsky affair had dominated the media in a way not seen since Watergate. It did so in a media landscape that was reconfiguring itself alongside significant and complementary, polarizing tendencies within the two main parties. In key respects, the Clinton impeachment was a watershed for presidential scandals.

Despite the approval ratings and the recognition that the outrage at the Lewinsky affair was contrived, Bill Clinton did leave the presidency changed in terms of its intrinsic legitimacy. With partisan affiliation as the key variable, it made Americans more cynical about their president. Already, there were cohorts of voters who questioned the value of their vote in a system that seemed driven by PR spin rather than a commitment to the common good. The 2000 election deepened this crisis of legitimacy by sowing doubts about the electoral process itself. The US Supreme Court's majority ruling in *Bush v. Gore,* which ended the Florida recount and thus handed the presidency to George W. Bush, may have been rooted in the letter of the Constitution insofar as the adjudication of voter intent on disputed ballots could not conform with the principle of equal protection under the law that was required by the Fourteen Amendment. But in practice, the decision left many groups with a heightened mistrust of the electoral machinery. The subsequent switch to computerised voting machines, while it improved the count, left many Americans cynical about subsequent elections, as well as about politicians and political candidates more generally.

By 2016, the simmering discontent among a diverse group of mainly white, rural, blue-collar voters was transforming the Republican Party in a way that enabled Donald Trump, a man mainly known as "The Boss" on the hit-show *The Apprentice* to become the GOP nominee. In a crowded field of contenders for the GOP nomination, Trump emerged as the candidate most adept at channelling the anger of these voters against Democratic opponent Hillary Clinton. Trump's scandal-littered past – dubious business deals and tabloid-rich stories of divorce and philandering – were metamorphosised into badges of authenticity. Whereas conventional politicians buried their skeletons in the closet, Trump seemed to wear them on his sleeve. He also was the ironic beneficiary of the principle of "balance" in the established media. This saw pieces critical of Trump balanced by pieces probing Hillary Clinton, whose decades in politics left ample scope for negative comment. Although there were plenty of articles warning that Trump was not well qualified for the office of president, it was easy for his supporters to dismiss this as "fake news." In most cases, such critiques would be read by the already converted on both sides deepening the pre-existing gulf between them. One side could shake their scandalized heads at Trump's boast of being able to grab women "by the pussy" because he was a celebrity and insist that Trump's refusal to honour the convention that presidential candidates should publish their tax returns was obviously due to his desire to conceal the truth about his finances. The other could chant "lock her up" in response to the use of Hillary's private email account or feel outrage at being labelled a "deplorable" or at the leaked details of her campaign's strategizing or the money she was happy to take from Wall Street. One side could ponder why Trump was apt to praise Putin, while the other could consider if Hillary had any real understanding of who they were and why they loved Trump. Each side had scandals and it seemed their own versions of truth.

The conduct of the new Trump administration gave momentum to the Russia scandal. The fact that the meeting in Trump Tower did not yield damaging revelations about Hillary Clinton did not diminish the

Democrats' clamour for its investigation. The firing of James Comey and the appointment of Robert Mueller as Special Prosecutor fed the expectation that Trump would be held accountable at the same time as it intensified the conviction among Trump supporters that the investigation was a "witch hunt" designed to deny Trump the spoils of victory. In the end, the fixation on whether Mueller would deliver a "gotcha" moment akin to the "smoking gun" Watergate tape that captured Nixon's instruction to use the CIA to block investigators served to deflect public attention from Mueller's most significant finding. Russia had actively and systematically interfered in the 2016 presidential election to block the election of Clinton and to foster division and recrimination within the United States, and it had succeeded.

Once the Mueller Report failed to deliver the basis for Trump's impeachment, the polarization generated a fresh scandal. An angry Trump wanted the Ukraine government to investigate Democratic scandals as payback, and angry Democrats wanted to use Trump's *quid pro quo* phone call as the basis for his removal from office. The picture that emerged of an administration that seemed driven by narrowly defined self-interest, by a conviction that opposing arguments were driven by disloyalty rather than principle, and by a belief that back-channels got the job done better than the formal institutional routes, all echoed Watergate and Iran-Contra style arrogance of power. The 2018 mid-term elections had given the Democrats control of the House but not the Senate. Speaker Pelosi was impelled to back impeachment by the need to placate progressive demands, even though she knew that the Senate votes were not there to achieve conviction. Senate Majority Leader McConnell knew that the President's mass following inside the GOP and the currently strong economy made backing Trump the politically astute path, even if privately he echoed concerns about the President's limited knowledge and competence and crude style.

The failed first impeachment became yet one more episode in the Trump show, a spectacle that the divided media landscape could use to service widely separated audiences. The old mainstream media could use the Watergate model of unfolding scandal that threatened Trump's survival and they could stress his weak approval ratings nationally. Trump's average Gallup approval rating over the course of his term was 41 percent and never exceeded 49 percent. But even during his impeachment in December-

January 2019-20, this figure contained a marked partisan disparity. When impeachment failed in February, 93 percent of Republicans polled approved of Trump's performance compared to just 6 percent of Democrats. His standing among so-called independents which had stood at 42 percent when impeachment was considered in the House was back at that level in February after his acquittal. Thus, scandal did not move the nation.

February 2020 marked the beginning of the COVID-19 outbreak in the US and this event rather than any personal scandal played the largest role in Trump's failure to be re-elected. At other points in the previous chapters, we have noted that in some respects scandals erupt via incompetence. Trump's blundering performance in televised briefings about COVID-19 damaged his electoral prospects, and his lack of empathy alienated some independent voters. His approval ratings had peaked at 49 percent in April 2020 around the time that he signed legislation to give federal aid to address the impact of the pandemic and announced an executive order suspending immigration to the United States as a health measure. However, on 23 April, Trump speculated on television about the efficacy of bleach as a cleansing agent for COVID-19. By early June with infection and death rates high in the US and racial tensions escalating after the 25 May police killing of George Floyd, his ratings had fallen to 39 percent; still high among Republicans (91 percent) but far lower with Independents (33 percent). Then, in the summer of 2020 as states eased restrictions on voting by mail to enable the election to occur in the context of the pandemic, Trump pushed the idea that the election might be stolen. Without proof, he equated mail-in voting to voter fraud.

In contrast to the 2000 election, the 2020 election was in many ways the most secure election ever, and one that saw the highest turnout this century (66.9 percent of eligible voters). Given the problems that persist in relation to in-person voting and voting restrictions, the switch to mail-in ballots was probably an improvement. This is, of course, the opposite of what Donald Trump has claimed, and his refusal to accept the result and his active attempts to orchestrate resistance to the peaceful transfer of power is likely to remain the enduring scandal of his presidency. It culminated in the attack on the Capitol Building on 6 January 2021 intended to prevent the ratification of the Electoral College votes by Congress, and that, in turn, led to Trump's unprecedented second impeachment. Trump's second acquittal, despite the 57-43 vote to convict, was due to the constitutional requirement of a two-thirds majority (67). Republicans who voted to acquit were able to use the excuse that Trump had already left office so the impeachment process was redundant. However, all this did was to reinforce the perception that Trump would not be held accountable for what many saw as scandalous presidential conduct.

Presidential scandals are intrinsically both political and media phenomena. As we argued in the introduction, scandal combines outrage and entertainment with the latter an important element in its appeal for commercial news outlets. The Watergate scandal was fundamentally political in the sense that the outrage it generated stemmed from the recognition that Richard Nixon's vision of government was dangerously amoral. He himself summed up the philosophy when he told interviewer David Frost that "when the President does it... that means it is not illegal." The Iran-Contra episode was similarly a scandal with grave political dimensions that exposed a rejection by some of Reagan's inner circle of the principle that Congress could limit the authority of the president in the conduct of foreign policy. It foreshadowed the growing partisan polarization since Republicans characterized the exposure and investigation of the episode as a *weaponization* of the legal process. The initial scandals of the Clinton administration retained this partisan dynamic but with an incipient prurient element that fed tabloid interest in the investigations via gossip about Bill's womanizing. This culminated in the Lewinsky affair and the Starr Report's exposure of his perjury and inducement of perjury by others. But the balance between outrage and titillation had been reversed. Therein lay a paradox. On the one hand, the apparent sophistication of the American electorate that seemed able to separate the moral failings of Clinton the man from the assessment of his conduct as President seemed to suggest that political manipulation of personal scandal had become less effective. On the other, the growth of media outlets and the ready circulation of scandalous accusations simultaneously marked a new era of scandal as a weapon.

The 2000 election diminished the public's faith in the election process itself, but it exposed what was as much a scandal of incompetence as of political manipulation and maladministration. It left both Democrats and Republicans mistrustful of electoral outcomes. Ironically, Democratic insistence that Donald Trump's surprise victory in 2016 could be questioned based on his campaign's interaction with Russian interests misdirected attention. The outrage that should have focused on Russian state actions was diffused to the Trump campaign who may still have benefitted without active engagement with Putin's regime. The sheer frequency of scandal as a label attached to a Trump action or tweet has served to mutate the meaning of scandal. Precisely because it outrages his Democratic opponents, it entertains his loyal followers. Its binary quality makes it rich material in the segmented media marketplace. As the Dominion lawsuit deposition of *Fox News* executives has made public, even when Trump's statements were recognisably false or when his actions were genuinely reprehensible, it was deemed commercially advantageous to frame any accusation of scandal as simply a political jibe. Thus, as Rudy Giuliani insists: "truth isn't truth," and certainly a newspaper scandal story can no longer easily expose falseness. It remains to be seen whether Trump's time as president proves an aberration, or whether the political assumption that scandal is dangerous and needs to be avoided at all costs is restored. The Republican-controlled House has pressed for thorough investigation of Hunter Biden and the Justice Department has appointed a Special Prosecutor to investigate. But this hasn't stopped Trump loyalists bemoaning the *weaponization of justice*. Nonetheless, the Biden presidency itself is proceeding along a more conventional course with far less noise and animus. The new Republican majority in the House has established an investigative committee which is clearly intent on finding scandals that may offer political capital; Trump militants have even introduced resolutions to impeach Biden. But despite these excesses, there seems a drift back to normality; a normality that regularly finds scandal but can only feign outrage.

A Guide to Further Reading

The Presidency

The powers of the President are laid out in the US Constitution. There is a very helpful online guide at https://constitution.congress.gov/constitution/

This offers access not just to the text but to annotations that explain the significance of each article and clause. The powers of the executive and procedures for election and impeachment are all outlined in Article II.

There is a vast library on the modern presidency. Here are a few places to learn more.

James M. Banner, Jr., *Presidential Misconduct: From George Washington to Today*, New York: The New Press, 2019.

This is an update on a report commissioned by the US Congress when it was considering the possible impeachment of Richard Nixon and it was revised in 2019 when it was still believed that the Mueller Report might result in the impeachment of Donald Trump.

Several other classic studies will need an update after Trump, but much can be still learned from them in the meantime. I recommend:

James D. Barber, *The Presidential Character: Predicting Performance in the White House*, London: Routledge, 2019.

Fred Greenstein, *The Presidential Difference: Leadership Style from FDR to Barack Obama*, Princeton: The University Press, 2009.

Lori Cox Han & Diane Heith, *Presidents and the American Presidency*, New York: Oxford University Press, 2022.

Stephen Skrowronek, *Presidential Leadership in Political Time: Reprise and Reappraisal*, Lawrence: University of Kansas Press, 2011.

Watergate

Fifty years after the event, there is a vast library of books and scholarly articles on Watergate, and it features in several archival collections. The US National Archives, for instance, as part of its material for teachers and students has a page that reproduces the memo assessing the wisdom of prosecuting Nixon; see https://www.archives.gov/education/lessons/watergate-constitution

Even the Nixon Presidential Library has extracts from the tapes: see https://www.nixonlibrary.gov/watergate-trial-tapes

It is also worth visiting the Frost-Nixon interviews of 1977 available at https://teachingamericanhistory.org/document/transcript-of-david-frosts-interview-with-richard-nixon/

The classic journalistic account remains Bob Woodward and Carl Bernstein, *All the President's Men*, London: Pocket Books, 2006 [original edition 1974].

The most comprehensive recent treatment is Garrett M. Graf, *Watergate: A New History*, New York: Avid Reader Press (Simon & Schuster), 2022. It fills in many details of the underlying scandals, notably those related to CREEP's money-raising operations.

From the older, classic accounts, two stand out:

Fred Emery, *Watergate: The Corruption of American Politics and the Fall of Richard Nixon*, New York: Touchstone (Simon & Schuster), 1995.

Stanley I. Kutler, *The Wars of Watergate: The Last Crisis of Richard Nixon*, New York: W.W. Norton, 1990.

Iran-Contra

Thanks to the Freedom of Information Act, and scholars who have used it, we continue to learn more about this episode. A major repository is the National Security Archive at George Washington University. A summary of their work as of 2016 with documents available at the bottom of the page (keep scrolling) is available here: https://nsarchive.gwu.edu/briefing-book/iran/2016-11-25/iran-contra-affair-30-years-later-milestone-post-truth-politics#docs

Several senior figures in the Reagan administration gave oral histories to the Miller Center for the study of the Presidency at the University of Virginia. They include Ed Meese, George Schultz, and Caspar Weinberger. See https://millercenter.org/the-presidency/presidential-oral-histories/ronald-reagan

The official record includes Lawrence Walsh's *Final Report of the Independent Counsel for Iran-Contra Matters*, (3 volumes), filed with US Court of Appeals for the District of Columbia Circuit, 1993. It's available for free download at Google Books. Walsh documents his struggle to secure the materials he needed in *Firewall: The Iran-Contra Conspiracy and Cover-Up*, New York: W.W. Norton, 1997. Alongside Walsh, there is the Tower Commission, whose *Report of the President's Special Review Board*, was published by the US Government Printing office on 26 February 1987. There are also the multiple reports of the House and Senate Committees for Foreign Relations and the Iran-Contra Committee itself between 1986 and 1989. They, too, are downloadable from Google Books.

My own account draws largely on the following:

David M. Abshire, *Saving the Reagan Presidency: Trust Is the Coin of the Realm*, College Station: Texas A&M University Press, 2005.

Malcolm Byrne, *Iran-Contra: Reagan's Scandal and the Unchecked Abuse of Presidential Power*, Lawrence: University of Kansas Press, 2014.

Ronald Reagan, *The Reagan Diaries: Unabridged*, edited by Douglas Brinkley, 2 vols, New York: Harper-Collins, 2009.

Clinton Scandals

If you want to explore the minutiae of the Whitewater scandal, a key text is *Investigation of Whitewater Development Corporation and Related Matters: Document production in response to S. Res. 120.* United States, U.S. Government Printing Office, 1997.

Similarly, the failure of the Madison Guaranty S & L that also drew suspicion was examined in *The Failure of Madison Guaranty Savings and Loan Association and Related Matters: Hearing Before the Committee on Banking and Financial Services, House of Representatives, One Hundred Fourth Congress, First Session. United States,* U.S. Government Printing Office, 1996.

Both are available for download from Google Books.

In contrast, the final Independent Counsel report remains a marketable text; see Kenneth Starr, *The Starr Report: Referral from Independent Counsel Kenneth W. Starr Regarding President Clinton*, Rocklin, CA: Forum Press 1998.

My own account draws on a cross-section of the polarized literature about the Clintons which left me less sympathetic to them at the end than I was at the outset. The main texts consulted included:

Joe Conason and Gene Lyons, *The Hunting of the President: The Ten-Year Campaign to Destroy Bill and Hillary Clinton*, New York: Thomas Dunne, 2000.

Ken Gormley, *The Death of American Virtue: Clinton vs. Starr*, New York: Random House, 2011.

Christopher Hitchens, *No One Left To Lie To: The Triangulations of William Jefferson Clinton*, London: Verso, 1999.

Michael Isikoff, *Uncovering the Clintons: A Reporter's Story*, New York: Crown Publishers, 1999.

Malvin L. Kalb, *One Scandalous Story: Clinton, Lewinsky and Thirteen Days That Tarnished American Journalism*, New York: Free Press, 2010.

Richard A. Posner, *An Affair of State: The Investigation, Impeachment and Trial of President Clinton*, Cambridge, MA: Harvard University Press, 1999.

Nicol. C. Rae, *Impeaching Clinton: Partisan Strife on Capitol Hill*, Lawrence: University of Kansas Press, 2004.

James B. Stewart, *Blood Sport: The President and His Adversaries*, New York: Touchstone (Simon & Schuster), 1996.

2000 Election

An interesting collection of documents relating to the election and the disputes it gave rise to is available from the American Presidency Project at the University of California Santa Barbara; see https://www.presidency.ucsb.edu/documents/presidential-documents-archive-guidebook/presidential-campaigns-debates-and-endorsements-1

A useful discussion of the basis for the US Supreme Court's decision in *Bush v. Gore* 2000, which effectively gave the presidency to Bush is presented on the website of the Constitution Center and it includes extracts from the dissenting opinions; see https://constitutioncenter.org/the-constitution/supreme-court-case-library/bush-v-gore

There is a specialist literature on election administration in the United States. I was guided by:

R. Michael Alvarez and Bernard Grofman, eds., *Election Administration in the United States: The State of Reform After Bush v. Gore*, Cambridge: Cambridge University Press, 2014.

Costas Panagopoulos, *Bases Loaded: How U.S. Presidential Campaigns Are Changing and Why It Matters*, New York: Oxford University Press, 2021.

Roy G. Saltman, *The History and Politics of Voting Technology*, New York: Palgrave Macmillan, 2006.

U.S. Commission on Civil Rights, *Voting Irregularities in Florida During the 2000 Presidential Election* available at https://www.usccr.gov/files/pubs/vote2000/report/exesum.htm

2016 Election

The controversy surrounding the 2016 election gave rise to the Mueller Report which, in its first volume, documented the scale of Russian interference; see *Report on The Investigation into Russian Interference in the 2016 Presidential Election* Volume I of II; available for download at https://www.justice.gov/archives/sco/file/1373816/download

Similarly, the Senate's investigation into Russian interference is available. The general website for access is govinfo.gov. This allows you to browse documents by committee. You can therefore find the Senate Select Committee on Intelligence. Find the tab for Hearings during the 115th Congress. Listed is the open hearing on Russian interference. You can then download a PDF file.

The secondary question as to whether the meeting at Trump Tower between members of the Trump campaign team and Russian operatives was part of a wider conspiracy was not confirmed by the Mueller Report. My account of the episode draws on the following:

Michael Isikoff and David Corn, *Russian Roulette: The Inside Story of Putin's War on America and the Election of Donald Trump*, New York: Twelve, 2018.
Craig Ungar, *House of Trump, House of Putin: The Untold Story of Donald Trump and the Russian Mafia*, New York: Dutton, 2019.
Michael Wolff, *Fire and Fury: Inside the Trump White House*, London: Little, Brown, 2018.
——, *Siege: Trump Under Fire*, New York: Henry Holt, 2019.
Bob Woodward, *Fear: Trump in the White House*, New York: Simon & Schuster, 2018.
Zirin, James D. *Plaintiff in Chief: A Portrait of Donald Trump in 3,500 Lawsuits*, New York: St. Martin's Press, 2019.

My overall impression of Trump is informed by Maggie Haberman's *Confidence Man*, London: Mudlark (Harper Collins) 2022. She makes a strong case for Trump in the White House remaining the creature of 1980s New York City boss-machine politics with all the corruption that implies. For those bemused by Trump's ability to win over millions of Americans with a style that is the opposite of eloquence, see Jennifer Mercieca, *Demagogue for President: The Rhetorical Genius of Donald Trump*, College Station: Texas A&M University Press, 2020. She takes a formal academic approach but links Trump's style to well-known rhetorical tricks. If you, like me, remain puzzled by Trump's psyche, you may find Daniel Drezner's *Toddler in Chief* (Chicago: University of Chicago Press 2020) edifying, if nonetheless alarming.

First Impeachment over Ukraine

The case against Donald Trump's behaviour towards Ukraine is laid out by the House Permanent Select Committee on Intelligence in the *Trump Ukraine Impeachment Inquiry Report* of December 2019. Available online at https://www.justsecurity.org/wp-content/uploads/2019/12/impeachment-report-majority-schiff-intelligence-december-3-2019.pdf

The same *Justsecurity* website has a much fuller list of relevant documents including the Senate trial proceedings at https://www.justsecurity.org/67076/public-document-clearinghouse-ukraine-impeachment-inquiry/

The website govinfo.gov cited above also allows you to browse A-Z and thus quickly find Impeachment related materials.

Understandably most of the books on the subject are by journalists. The *Washington Post* reporters Kevin Sullivan and Mary Jordan have published *Trump on Trial*, New York: Scribner's, 2020. A further two *Washington Post* journalists, Philip Rucker and Carol Leonnig, address the impeachment in the conclusion of their *A Very Stable Genius: Donald Trump's Testing of America*, New York: Random House, 2020. Lawyer and *CNN* analyst, Jeffrey Toobin, offered an account that linked the impeachment to the Mueller investigation in *True Crimes and Misdemeanors*, New York: Random House, 2020. It should be conceded that pro-Trump activists will have none of it; see Dan Bongino, *Follow the Money: The*

Shocking Deep State Connections of the Anti-Trump Cabal, Nashville, TN: Post Hill Press, 2020. Its subtitle gives a clue as to its approach.

The COVID-19 Pandemic

For an early scholarly appraisal of the Trump administration's response to the pandemic, see:

Parker, Charles F. and Eric K. Stern. "The Trump Administration and the COVID-19 crisis: Exploring the warning-response problems and missed opportunities of a public health emergency." *Public administration*, 10.1111/padm.12843. 29 Mar. 2022, doi:10.1111/padm.12843

My own account draws on Lawrence Wright, *The Plague Year: America in the Time of Covid*, New York: Alfred A, Knopf, 2021. You can also listen to Bob Woodward's audiotape book of interviews, *The Trump Tapes*, New York: Simon & Schuster, 2022 via various audiobook providers. Woodward is one of several journalists who explain that Trump was far more ill than the White House initially conceded, see Woodward and Robert Costa, *Peril*, New York: Simon & Schuster 2021.

2020 Election and Second Impeachment

The American Presidency Project at the University of California Santa Barbara cited above with reference to the 2000 election has already created a webpage of campaign and transition documents for 2020, see https://www.presidency.ucsb.edu/documents/app-categories/elections-and-transitions/campaign-documents

As previously indicated you can also find documents on govinfo.gov.

My own account draws on the following:

Michael Bender, *Frankly, We Did Win This Election: The Inside Story of How Trump Lost*, London: Hachette UK, 2022.

Mark Bowden and Matthew Teague, *The Steal: The Attempt to Overturn the 2020 Election and the People Who Stopped It*, London: Grove Press, 2022.

Jonathan Karl, *Betrayal: The Final Act of the Trump Show*, New York: Dutton, 2021.

Mark Leibovich, *Thank You for Your Servitude: Donald Trump's Washington and the Price of Submission*, New York: Penguin, 2022.

Carol Leonnig & Philip Rucker, *I Alone Can Fix It: Donald Trump's Catastrophic Final Year*, London: Bloomsbury, 2021.

Michael Wolff, *Landslide: The Final Days of the Trump Presidency*, London: The Bridge Street Press, 2021.

The still unfolding lawsuits against Trump draw regular coverage in the main US newspapers such as the *Washington Post*, *New York Times*, and news agencies such as Reuters.

Index